Country Seats & Modern Dwellings

Two Victorian Domestic Architectural Stylebooks by Henry Hudson Holly

With a new Introduction & Index by
Michael Tomlan

ৡ

Library of Victorian Culture

Watkins Glen, New York

© American Life Foundation, 1977

ISBN   0-89257-013-x

The American Life Foundation & Study Institute, Watkins Glen,
New York 14891 published and distributes this book for
THE LIBRARY OF VICTORIAN CULTURE

Second printing, 1980

THE DOMESTIC ARCHITECTURAL STYLEBOOKS
OF
HENRY HUDSON HOLLY

THE REPUBLICATION of these two books provides an opportunity to follow in the work of one architect-author, Henry Hudson Holly, the stylistic development of domestic American architecture over a period of about fifteen years. In the first book, *Country Seats* (1863), the picturesque villas and cottages of the "Hudson River bracketed" style predominate; while in the second, *Modern Dwellings* (1878), what is loosely termed the "Queen Anne" mode has supplanted all else. It is in the latter book that the author's concern is extended beyond the façade to include the design of interiors—dictating even their furnishings. Both books are reflections of their times and both mirror their author's particular background and his biases.

As with the lives of so many mid-nineteenth century architects, Holly is known more from his published works and secondary sources than from any surviving documents. "Born and bred," as he tells us,[1] in New York City, Henry Hudson was the seventh of nine children of William Welles Holly, a merchant turned politician, who became an alderman of some note in the 1830s.[2] While no family records have been found, the Hollys probably lived in considerable comfort, for the grounds of the family estate on Fifth Avenue between Fifteenth and Sixteenth Streets were sufficiently impressive to be noted years later in the architect's obituary.[3]

In 1854, Henry Hudson Holly began two years of architectural study in New York City with the Englishman Gervase Wheeler,[4] who had only recently moved to that city.[5] While he had already been introduced to the American reading public, and perhaps to Holly, in the pages of A. J. Downing's *Horticulturist*,[6] Wheeler had certainly become better known with the publication of his first book, *Rural Homes: or, Sketches of houses suited to American country life*, in 1851. When Holly entered his office, Wheeler was probably already involved with his second work, *Homes for the People*, which was first published in 1855. It is also likely that Holly's visit to England in 1856, to complete his studies,[7] was made at his mentor's urging. Upon his return, made by the following year, Holly opened an office in Manhattan and began his own practice as an architect. However, he continued to reside for some time in Stamford, Connecticut, where the majority of the Holly family had been prominent since the early seventeenth century.[8]

Against this background, Holly's first book, *Country Seats*, prepared before the "War for the Union," [9] is all the more understandable. Not only the format of the book, but also its organization and content reflect to a considerable degree the Wheeler publications, although many of the design ideas can be found in other contemporary architectural books as well. The works of Calvert Vaux, Henry W. Cleaveland and the Backus Brothers, Lewis Falley Allen, and of course, A. J. Downing are most closely related.

A number of allusions to significant developments in American architecture will also be apparent to the reader. For example, the dedication to the newly-formed American Institute of Architects is important for it indicates the author's respect for that institution and his awareness of the rising standards of professionalism, a matter of great concern to the early membership. Holly had only recently, in December, 1858, been unanimously elected to that body, and he was probably its youngest member at that time.[10] Continually involved in the fellowship of the Institute, Holly's office was, from 1862 onward, in the Tribune Building at 111 Broadway, the address of many of the leading architects of the day, including Richard Upjohn, first president of the A.I.A. Turning to Holly's "Preface," mention is made of a professional in another field: George E. Waring. A well-known drainage and sanitary engineer,[11] Waring was both a friend and an associate of Frederick Law Olmsted in the creation of Central Park,[12] and was himself once a resident of Stamford.[13] He was to have provided for *Country Seats* a "Treatise on Landscape Gardening," a project abandoned because of his participation in the Civil War.

Opening with "An Account of the History of Architecture," *Country Seats* begins in a more historical and analytical manner than most of the American books of the period. Holly quite deliberately presents this historical overview, weighted in favor of the "mother country," [14] in order to properly establish the place of American architectural development. There follows a clarion call to enjoy the advantages of country life in the English manner, a theme which continues throughout the book, heavily emphasized at times, such as when he provides an extensive list of English country seat names.[15] The author may well have viewed his own situation in a similar manner, as he undoubtedly commuted from a gentleman's estate in the suburbs to his place of business in the city.[16]

Holly proudly sets forth some of his earliest commissions.[17] Beginning with a modest gate lodge and the remodelling of a country cottage, he proceeds to larger designs in the "half-timber style," or of "an irregular Italian character," and then elaborates on some of his most romantic notions: an old sawmill which might become a Swiss country pleasure pavilion, and a tasteful little railroad station, like those "dotted along the railway web of Great Britain and the Continent." [18] He also seems to have a considerable interest in materials, particularly slate and stone, and in technical innovations. His position, however, is neither consistently *avant garde* nor *retardataire*, for he is as quick to laud Foster concrete bricks [19] as he is to condemn the use of gas for lighting.[20]

Far from a technical treatise, *Country Seats* is primarily a popular literary effort. A benchmark in his professional life, the book may also be considered in relation to his personal affairs, particularly his marriage, in the mid-1860s, to a young authoress of children's stories, Sarah L. Barrow, known to her numerous little readers as "Aunt Fanny's daughter." [21] Holly, too, could claim to be as much an author as an architect, especially after his second work, *Church Architecture*, was published in 1871. While the author's obvious intention was the exposition of the latest ecclesiastical style, the prose was not directed to the professional, but seemingly to the naive members of a church building committee, providing them with a guide to the principles of good construction.[22]

Holly addressed himself to a larger popular audience when he began, in the May, 1876, issue of *Harper's New Monthly Magazine*, the first of a series of articles entitled "Modern Dwellings, Their Construction, Decoration and Furniture." The reviewer for the *American Architect and Building News* was obviously impressed with the first contribution, for he hailed it as [23]

The best article of the kind, that we have seen lately, ... It contains a good many suggestions of practical and artistic value, for the planning of country houses, with half a dozen plans, for the most part ingeniously and effectively arranged. The exteriors which accompany them are attractively picturesque, and show, much more than is usual in such articles, the freedom and sureness of the practiced professional hand.

In contrast, the next review printed by the *American Architect* was anything but favorable. Holly's second article, which appeared in the June number of *Harper's*, was found to contain only "vague generalizations on common doctrines of color-decoration based solely on lately abandoned theories of the composition of light." [24] The real basis for the *American Architect's* dissatisfaction, however, was a letter which another architect had written to the editor of the *Nation*, claiming that Holly's article was "essentially derived from Mr. Eastlake's work," and "contained passages derived from it with but trifling variations," [25] for the most part unacknowledged. The *American Architect* had found this charge true, and further held that Holly had drawn on Messrs. Cox and Sons catalogues for illustrations, without giving them credit. The reviewer concluded, "It is difficult to believe that he expected to 'convey' these illustrations without detection, it looks more like carelessness." [26] "Inadvertance" was the keynote of Holly's apology, printed a few weeks later,[27] and he concluded the series without further criticism.

Collecting and enlarging upon these articles, Holly composed his third book, *Modern Dwellings in Town and Country*, published in 1878. Bearing in mind the earlier criticism, the author took care in his preface to briefly acknowledge his sources, although the astute reader will have no difficulty in recognizing in the text the pastiche of quotes from Eastlake, the *American Architect*, and the London *Building News*, as well as fragments from the eight trade catalogues mentioned in Part II, "Furniture and Decoration." Perhaps more surprising is the degree to which Holly adapted and incorporated portions of his first work, *Country Seats*, in this, his second book on domestic architecture. In fact, by close examination, it is possible to suggest which of Holly's architectural ideas have changed and which have remained the same.

Despite its reliance upon the earlier publication, *Modern Dwellings* clearly contains a new message. Here Holly presents a vernacular style, the free classic, or "Queen Anne," which he claims best expresses real domestic needs. The author makes no effort to conceal his admiration for the fashionable country house designs of the English advocates of this style, architects R. Norman Shaw and J. J. Stevenson, nor to hide his desire to become the spokesman for the translation of their ideas into an American idiom. Most of Holly's designs are of this English inspiration; only occasionally does he copy a French sourcebook, such as *Habitations Modernes* (1875-1877), by Eugène Emmanuel Viollet-le-Duc,[28] itself actually a compilation of the designs of many authors. (Fig. 1)

Well-advertised and widely distributed, *Modern Dwellings* soon became Holly's best known book. An impressive source to many, especially to those untutored in the fine points of the architectural fashion of the day, the book could have been responsible for Holly's more distant commissions, conducted through the mails. Indeed, his practice relied not only on his reputation and personal connections in the New York-Stamford area, but also on his published work and advertisements in such nationally recognized periodicals as the Anglican newspaper, *The Churchman*. Providing designs and working drawings by mail was a means of practice well-accepted in the days when architects in small towns were few and distances were longer than they now seem to be. Then, such a book as *Modern Dwellings* was often sufficient recommendation in itself, and might easily lead the prospective client or the secretary of the building committee to write a letter of inquiry.

The inherent limitations of the design-by-mail practice occasionally became evident. In providing the drawings for St. Luke's Memorial Hall, the department of theology building at the University of the South at Sewanee, Tennessee, for example, unforeseen problems arose primarily because Holly had never visited the site, and had no knowledge of the relatively low compressive strength of the local building stone. (Fig. 2) As a result, walls had to be rebuilt, and the negotiations for a settlement continued for years afterward. But Sewanee was proud of her new building, and the architect's practice continued, unaffected.[29]

Unfortunately, few of Holly's buildings still stand and even fewer remain unaltered. Perhaps this is due in part to their siting, often along principal roadways, railroads, and streetcar lines, on land subject to great redevelopment pressures. Certainly the limited recognition accorded the period by architectural historians until

Figure 1: "Villa à Houlgate (Calvados)," M. Aubertin, Arch. From E.-E. Viollet-le-Duc, *Habitations Modernes*. Compare with Design No. 19, p. 120, of *Modern Dwellings*.

Figure 2: St. Luke's Theological Memorial Hall, Sewanee, Tennessee, as first proposed. From David Greene Haskins, *A Brief Account of the University of the South*.

Figure 3: "Residence of Mr. Henry C. Pedder, Llewellyn Park, Orange, N. J.," later home of Thomas A. Edison. From *American Architect and Building News*, August 27, 1881.

Figure 4: "Rockland," residence of Mr. Henry R. Towne, Atlantic Street. From Edward T. W. Gillespie, *Picturesque Stamford*.

only very recently permitted demolition to proceed unhindered. Of the remaining Holly designs, the best known has become famous more because its second owner—Thomas A. Edison—lived there, than for its superior architectural merit. (Fig. 3) While it is protected, as a National Park Service property in Llewellyn Park, New Jersey, a number of equally splendid "country houses," such as "Rockland," the Stamford residence of Henry R. Towne, President of the Yale and Towne Manufacturing Company, have been destroyed almost without notice. (Fig. 4)

Both *Country Seats* and *Modern Dwellings* are important not only for the light they shed on the stylistic evolution of domestic American architecture, and for the suggestions they give of a growing professional awareness, but also because so little is known of Holly's buildings themselves. Both books were as much a portfolio of designs as they were polite forms of advertisement. Together they represent Holly's principal contribution to American architecture: the introduction of the latest ideas for domestic construction, presented from a professional's viewpoint in a popular, literary fashion.

Michael A. Tomlan
Ithaca, N. Y.
January, 1977

FOOTNOTES

1. Henry Hudson Holly, *Modern Dwellings in Town and Country* (New York: Harper and Brothers Publishers, 1878), p. 152.

2. Charles Moses Holly, *Record of the Holly Family in America* (Stamford, Conn.: By the Author, 1861), p. 86. According to this source, Holly was born October 8, 1834.

3. Periodicals such as the *American Architect and Building News, Architecture and Building, Carpentry and Building* and the newspaper, the *Stamford Advocate*, all carried obituary notices, but the most complete account of the circumstances surrounding Holly's death was published in the *New York Daily Tribune*, Wednesday, September 7, 1892, p. 7. It notes that Holly "died on Monday in his home, this city. The cause of his death was dropsy and liver and spinal disorders resulting from a fall three years ago in a building the construction of which he was supervising." Holly's partner, Horatio F. Jelliff, died less than a month later; John A. Holly continued to practice from the same office for a few years.

4. "A Group of American Architects," *American Architect and Building News* XV, no. 424 (February 16, 1884), p. 76.

5. Gervase Wheeler is first listed in *Trow's New York City Directory for the Year Ending May 1, 1854* (New York: Trow Directory and Bookbinding Company, 1854), p. 134.

As little is known of Wheeler, the following discussion may be helpful to the reader. A copy of *The Architect's, Engineer's and Building-Trades' Directory* (London: Wyman & Sons, 1868, p. 143) in the RIBA library notes that Wheeler was "a pupil of Richard C. Carpenter, Esq.," and that his works included "railway buildings, banks, churches, and private residences in the United States and England." (Among his known commissions in this country are the Henry Boody House, Brunswick, Maine; the Patrick Barry House, near Mt. Hope Cemetery, in Rochester, New York; and Goodrich Hall, Williams College, Williamstown, Massachusetts.) Wheeler was "also engaged in laying out lands, and in sanitary appliances," and had "contributed papers to the *Builder* and some American publications." His nomination as a Fellow of the Royal Institute of British Architects, recommended by Fellows William Slater, George Godwin and H. A. Darbyshire, took place on January 26, 1867, and his election on March 11 of the same year (*Nomination Papers*, 1867 volume, p. 36). At the Ordinary General Meeting of February 3, 1868, he displayed his familiarity with building characteristics and conditions throughout the northeastern United States in a paper entitled "Peculiarities of Domestic Architecture in America." Wheeler's last known work, *The Choice of a Dwelling* (London: John Murray) went through two editions, in 1871 and 1872. He seems to have failed to continue to fulfil the membership requirements for the RIBA however, for he was dropped from a list of fellows published in April, 1873. I thank my wife, Mary Raddant Tomlan, for her assistance in bringing this material to light.

6. Gervase Wheeler, Architect, Hartford, Ct., "Design and Description of an English Cottage," *The Horticulturist and Journal of Rural Art and Rural Taste*, A. J. Downing, ed., IV, no. 2 (August, 1849), p. 77.

7. *American Architect, op. cit.*, p. 76.

8. Edward T. W. Gillespie, *Picturesque Stamford, 1641-1892* (Stamford, Conn.: Gillespie Brothers, 1892), p. 50.

9. Henry Hudson Holly, *Country Seats: Containing Lithographic Designs for Cottages, Villas, Mansions, Etc., with Their Accompanying Outbuildings* (New York: D. Appleton and Company, 1863), p. v.

10. The *AIA Proceedings, 1857-1871*, the official, handwritten accounts of the Institute, held in its Washington archives note that at the meeting of December 7, 1857, Henry Hudson Holly was unanimously elected to membership. He does not seem to have attended any regular meetings, however, until June 5, 1860. I am indebted to Mr. George E. Pettengill, Hon. AIA, Librarian Emeritus, for his assistance in this matter.

11. James H. Cassedy, "The Flamboyant Colonel Waring," *Bulletin of the History of Medicine* XXXVI (March-April, 1962), pp. 163-176.

12. Laura Roper, *FLO: A Biography of Frederick Law Olmsted* (Baltimore: Johns Hopkins University Press, 1973), p. 361.

13. Edward T. W. Gillespie, *Picturesque Stamford, op. cit.*, p. 137.

14. Henry Hudson Holly, *Country Seats, op. cit.*, p. 12.

15. *Ibid.*, p. 56.

16. Later New York City directories list Holly's home as Rye, New York, and Montclair, New Jersey.

17. See the *Stamford Advocate*, April 27, 1858, p. 2, for a few other residences designed by Holly in his early years.

18. Henry Hudson Holly, *Country Seats, op. cit.*, pp. 61, 97, 160, and 170.

19. *Ibid.*, p. 118.

20. *Ibid.*, p. 99.

21. Sarah L. Barrow was the daughter of Mrs. Francis E. Mease Barrow, or "Aunt Fanny," the celebrated authoress of at least two dozen children's stories. "Aunt Fanny's daughter" also had completed an impressive number of books before her marriage, including the six volume "Sock Stories," and she continued writing after her child-bearing years. In 1880-81, for example, she co-authored with her mother the "Twelve Little Sisters" series. It is also noteworthy that Sarah's aunt, Alexina Mease White, also a writer, was the mother of the architect Stanford White.

22. For a rather incisive contemporary review, see *The Architect* (London) VII (May 18, 1872), p. 261.

23. *American Architect and Building News* I (May 13, 1876), p. 154.

24. *Ibid.* (July 8, 1876), p. 217-18.

25. See also *The Nation* XXI, no. 754 (June 29, 1876), p. 414.

26. *American Architect and Building News* I (July 8, 1876), p. 218.

27. *The Nation* XXII, no. 577 (July 20, 1876), p. 40, reprinted in the *American Architect and Building News* I (July 22, 1876), p. 234.

28. Eugène Emmanuel Viollet-Le-Duc, *Habitations Modernes* (Paris: A. Morel, 1875-76) I, p. 17 and plates 50 and 51.

29. St. Luke's Memorial Hall was the second of two buildings designed for the University of the South, the other being the Hodgson Library, which has not survived. These buildings are undoubtedly among those to which Holly refers on page 45 of *Modern Dwellings*. See David Greene Haskins, *A Brief Account of the University of the South* (New York: E. P. Dutton & Company, 1877), pages 15-18; further material may be found in the archives of the University of the South.

NOTE: CERTAIN LINES OF TEXT AND ILLUSTRATIONS IN *Country Seats* HAVE BEEN REPOSITIONED, AS FOLLOWS:

—Four lines of text on page 44 have been repositioned at the bottom of page 43, thereby making room for the plate to Design No. 4.
—The plate illustrating Design No. 6 will be found at the end of the article, facing page 58.
—The plate illustrating Design No. 8 will be found at the end of the article, facing page 64.
—Four lines of text on page 68 have been repositioned at the bottom of page 67, thereby making room for the plate to Design No. 10.
—The plate illustrating Design No. 12 will be found at the end of the article, facing page 82.
—The plate illustrating Design No. 15 will be found at the end of the article, facing page 96.
—The plate illustrating Design No. 19 will be found at the end of the article, facing page 112.
—The plate illustrating Design No. 22 will be found at the end of the article, facing page 124.
—The plate illustrating Design No. 25 will be found at the end of the article, facing page 136.
—Page 137 has been renumbered page 138, thereby making room for the two plates to Design No. 26.
—The plate illustrating Design No. 27 will be found at the end of the article, facing page 146.
—The plate illustrating Design No. 31 will be found at the end of the article, facing page 160.

HOLLY'S

COUNTRY SEATS.

HOLLY'S

COUNTRY SEATS:

CONTAINING

LITHOGRAPHIC DESIGNS

FOR COTTAGES, VILLAS, MANSIONS, ETC., WITH THEIR
ACCOMPANYING OUTBUILDINGS;

ALSO,

𝕮𝖔𝖚𝖓𝖙𝖗𝖞 𝕮𝖍𝖚𝖗𝖈𝖍𝖊𝖘, 𝕮𝖎𝖙𝖞 𝕭𝖚𝖎𝖑𝖉𝖎𝖓𝖌𝖘, 𝕽𝖆𝖎𝖑𝖜𝖆𝖞 𝕾𝖙𝖆𝖙𝖎𝖔𝖓𝖘,

ETC., ETC.

BY

HENRY HUDSON HOLLY.

ARCHITECT.

NEW YORK:
D. APPLETON AND COMPANY, 443 & 445 BROADWAY.
1863.

TO

The American Institute of Architects,

THIS BOOK IS

RESPECTFULLY DEDICATED,

BY

THE AUTHOR.

HENRY HUDSON HOLLY,

ARCHITECT,

111 Broadway, New York.

———◆◆◆———

CHARGES

On Contracts exceeding $3,000.

For Plans and Specifications, 2½ per cent.
For Detail Drawings, . . 1 "
For Superintendence, . . 1½ "
Surveys of Old Buildings, . 25 dollars.

Expenses added.

PREFACE.

THIS work was fully prepared for the press some two years since, and was about being put into the hands of publishers, when the "War for the Union" broke out, and seemed for a time to paralyze any new enterprise; the author, therefore, thought proper to postpone the publication, until affairs should be in a more settled state, which, although not fully realized at the present time, yet as business has so far become based upon a war footing, the ball is kept rolling, and fortunes appear to be made even faster than in times of peace.

We did intend, as hinted in Design No. 1, giving with this work a Treatise on Landscape Gardening, which, with maps, was commenced under the auspices of Mr. George E. Waring, jr., late of the Central Park; but that gentleman having accepted a commission in the army, the plan was unfortunately abandoned.

The lithographic views, which are signed by Paul Schulze, were in no way designed by him, but simply copied on stone from drawings by the author. One or two of these, in a few of the copies, have a slight mistake in the ground plans, which was not discovered until a small number were printed.

HENRY HUDSON HOLLY,
Architect.

NEW YORK, *Jan. 1st*, 1863.

CONTENTS.

———•••———

CONTENTS.

CONTENTS.

CONTENTS.

CONTENTS.

CONTENTS.

DESIGN No. 33.

HOLLY'S

COUNTRY SEATS.

SOME ACCOUNT OF THE HISTORY OF ARCHITECTURE.

ARCHITECTURE, "the first and noblest of the arts," arose with the first wants of mankind. With their earliest ideas of self-dependence, we may reasonably suppose men began to look around them for shelter and protection alike from heat and cold. The refuge of caves and natural excavations could suffice for their uses only while in the most savage state. The first step toward civilization was to create artificial habitations—to build. How rude and insufficient must have been these first attempts we may well judge, when we consider what structures sheltered the descendants of these primeval builders even within the memory of history, and the cabins and huts even now dwelt in by some remote tribes of the wilderness. What plans they adopted, what systems of construction, if any, they pursued, can only be conjectured. The origin of architecture, like all other antediluvian sciences, is involved in obscurity. We know from its nature that it is eminently a progressive science; and, tracing it backward, step by step, we may arrive at an approximate idea of its earliest feeble efforts. Such a retrospect is not only instructive, but encouraging, reminding us, as it does, of the errors of the rude infancy of architecture, and compelling us to respect the innate strength and manifest destiny of an art which, through innumerable difficulties, could steadily advance from primeval simplicity to its present perfection, where it claims the highest rank among the noblest of human sciences, and points to monuments of its success, not surpassed in excellence by those of any sister art.

The probability is, that nothing more substantial than wood, the skins of beasts, or other equally simple materials, formed the primitive dwellings of mankind. Scripture informs us that Cain built a city; but that it was constituted of anything more permanent than tents is doubtful. Not till the building of the Tower of Babel, do we hear of the use of any more noble material. In this case we are told that burnt brick and slime were used, and it is probable that some previous experience in the working of these materials had been obtained in the erection of less important structures. We next read of the city of Babylon; but the account is brief and unsatisfactory, throwing no light upon the subject.

The next styles which arose were the Persian, Egyptian, and Indian, the former of which is sometimes called Persepolitan, from Persepolis, in which city are found the principal remains of this style. It bears some resemblance to the other two in general character, but differs materially in detail. In each country we find temples of considerable extent, and sepulchral chambers, or catacombs, hewn out of the solid rock, and the walls adorned with hieroglyphics, the records of an advanced state of civilization. In Egypt these structures contain numerous apartments, while in Persia they are comparatively small, but excel in elaborate porticos richly embellished with sculpture. Another similarity consists in the massive proportions of these rock-hewn temples and tombs, all seeming to point to a common origin. The sculpture of Persia and Egypt is also of like character—stiff, formal, and exceedingly laborious; and this fact, in connection with the arrow-headed characters common to both styles, presents a good argument in favor of their relationship.

Egypt, like other primeval nations, has its history shrouded in mystery, and, like that of early Rome, so entangled with the web of mythology, that it is impossible to distinguish truth from fable. It is, therefore, a matter of uncertainty which of these nations should receive the credit of the earliest attention to architecture; but, judging from the specimens found in the ruins of Babylon, it would seem to be due to that city—these being of a ruder construction than those of Egypt and India, and bearing intrinsic evidence of greater antiquity. For the same reason we would place Egypt second in point of time.

Manetho informs us that the irruption of the *Hyksos*, or shepherd-kings, into Egypt, is supposed to have occurred at about the close of the sixteenth dynasty, and that the seventeenth was under these monarchs. It is at this time that the erection of extensive edifices is presumed to have begun. The usurping shepherds were overpowered by the Pharaohs about 2,000 years B. C., and then commenced the rebuilding of those temples, the magnificent remains of which are the wonder and delight of the traveller even to the present day.

The most noted erections are those whose remains are found in the Egyptian cities along the Nile, and of these, especially Thebes and the Island of Pytæ; yet all contain most interesting specimens of temples, monuments, tombs, sphinxes, and pyramids, delicately sculptured in the hardest granite, and ponderous and herculean beyond any subsequent efforts of the chisel.

The next system, in chronological rotation, appears to be the Grecian, the origin of which is almost as obscure as that of the nation itself. Many authors claim for the Greeks great originality of design; yet there is much reason to suppose them indebted for their first inspirations to the sources we have specified. While denying, however, their originality in architecture, we must admit that in their hands it attained its highest degree of purity, chastity, and grandeur; so that even to the present day their architectural details are imitated, as far more refined and beautiful than any which have since been invented. To this wonderful nation are attributed the three principal orders of architecture, the Doric, Ionic, and Corinthian.

The proportions of the first, we are told, were taken from the figure of a man, its height being six times its diameter—the same ratio that a man's foot bears to his height. This order differs from the other two in the absence of a base. Vitruvius fancifully says that the base was introduced into the Ionic order to represent the sandal, or covering of a woman's foot, and that to the Doric, which represents the strong, muscular, barefooted man, this member is inappropriate.

It is not surprising that a people like the versatile and elegant Greeks should soon weary of a single stereotyped style, repeated with but slight modifications in all their buildings, and long for a change in both order and design. It was to meet this demand that the Ionic order arose. It was invented by the Ionians, as its name implies. The Vitruvian account, sufficiently poetical to be exceedingly improbable, is, "that in erecting the temple of Diana, the proportions and dress of the Goddess were studied. The diameter of the columns was made an eighth part of their height; the base, with folds representing the shoe; the capitals, with volutes, in form of the curled hair worn upon the right and left; and the cymatium, for the locks pending on the forehead from the crown; the flutes in the column are supposed to represent the folds in the drapery." Yet *motives* for all these features are found in the remains of Persepolis and Egypt.

Although there are extant no examples of the Corinthian order at Corinth, yet its name would seem sufficient to entitle that city to the honor of its birthplace. Vitruvius' account of the origin of its capital is a well-known and pretty fable: "Callimachus, an Athenian sculptor, passing the tomb of a young virgin, observed an acanthus growing around the sides of a basket, covered with a tile, and placed upon the tomb; and seeing that the tops of the leaves were bent downward, in the form of volutes, by the resistance of the tile, he took the hint, and executed some columns with foliated capitals, near Corinth, of a more slender proportion than those of the Ionic, imitative of the figure and delicacy of virgins." Unfortunately, however, Egypt is full of the prototypes of this composition.

These three may well be called the basis of all trabeated and columnar architecture; for, whatever changes have been wrought upon them—however much the originals may seem to be lost from view in the multitudinous fancies of subsequent artists, still, divested of all their superfluities, the later productions invariably reduce themselves to one of these.

In this connection it may not be inappropriate to speak of a most remarkable fact in this art. The earliest monuments of the sister arts have passed away; nothing is left, save tradition, by which to judge of the first stages of their existence. The Grecian and Roman empires, where the arts were most cultivated, have declined and fallen, and with them a great part of their history. Little remains even of description, and still less of reality, to guide us in the study of their great achievements. But Architecture nevertheless has survived, an indelible, majestic, and authentic record of their intellectual and moral culture, and the progress of their civilization. It is an art which most closely and intimately unites the beautiful with the useful—a deliberate growth out of the necessities of nations. Were its only object an æsthetic one, its earlier monuments would long ago have disappeared; for it is not in the nature of man habitually to render immortal the "unsubstantial pageants" of the mind. They will not build for beauty, but rather beautify in building. Therefore the adaptation of architecture to the wants of mankind is not only the secret of its beauty, but of its durability also. We may confidently expect that hereafter, as hitherto, this great art will keep pace with the growing grandeur and magnificence of nations, and we may anticipate architectural achievements which, in refinement, splendor, and dignity, will surpass all that our researches in the past can give.

During the administration of Pericles, art made rapid strides. His character, as described by Plutarch, coincides most remarkably with the style of the temples erected by him. He is represented as exhibiting " an elevation of sentiment, a loftiness and purity of style, a gravity of countenance, jealous of laughter, a firm and even tone of delivery, and a decency of dress which no vehemence of speaking ever put in disorder." Athens was at this time nominally a republic, but Pericles was in fact a king; and when the people complained of his lavish expenditures, he replied, " Be mine, then, alone the cost; but, mark ye, be mine alone the glory. Not an Athenian shall be praised, not an Athenian obtain the homage of worship by posterity, when it contemplates these enduring monuments. Not to Athens shall belong the praise of those temples raised to the honor of her deities. No; my name alone shall be inscribed on them, and the city Athens shall live only in the fame of the citizen Pericles." " No! " exclaimed the united voice of the people; " be yours and ours the glory. Draw on the treasury as you will." This anecdote well serves to illustrate the spirit which animated the Grecian architect.

But it is in ancient Rome we must look for the greatest variety and magnificence in architecture. In the time of Romulus, the dwellings of the inhabitants were of the rudest description. Ancus Martius was the first king who commenced work on a larger and more substantial scale. All succeeding rulers bestowed more or less attention upon this art. When Greece was overrun by Roman legions, the conquered provinces retaliated with their architecture, and in a short time overturned all previous systems in Italy, and became in art the masters of the conquerors. Augustus may be called the Pericles of Rome. He it was who conceived the idea of making it the most splendid city in the world ; and in his day she attained her highest point of glory in this art. Architects flocked from Greece to tender their services in beautifying the city, and, by their aid, Augustus was able to see the realization of his dreams, and to boast "that he found Rome built in brick, and left it in marble." After Augustus architecture fell into a decline, and did not revive until the reign of Vespasian. The Coliseum, which was begun by him and finished by Titus, still stands as one of the wonders of the world. Of all the buildings of ancient Rome, the Pantheon is perhaps most worthy of note. It was erected by Agrippa, and, as the name indicates, was dedicated to all the gods. This building will serve as an illustration of some principles of Roman architecture, as distinguished from Grecian. Its decorations are of the Corinthian order, and the interior is about 140 feet in height and diameter. The roof is vaulted ; and it is in this system of construction— that of the arch—that Rome can claim its only title to originality. The dome is constructed of brick, rubble, and pumice stone, and has a clear internal diameter of 140 feet, with a circular aperture at the top of 30 feet diameter, which supplies the whole building with light and air, there being no windows. Around the inside walls are several niches, each adorned with two columns composed of antique yellow marble, and the whole interior lining of the walls, as far as the springing of the dome, is of the finest marble.

Writers, in speaking of the Grecian orders, generally add to them two others, said to have originated in Rome, viz., the Tuscan and the Composite. The former, of Etruscan origin, is in reality no more than a clumsy imitation of the Doric, before the Greeks came to teach Rome the true principles of that style ; and the latter is a combination of the Ionic and Corinthian. The chief, if not the only merits of the old Roman architecture, are its variety and magnificent extent. It possesses little of that strong, meaning, and simple elegance, that refined dignity, so characteristic of the Greek school. Constructive expression and architectural truth were evidently not its aims; and the noble columns supporting massive entablatures in Greece, became here merely ornamental appendages. The arch sustaining all the weight, the columns stand idle and useless on either hand. Of the Romans it has been said, "They emblazoned their imperial city with a thousand splendid errors." Roman architecture typifies Roman pride and ostentation. Here are triumphal arches with bas-reliefs, commemorative of the triumphs of kings and conquerors, and designed to perpetuate their fame, but subserving no loftier purpose; columns, to support only the memory of barbarous conquests; theatres, stadia, and basilicas, to make more magnificent the daily life of a presumptuous and tyrannical people.

It has been said, and not without truth, that the arts are a mirror in which we may see reflected the character of a people; and indeed, as regards architecture, it is an indelible reflection. Every great era in the world's history has left its lasting image on the mirror of this art. If we would know the secrets of the past, we have but to look on the monumental records of Architecture, Sculpture, and Painting. But, among all political changes, none has had a more marked influence on every department of art than the introduction of Christianity. On architecture, especially, has it left its indelible impress; and, through its inspiration, mediæval builders in the midst of Dark Ages built temples of worship so full of beautiful persuasion, that the people entered these gates of promise and joyfully received the baptism of the new faith. Religion, indeed, had always been the principal source—except, perhaps, in Rome—of the highest architectural efforts; and in the idolatrous temples of Greece, Egypt, and India, we may behold the most sumptuous expressions of human intellect in art. But it was reserved for Christian architecture to symbolize a higher aspiration, which only a faith revealed from the Deity himself was capable of conceiving.

Thus originated what is called the Gothic, the first stage of which, from its close relationship with Roman precedents, was known as the

Romanesque, including the Byzantine, Lombardic, Saxon, and Norman, each of which we propose very briefly to describe.

Constantine was the first of the Roman emperors to embrace Christianity ; and, that he might with more freedom establish the new religion, he transferred the seat of government to Byzantium. Here, in the effort to throw off all influence of paganism, and to disclaim all connection therewith, a new order of architecture was instituted. Christianity rapidly achieved new triumphs, and spread far and wide, so that in a little more than two hundred years, from Constantine to Justinian, eighteen hundred churches were erected. Christianity soon extended through the entire Eastern Empire, and everywhere this style of architecture, which was the symbol and expression of the new dispensation, accompanied its triumphant progress.

In the reign of Justinian, the Ostrogoths were driven out of Italy, and, the Eastern and Western Empires being thus brought under the rule of one sovereign, the way was opened for the introduction of Byzantine architecture, which, however, did not gain a firm footing in the West till the building of the famous basilica of St. Mark in Venice, in the latter part of the tenth century, though Byzantine builders had been employed in Italy, in works of less importance, many years before this. It is a common error to suppose that Byzantine architecture ever became thoroughly acclimated in Italy. We do not think its efforts were ever very strongly felt outside of Venice, except, perhaps, in some matters of detail. A natural confusion arises from the neglect of the fact, that both Byzantine and Lombardic had a common origin, and therefore in many points were identical. The pure Byzantine seems to have held sway in the East until the invasion of the Ottomans.

Mr. Hope, in speaking of the churches of Byzantium, says : " Arches rising above arches, and cupolas over cupolas, we may say that all which in the temples of Athens was straight, angular, and square, in the churches of Constantine became curved and rounded, concave within and convex without."

The plan of the Byzantine church is what is called a Greek cross ; that is, having the arms of equal length. A double dome is placed over the intersection of these arms, the ends of which are covered with conchas, or semi-domes, abutting against the main central cupola. The porticos are invariably omitted, and semicircular arches are everywhere prevalent.

The Lombardic, which, like its rival, the Byzantine, had its origin in the same early Christian Romanesque, derived its name from the circumstance of its prevalence during the supremacy of the Lombards in Italy, and not from its invention being due to them ; since it was developed by the native architects of Italy, and was most in vogue from the seventh to the thirteenth century. The arts flourished in Italy under the Lombardic government, which continued till the time of Charlemagne (A. D. 774), during which period Central Italy became studded with churches and baptistries. This style does not appear to have obtained in Rome. Architecture received a severe check from the incursions of the Saracens from the south, and the discords of rival princes of the north, and did not recover until the eleventh century. From this, until the pointed style was introduced in the thirteenth century, the Lombardic, though somewhat modified, especially prevailed. There are two features which principally distinguished this from the Byzantine, viz., the bell tower, or campanile, and the substitution of the Latin for the Greek cross, as a characteristic form.

The Saxon was the first system of any importance in England, and prevailed from the time of the conversion of the Saxons until the Norman conquest. Doubtless it had its source in the style introduced during the Roman supremacy, as it is hardly to be presumed that either Britons or Saxons had any architecture of their own.

Gregory the Great is believed to have been the first to encourage Christianity in England. We are told he gave permission to St. Augustine to use the pagan temples for purposes of Christian worship.* Within less than fifty years after the death of this great and successful propagandist, the great cathedrals of London, Rochester, and York, and the Abbey of Westminster, were erected, and the more modern structures now occupying the sites of these cathedrals are dedicated to the same saints. The foundations still bear traces of the antique Saxon masonry.

---

* It is well to observe here, that all the earliest Christian temples of worship in Rome were originally the ancient basilicas, or courts of justice, which were admirably suited for the forms of the early ritual of the Church. From these basilicas are directly descended the later cathedral plans with which we are familiar.

The Norman was the Lombardic transplanted into the north of France, and there receiving characteristic modification from the manly energy of the people, and the necessities of the ruder climate. It went over to England with the conquerors, and soon prevailed everywhere throughout the island, absorbing those features of the Saxon style which had in them enough of the elements of life to render them worth preserving. It much resembles the Lombardic, differing from it especially in the absence of the dome or cupola, nor has it the low pedimental roof extending over the whole facade. The sloping arcade in the gable is absent, as likewise the tiers of external galleries or arches. Circular windows are more common, nor do we meet with the peculiar projecting porch, having its columns resting on the backs of animals. Other of its details agree with the Saxon in its massive proportions, the shape of its arches and piers, and its general construction. It is, however, a much more cultivated style than any of the Romanesque schools. It flourished in England from the middle of the eleventh to the end of the twelfth century. After the arrival of William of Normandy, churches were erected in almost every city, village, and hamlet, throughout the island. The latter period of this style has been termed the Semi-Norman, and is important as forming a connecting link between the Romanesque and the Pointed, or Gothic, its principal medium being the pointed arch, which was first introduced about the time of Richard I., when the Crusaders, who are sometimes supposed to have brought this arch from the East, gave a new impulse to Christian architecture. The origin of this pointed arch has for a long time been a subject of controversy; and the minds of archæologists appear now to be pretty generally inclined to the belief that it was not an importation, but a natural constructive development from the old round arch, dimly foreshadowed, a century before it prevailed, so extensively as to be the leading feature of a new system of architecture.

This Gothic or Pointed style, which grew out of and immediately succeeded the Semi-Norman, was expressive in the highest degree of the then prevailing religion. All lines now tended upward, and each member appeared expressive of some mark of the Christian faith. The plan of the church was a cross, which also appeared conspicuous in its various details. Trefoil arches and panels, typifying the Trinity, soon became prominent. The substantial buttress, which gave strength to the walls, now ran above the roof, and finished with a pinnacle. Instead of heathen domes, the Christian spire towered upward, pointing to the heaven of which Faith whispers. Mr. Wightwick, in alluding to this beautiful thought, says: " All that you saw ere you entered the gate of Constantinal Rome, only sought to inform you of the grandeur and the grace belonging to those idolatrous creations, which, however lofty, still maintain but a horizontal course with Earth : nor was it till the genius of Pointed Design expanded itself in the glowing atmosphere of Christianized Europe, that Architecture aspired to raise the eye above the level of mere human perfection, and to give it a ' heaven-directed ' aim. Then sought she, in the long vistas and mounting spires which distinguish the wondrous temples of Germany, France, and Great Britain, to symbolize the ever-vanishing perspective of Eternity, and the infinite altitude of the Creator above his creatures. Their lofty pillars seemed rather to spring *from* the earth, than to rest *upon* it ; their aspiring arches, instead of downward pressure, expressed upward continuity ; and those windowless walls, which in the Heathen temple remained in stubborn solidity to exclude the light, were now pierced on all sides to admit the beams of divine day. Now sought they to typify, by the sobered splendor of emblazoned glass, how, through the many-colored medium of mystery, heaven poured its dazzling rays, in mercy dimmed for mortal eyes. Now, sought they, in their cruciform plan, to exhibit a symbol of the Everlasting sacrifice, and in their central crowning tower, an abiding monument of Salvation ; whilst, like ever-soaring piety, upward and still upward rose the ' star-y-pointing' spire, to seek its *finial* in that heaven where alone the soul's consummation *can* be sought."

The words of Coleridge, in comparing the Classic and Gothic modes of architecture, are remarkable : " The Greek art is beautiful. When I enter a Greek church, my eye is charmed, and my mind elated ; I feel exalted, and proud that I am a man. But the Gothic art is sublime. On entering a cathedral, I am filled with devotion and with awe ; I am lost to the actualities that surround me, and my whole being expands into the infinite ; earth and air, nature and art, all sweep up into eternity, and the only sensible impression left is, that I am nothing."

If, in describing the various eras of Gothic architecture, we seem to lay too little stress on its continental developments in France, Germany, and Italy, we are not to be understood as undervaluing the latter. On the contrary, we are ready to state that these continental developments were always in advance of the English a quarter of a century or more, and in quality and quantity perhaps, in magnificence and costliness, far surpassed those of our mother country. But the limit to which we have restricted ourselves in this brief historical sketch, scarcely permits our following the progress of architecture everywhere, and so we have thought proper to confine our attention to the English, as being nearer our own sympathies, less likely to confuse our readers with a multitude of examples, and, at the same time, containing all the essential characteristics, signally expressed, which constitute mediæval or Gothic architecture.

It is the custom to divide English Gothic as follows : *Early English*, from A. D. 1189 to 1307, or during the reigns of Henry II., Richard I., John, Henry III., and Edward I. *Decorated English*, from A. D. 1307 to 1377, or during the reigns of Edward II., Edward III., and Richard II. *Perpendicular English*, from A. D. 1377 to 1460, or during the reigns of Henry IV., V., and VI.

The first of these, which we shall call the style of the thirteenth century, is distinguished by long and narrow lancet-headed windows, employed singly or collectively ; being in the latter case separated by narrow piers. The heads are decorated with concentric tables or dripstones. The buttresses have much greater projection than in the Norman examples, where they were rarely larger than the pilasters of the classic temples. Large columns of this style are seldom seen, save in the form of a series of small ones clustered. Examples of this period are exceedingly beautiful, simple, and elegant in design, and delicate in execution, equally applicable to the modest village church and the noble abbey or cathedral ; remarkable in the one case for unpretending simplicity, and in the other for solemn and majestic grandeur.

The second of these divisions, which is called the Decorated, or middle pointed Gothic, may be classed as the style of the fourteenth century. This period excels all the others in point of beauty. It not only rivals the preceding in chastity, but surpasses it in richness, without being overburdened with the extravagant and unmeaning ornamentation of the styles which followed. In this the narrow, lancet-headed windows, grouped together, as in the former style, and separated by narrow piers, are clustered into one imposing window, with one arch surmounting the whole and filled up with tracery, composed in the most graceful combinations, in which are introduced cuspidations or foliations in nearly every possible variety. The increased richness of these windows warranted a corresponding decoration of the entire building. Enriched crockets, or bunches of carved leaves, were soon employed, running up the sloping angles of gables and spires, and terminating in an ornamental finial which surmounted the whole.* These ornaments, though chaste, were still superfluous, and soon degenerated into extravagant, unmeaning decoration, the invariable precursor of declining art. This was soon evident in the Perpendicular, whose origin dates at the close of the fourteenth century, and which prevailed till the almost total disuse of Gothic architecture in England. It was characterized by its excess of ornaments, forming a marked contrast with the former styles. The term Perpendicular was given it on account of the peculiar arrangement of the tracery in the window heads, and in the panels with which every surface was filled, this tracery being composed exclusively of upright bars connected by foliated heads. This name has, however, been objected to as of only partial application, and the term Horizontal suggested as more appropriate and significant of the general tendency of the style ; and this idea seems well founded, for here, instead of the uplifted arch and the uniform upward tendency, alluded to as features of the preceding styles, we have the depressed arch, low roof, square-headed windows and doorways, square hood mouldings and horizontal transoms, all imparting a flat and level appearance. Even spires were abandoned, elaborately finished towers being substituted, which were sometimes surmounted by lanterns.

King's College Chapel, Cambridge, and Henry the Seventh's Chapel at Westminster, are the most elaborate examples in England of the Perpendicular system. It is worthy of note that this style is so prevalent among the collegiate buildings of England, especially at Oxford and Cambridge, as, through association, to have become almost classic. Few eras

* For an early English design of the thirteenth century, see No. 32 ; while Design No. 33 is of the Decorative, or fourteenth century.

of building are so open to criticism as this; but its practical results are such that, perhaps, no other one is so endeared to the hearts of the English people. This may be owing partly to the fact that the Perpendicular, unlike the other styles, was not derived from the Continent, but is exclusively English in all its characteristics; the contemporary style in France being the Flamboyant, where the tracery seems to wave and flare like the wildest flames; and in Germany, the Geometrical, the tracery being composed merely of geometrical lines, infinitely combined from angular and circular elements, and foliated. The cathedrals of Beauvais, St. Ouen, and part of Rouen, may be considered the representative buildings of the Flamboyant; while those of Cologne and Strasburg occupy the same position in the geometrical style of Germany.

Domestic architecture in England may be said to have arisen in the time of Henry VII. With his reign was inaugurated an entire change in the life and habits of the English people. With his marriage the feuds of York and Lancaster ceased, and a long season of peace seemed about to follow the internal discords which had distracted the reigns of his predecessors. Previous to this period, domestic architecture had scarcely an existence, save in the form of fortified castles. Henry VIII. did much to revolutionize the art, for during his reign the Reformation was established in England, and the sacrilegious plunder and destruction of monasteries and religious houses, carried on under his orders, discouraged the erection of new, while it removed the old examples. But, while he was thus a destroyer of the works of antiquity, he was a liberal patron of the new architecture, and erected many palaces and civic buildings.

It is not surprising that, when a monarch initiated a movement of this kind, his subjects should continue it. Foremost in such works, therefore, was the great Cardinal Wolsey, by whose power and lavish expenditure were built some of the noblest residences and collegiate buildings in England.

Many novel features were introduced into domestic architecture to meet the new exigencies of the improved social life of those days: among the most prominent of these are bay and oriel windows, chimney stacks, roof ceilings, and panelled wainscots around interior walls.

The Italian style did not prevail extensively in England until some time after it had been established in France under Pierre Lescot, Philibert, Delorme, Jean Bullaut, and other architects of celebrity. In the reign of Henry VIII., and more especially in that of Elizabeth, owing to the increased intercourse with the Continent, Italian details began to work their way into English architecture. It was evident which way the finger of art was pointing. As the mixed architecture of Constantine formed a connecting link between heathen " classic " and Christian " Gothic," so the Elizabethan stood between Christian " Gothic " and the revival of the old classic forms. It has been remarked that, in the mausoleum of Westminster, the pointed style expired in a blaze of glory. It was like the setting of the sun, whose lingering rays play around and illuminate the mountain tops, when their great source has sunk below the horizon.

Holbein initiated the fashion for reviving the styles of Italy in England; and when Elizabeth ascended the throne she found her architectural realms distracted by a most fierce civil war. The buildings erected in her time are but so many lasting records of desperate actions between the antagonistic principles of the Gothic St. Peter's at York and the classic St. Peter's at Rome.

Perhaps the first indication of a tendency to revive the classic orders was exhibited by *Arnolfo di Cambio da Colle*, in his design for the Cathedral of Florence, which, however, is essentially an Italian Gothic composition in sentiment. But little progress was made in this direction till the time of Brunelleschi, who built the famous dome over that cathedral, and who may be said to be the father of the Italian style. From this period, the beginning of the 15th century, this style extended rapidly throughout Italy.

Italian Renaissance may be divided into three classes, named, from the cities in which they prevailed, Florentine, Roman, and Venetian. That of Florence is peculiar, especially that of her palaces. Strong, massive, and severe, they are rather fortresses than the residences of peaceful merchants. Nor was this appearance needless and deceitful; for the strength of these mansions was requisite for defence in the midst of the civil strifes and commotions which disturbed the peace of the State until the time of the Medicis. Florentine buildings excel in dignity those of Rome and Venice, but fall far short of them in lightness and elegance; they are inferior in refinement of detail, but surpass all others in imposing boldness.

" The buildings of Florence," says a French author, " appear to be not the work of ordinary men. We enter them with respect, expecting to find them inhabited by beings of a nature superior to ourselves. Whether the eye is arrested by monuments of the age of Cosmo de Medici, or of the times which preceded or followed it, all in this imposing city carries the imprint of grandeur and majesty. Frequent revolutions oblige the chief parties to consider their personal safety, along with the magnificence of their dwellings. Externally, they are examples of skilful union of grace with simplicity and massiveness. After Rome, Florence is the most interesting city to every artist."

The edifices of modern Rome are of a very different character from those of Florence ; they do not possess the massive appearance of the latter, but are distinguished for an air of lightness and elegance. This style forms a connecting link between the Florentine and Venetian ; for, while on the one hand it is less heavy and severe than the former, it is, on the other, not so gay and slight as the latter. Bramante, perhaps, was the founder of this style, and the principal examples are the great basilica of St. Peter's and the Farnese palace ; the former of which may justly be considered the great achievement of Renaissance. The original design was furnished by Bramante, but was altered by almost every architect employed upon the building. Bramante commenced the erection, but did not proceed far with the work ; the body of the church being the work of Peruzzi and San Gallo ; the dome, of Michael Angelo and Fontana ; the nave and west façade, of Carlo Maderno ; the colonnades, of Bernini. The plan was originally a Latin cross, which was changed by Michael Angelo into a Greek cross, and again to the Latin form by Carlo Maderno, called by an indignant and caustic critic, " the wretched plasterer from Como." A few of the dimensions of this building may not be uninteresting, and, in giving them, we shall compare them with those of St. Paul's, of London.

	ST. PETER'S.	ST. PAUL'S.
Whole length of church and porch,	729 feet.	500 feet.
Breadth of front with turrets,	364 "	180 "
Diameter of cupola,	189 "	145 "
Height from ground to top of cross,	437½ "	370 "
Top of highest statue on front,	175 "	135 "

As before stated, the Venetian Renaissance is characterized by its preëminent lightness and elegance. San Michele or Sansovino may be said to have been the founder of this school, and they were followed by Palladio, Scamozzi, &c. Good examples of these are the Library of St. Mark, the Pamphili palace, Verona, and the Chapel of St. Bernardino.

But Palladio is our model among Italian artists. His style, termed the Palladian, was soon adopted throughout a great part of the Continent, and introduced, in the reign of James I., into England by the celebrated Inigo Jones. In the early part of his practice, this architect had followed the mixed style before described as the Elizabethan, but on his return from a journey to Italy in 1619, he brought back with him the manner of the Palladian school, in which his principal works were executed, as the portico of old St. Paul's, Whitehall palace, York stairs, and the church of St. Paul, Covent Garden. Few of the works of his genius now remain; most of them having been destroyed by the great fire of 1666, or removed to make way for succeeding improvements. This great fire gave an opening for the newly adopted style of architecture, which perhaps would never otherwise have been obtained. Nor was it a small advantage that it received the favor of Sir Christopher Wren, who was undoubtedly a man of superior attainments in his profession.

Space will not allow us to enumerate the sixty churches, the palaces, and other public and private buildings erected by him; but we cannot pass over his *chef d'œuvre*, the Cathedral of St. Paul, without some brief description. This magnificent edifice not only furnishes us with a remarkable specimen of constructive skill, but with a grand example of Italian architecture, as applied to sacred purposes.

Tradition informs us that the site of this building was, at the time of the Roman rule in England, occupied by a temple dedicated to Diana. However this may be, it is certain that one of the earliest Christian churches in England was erected on this spot by King Ethelbert, who had been converted by St. Augustine. This church was destroyed by fire in 961, but was immediately rebuilt. In 1087 it was again consumed in a conflagration, which laid waste the greater part of the metropolis. At this time Maurice, Bishop of London, conceived the grand design of erecting the magnificent edifice which preceded the present cathedral. This was again much injured by fire in 1135, which consumed all of the building that was combustible. The enterprise of the age was not, however, to be repressed, even by such repeated disasters; for, in 1221, the central tower was finished, and in 1229 Bishop Niger undertook to rebuild the choir in a new style of architecture and with enlarged dimensions; this was completed in 1240. This edifice, previous to James I., had been twice struck by lightning and had undergone many changes and repairs; but in his reign it was found to be in a dilapidated condition, and, though large sums of money were collected and material provided for its repair, nothing was done till the reign of Charles I., when Inigo Jones was appointed to superintend the work, which was begun in 1633, and in the course of nine years a magnificent portico was erected on the west front, and the building newly cased in stone. During the time of Cromwell, however, the building was nearly ruined by being converted into stables and barracks. The regular government of the church being restored with the succeeding monarch, the Dean and Chapter proceeded immediately, under the direction of Sir John Durham, to remove all traces of the encroachments begun in 1663. Three years later, this unfortunate building again fell a prey to the flames, which consumed the roof, and so weakened the walls that they were deemed incapable of repair. It was determined to erect a new building, which was commenced in 1675, and in 1710 the last stone was laid by Mr. Christopher Wren, son of the architect. Thus, through a series of most unexampled misfortunes, this church was completed in thirty-five years, under the direction of one architect, and, by a remarkable coincidence, of one master mason, Mr. Strong, and under the auspices of one bishop of London, Dr. Henry Compton.

Of all Wren's pupils, only one attained great eminence, Nicholas Hawksmore, one of whose churches, that of St. Mary, Woolworth, is of considerable merit. The next architect of note, practising this style, was James Gibbs, the architect of St. Martin's-in-the-Fields and St. Mary's-le-Strand, both of which present many good features. Passing by many architects of less note, we may mention Sir William Chambers, who greatly excelled his contemporaries, and many of his predecessors of this school. His greatest work is Somerset House, a description of which we regret being compelled to omit.

Meanwhile, the French Renaissance was brilliantly developing itself in innumerable palaces and churches and civil buildings. In the palaces, especially, are displayed the most original invention and profoundest knowledge of the art of design ever lavished upon the Renaissance. It would be impossible to enumerate and detail all the examples of this era in France, but we would especially signalize the royal chateaux and palaces of Blois, Chambord, Chinonceaux, Fontainebleau, the Tuileries, and the extensions of the Louvre.

The London club houses exhibit some of the most happy attempts at Italian architecture, and are far preferable to ecclesiastical edifices built in this style; a fact arising not so much from the respective merits of the architects employed, as from the better adaptation of the style for that particular class of buildings. It has also of late been adopted for private mansions, both in town and country, for which it seems particularly fitted; but for ecclesiastical structures, colleges, &c., the Gothic designs are rapidly superseding the Italian, while for public buildings for government, and other secular purposes, the Grecian is generally regarded as preferable, though in the great Parliament Houses of London the Perpendicular style has been imitated by Sir Charles Barry.

Architecture, in our own country, has never taken any stand, or received especial attention till within the past few years. But in this brief time it has made unprecedented progress, and bids fair to advance at a much more rapid rate, so that before another century rolls by we shall undoubtedly be able to show an architecture which will be capable of taking its stand by the side of the great historical architectures of the world. To attain this end, we must not be mere copyists of those who have gone before. While we cull from the structures of all ages and countries those features which are applicable to our requirements, we must reject those which to us are without meaning or use, and, at the same time, add whatever may be suggested by the necessities of climate, habits, and education.

To us, then, architecture becomes the most important of the arts, as by it we are destined to express in monumental language our worthiness to occupy a place among the civilized nations of Christendom, and by every consideration, therefore, we urge that it receive, in our colleges and schools, that attention and cultivation to which it is eminently entitled. A knowledge of this art is abroad deemed no less essential than, among us, is that of music or any accomplishment.   In England, the youth who could not tell what style of architecture prevailed in any given country would be regarded as we would regard the American lad who is ignorant of an important era or event in our history.

Thus have we, briefly as might be, attempted some description of the rise and progress of this important art.   Its details are far too extensive to be more than glanced at in our space, and our only object has been to maintain and illustrate the idea that architecture is an art which, as its foundations are laid in utility, is eminently progressive.   A retrospect of its history cannot fail to impress the thoughtful student with the idea that its triumphs under so many and great difficulties demonstrate most satisfactorily its manifest destiny to continue its majestic growth and expansion, as we grow and expand in all the arts of peace and prosperity.   Conscious of our own inability worthily to display the beauties of our subject, we shall be amply repaid if by our effort any degree of attention may be attracted to this subject and, in the mind of our reader, our original position sustained, however imperfectly—that " architecture is the first and noblest of the arts."

ADVANTAGES OF A COUNTRY LIFE.

In this country, like those of Europe, more especially that portion inhabited by the Anglo-Saxon race, the inclinations of the people, save where perverted by unwholesome education, seem decidedly in favor of a rural life; already there are many families of culture and refinement who spend all their days in their country homes, or, if they leave them, they do so only for a few months in winter, when nature, disrobed of her more pleasing ornaments, with scourges of snow, and sleet, and bitter cold, drives even her most constant votaries to seek the social comforts of the city. But it is a source of rejoicing when they are reached by the march of spring from the dissipation and the artificialities of town life to the simpler and purer pleasures which she gives. There is another class, which, though compelled to spend the business hours of the day in the city, gladly hasten when these are over to peaceful homes, removed from the bustle and turmoil of the crowded town. This manner of living is becoming very popular, especially among the business community; and now that we have so many and ready means of communication between cities and their suburbs for many miles around, and at so trifling an expense, it is rather to be wondered at that more do not adopt it. The objection that too much time is thus lost in travelling to and fro is not well founded, since it actually requires but little more to reach a country place twenty miles from town than to go from an office in Wall Street to a residence in the upper part of the city.

It seems scarcely necessary at this day to bring forward any formal arguments in favor of country life. It has beeen the favorite theme of

philosophers and poets in all times. Its pure and elevating influences, its
comfortable ease, its simplicity and cheapness, have been urged again and
again in grave essays and pleasant pastoral and bucolic meditations. Yet
there is one consideration to which we, by permission, wish briefly to draw
the attention of our readers. We refer to that of health. It is often declared that the human race, at least in this country, is degenerating ; and
there appears to be some foundation for this remark as applied to our
large towns. We look at a tall, muscular, well-developed form, in all its
rare physique, rather as the heritage of some heroic past than an expression of life such as we now lead, which seems rather to produce a
weak-eyed, narrow-chested race, with sallow complexions, weak constitu-
tions, and, in short, but little physical force. We rather run to brains, and
are content to *read* the exploits of Achilles and Hector in our classics,
rather than emulate their strength and prowess. We touch with delicate
hands the great, rude armor in the Tower, and wonder at the huge-limbed
generation which wore it as we do our silk and broadcloth. We are thus
forced to inquire why so marked a deterioration has taken place. It has
been said that we Americans are not acclimated in this New World ; that
this decline has been constantly going on from the days of our forefathers.
But we need not go back far in time or deep in science to account for this
change. The secret lies in our artificial lives. We do not breathe enough
of the pure, fresh air of heaven ; the little exercise we take is spasmodic
and business-like ; and, worse than all, we are irregular in our habits, im-
prudent in diet and exposure, and indulge too freely in the well-known dissipations of city life. In many cases, perhaps in the majority, the leaving
of town in the summer is but another phase of the same life, with simply
a change of scene from the city to some fashionable watering place, with a
repetition of the routine of dress, suppers, and late hours. Such life is
unnatural and injurious, simply because it is artificial. If, then, we would
leave the city, not for fashion, but for prudence ; if we would really recupe-
rate our strength and energies, we must seek the repose of a genuine country home, and those remedies which nature provides with a lavish but
never-failing hand.

Let us presume that, influenced by these and the many other considerations which will suggest themselves to the intelligent reader, it is decided

to build a home somewhere in the country. Where shall it be? A homestead—for we would not build for ourselves alone, but for those who may succeed us—naturally suggests a place somewhat isolated and independent, rather than a residence on the street of a country town or village: it should be complete in itself, liberal in extent, and free from all intrusions—in fine, a little principality. Do not suppose that such a country home can be secured only by the wealthy, and that those of more moderate means can expect nothing better than a house, elbowed by neighbors, in the closer suburbs of a town, or at most a lot in a village, where one must be content with half an acre of land, and submit ease and domestic quiet to the scrutiny of tattling gossips and the curiosity of the vulgar. The inconveniences and petty annoyances of such life are so well known, that one of limited means, who would make himself a home in the country, would do well to inquire if it is necessary to submit to them, or if they cannot economically be avoided.

It is generally thought that the establishment of a country place, with several acres of land, involves a great original outlay and a large increase of taxes, which, added to the interest on the investment, makes a heavy rent; that a residence of this kind involves the necessity of keeping a horse and conveyance of some kind, and a man servant to take care of them. Now we reply by reminding our readers, that six acres in the country can generally be had for a smaller sum than half an acre in a village, with a proportional difference in taxes. Again, we may safely consider that the produce of a little farm, if prudently managed, will not only support both man and horse, but, with attention, can be made a source of profit, and supply to its owner many luxuries of a superior kind and at little cost. Moreover, in improving the place and elaborating its culture, he obtains a nobler profit than this—an inheritance of happiness and content for his children.

Our country abounds in most interesting and picturesque scenery, embracing ocean, river, lake, and mountain, easy of access, habitable and healthy; and, though filled with delightful villa sites, is too frequently suffered to remain neglected and unpeopled in its choicest nooks. Those proposing to build in the country, are much more likely to select some spot destitute of almost every natural embellishment. There appears to be little appreciative aptitude for the association of homes with natural beauty. If the ground is entirely level, free from rocks, hills, dales, water, and trees, it is claimed and occupied quite as readily as some site equally accessible and adorned with all the picturesque or gentle loveliness of nature—perhaps even more so. People like to *visit* such places, but they *will not live* there. A fine view and romantic scenery seem to be secondary considerations to other and less elevated advantages, such as neighbors, proximity to railway stations, &c. It must be granted, however, that rural taste has greatly improved since the days of Downing. Until the present time the professions of architecture and landscape gardening have been nearly new among us, and practised mostly by strangers; but now that so many young Americans of intelligence and culture are studying and assuming these professions, we may reasonably hope to see more interest taken in them, and the happy revolution, so long delayed, at length realized and effected.

Giving these reflections their due weight, let us now proceed to select a site. Accessibility, neighborhood, and health, are, of course, primary considerations, and in most instances it would be improper to sacrifice any of these, even to the desire to live in the midst of natural beauty. Fortunately, however, we are rarely obliged to go far before we find plenty of locations which combine natural beauty with all the practical advantages we can wish for. We are naturally attracted by fertility of soil; but if we do not propose to establish a productive farm, simply for the sake of its productiveness, it would be well to inquire, before settling in any such locality, about the healthfulness of it; for the most fertile spots are frequently the most insalubrious. Burton, in his "Anatomy of Melancholy," quaintly draws our attention to this fact. "The best soil commonly yields the worst air; a dry, sandy plat is fittest to build upon, and such as is rather hilly, than a plain full of downs; a cotswold country, as being most commodious for hawking, hunting, wood, waters, and all manner of pleasures." After enumerating many such tracts of land, he goes on to say that Stephanus, a Frenchman, agrees with "Cato, Varro, Columella, those ancient rusticks," in the idea that the front of a house should "stand to the south," and approves especially of "the descent of a hill south or southeast, with trees to the north, so that it will be well watered; a condition in all sites which must not be omitted, as Herbastein incul-cates."

It is an erroneous idea to suppose that your house must necessarily be approached by the highway. If you own to the main road, you may, of course, have your gate entrance on your own land ; if not, you have only to obtain a right of way from your neighbor, and continue your carriage road through his grounds. There is rarely any difficulty in the way of obtaining this privilege. In selecting a site, it is well to have higher ground on the northern and western sides to screen your house in winter from chilling winds. Do not allow picturesque rocks, or wild forest trees to influence your decision against any site, as, in case such features appear too rude for your notions of the elegant repose and gentleness which should surround your domicil, your landscape gardener can always reconcile them, domesticate them, as it were ; in short, make them beautiful and appro-priate ; and your architect, if a man of taste and education, can arrange your house to combine gracefulness with any peculiarities of country, and give it such character as will be congruous with surrounding scenery.

It is well to warn our readers against adopting any plan of a model house, or the design in some book, which there may present a pleasing ex-terior, without careful consideration of its adaptability to their grounds. Such designs may, perhaps, be suitable in every respect for their intended site ; but when placed on a different one, may be quite the reverse. In the one case, the kitchen, hall, and minor offices may occupy the least de-sirable exposures, and obstruct no views, but by their position shelter the house from wind and storm ; in the other, all may be changed. None of the advantages of the new situation will be improved. The drawing room, perhaps, looks out upon the farm yard ; the dining room, with a fine bay window, from which originally might have been enjoyed three distinct views, commands an uninterrupted prospect of the stable, the kitchen gar-den, or some low, flat, and uninteresting country ; while really the only pleasantly situated room is, fortunately for the servants, appropriated to their avocations. So, too, the external appearance of the house may be little fitted for its new position. It may be Italian in style, adapted to a level, grassy lawn, pleasantly shaded by majestic elms and maples. Your site, however, is perhaps picturesque, covered wildly with oak, and cedar, and larches, full of sudden surprises of form and color.   To place an Italian villa here, is like adorning a wigwam with the Venus de Milo.   Let us rather, for such a locality, adopt *motives* from the irregular Gothic, with its pointed roofs, lofty towers and chimneys, and varied outline; or from some other congenial styles.

Though architecture is comparatively so new, and has received so little earnest and serious attention from us as a nation, that we can scarcely be said to have any styles or systems peculiarly our own, yet there have grown out of our necessities certain idiosyncracies of building and design, which are doubtless in the way of establishing that long-dreamed-of aim, an *American style*.   In the absence of such a style, we have been too apt to borrow bodily and without change from those of foreign countries, which are the expressions of the especial needs and social conditions of those countries and those alone.   It is certainly our duty to introduce from abroad methods and manners of design, so far as they meet our wants.   But it would be worse than folly, in building an English cottage, for example, not to have a veranda, because its prototypes in England have none; we have an actual need for such an appliance in our dry and sunny climate, and it is out of such need that must proceed a distinctive feature of American cottage architecture.   While, therefore, we avail ourselves of all the good points of the different styles, and make ourselves familiar with them, we should not so venerate as to fear to change them when we find that our necessities require it.

Thus, doubtless, we are building up styles of our own, taught, as other founders of styles have been, by precedents in older countries or times.   Our climates, habits, and materials differ enough from those of Europe to demand different architectural arrangements and treatments. For instance, most of our country abounds in timber, a most excellent building material.   In this respect we differ from Europe, where wood is much more rare and expensive.   Yet, in our careless and blind way, we have proceeded to copy in this material, as exactly as we can, the details of foreign architecture, which were intended to express the constructive capacities of stone or brick.   The temples of Greece, built of marble, with their ponderous shafts, entablatures, and pediments, have all been repeated in this country in wood, painted white, and blocked in courses to imitate stone, and often sanded to perfect the intended deception. So, too, with the feudal castles of England; they are here revived, and, with their frowning battlements and towers, are built of the same improper material. The grand old massive cathedrals and churches of by-gone days have not escaped the same indignity. How absurd it must seem to a stranger to see a Roman arch, key-stone and all, imitated in wood, or a buttress of hollow woodwork, or a simple cottage painted to resemble stone. Fortunately, our people are awakening to the folly of this unmeaning imitation, and where stone is adopted it is treated as stone, and where wood is employed we are properly beginning to show details adapted to the material, such as projecting roofs and framed brackets descending from the rafters, with a lighter and more fitting construction of verandas and balconies.

But there are some portions of our country, as in most of the Eastern and Middle States, where wood is by no means abundant. In many localities we have barely enough left for shade, and some of the finest sites have been stripped of their luxuriant and noble growth of trees. We have been wastefully extravagant of our timber, and should now sometimes be at a loss for building materials, had not nature provided another near at hand, and in such profusion that we are really compelled to use it or to remove it from our way. This, we need hardly say, is stone, which is constantly growing in favor and use.

People who build in the country are often like those who plant trees, whose full luxuriance they themselves can never expect to enjoy; and the children who come after them reap the benefit of the generous forethought. When we have procured a rude piece of ground, cleared it, planted it, beautified it, constructed the roads, and erected house, stable, and all the fixtures of a homestead thereon, we cannot realize from its sale the value of our time, trouble, and outlay. The reward is in the comfort of our declining years, and the happiness of our descendants. A country house is a *cheap luxury*, which we buy, build, or inherit for ourselves and our children. Such being the intention, evidently it should be built of the most durable materials. Nor is stone so expensive when we regard its use in a proper light; nay, we may even say it is cheaper in the end. Take, for example, Design No. 9, which cost about $5,000. The owner says his house is perfectly dry, stands in the best manner, and requires much less fuel to warm it than he has been in the habit of using in frame houses of the same size. With this may be compared a house very similar and of about the same cost, but built of wood, whose owner declares that he is obliged to paint the outside every two or three years to preserve the woodwork and make it appear respectable. Frequent repairs are also necessary on the exterior; some of the timbers have sprung, the floors are uneven, and the walls and ceilings cracked. His roof, which is of shingles, he says frequently leaks, and a new one will soon be required. These repairs demand no small outlay each year, all of which, with the great attendent inconveniences, might have been avoided, had he built of stone with a slate roof. A prejudice has extensively prevailed against stone houses on account of their dampness; an objection which has not been unfounded, but which is now wholly removed by building the outside walls hollow; that is, using brick furring within a few inches of the external wall, and fastened to it by iron anchors. The old plan was to nail wooden strips to the inside of stone walls, and lath and plaster upon these; but this affords no protection from the dampness. Again, should the outside wall settle, the plaster must be cracked, while the brick furring would settle with the stone; so, too, the wood furring is apt to shrink from having the warm room on one side and the cold or damp wall on the other.

In Design No. 9, already alluded to, the brick furring is used, thus making it a house within a house; it has an outside stone wall 18 inches thick, a hollow space of 3 inches, and a brick wall of 4 inches. The plastering is done on the inside surface of the brick, consequently no lathing is required, and but two coats of plaster instead of three. This avoids the difficulties spoken of, and is proof from vermin and fire. The hollow space acts as a perfect ventilating flue throughout the house, and by having outside registers, which can be closed in cold weather, and a register at the floor and ceiling of each room, a constant circulation may be obtained. It is well to continue this hollow space up to the roof rafters, and the air, following the space between these rafters up to the scuttle between roof and ceiling, will keep the attic perfectly cool in summer.

As to the durability of stone, no argument is, of course, required. We have only to visit older countries to find walls which have stood hundreds of years, and there is no reason why we may not have them of equal durability. There is an air of dignity and stability about a stone structure, and age, so far from being destructive to it, serves only to increase its solidity and improve its appearance. What can be more beautiful and picturesque than an old stone edifice, overgrown with moss and shaded by noble trees, all indicating that time has but improved the work of art? What would be the case with a wooden structure under similar circumstances? "Decay's effacing fingers" are constantly at work, and walls of wood offer an effectual field for their labors. Frequent and expensive repairs present but feeble resistance to the progress of dilapidation. The building must crumble and fall in the process of a few generations. The wood rots, the roof leaks, the walls and ceilings are cracked by the shrinking and settling of the timbers. With such facts known to us, there can be no doubt which of these two materials is the most suitable and economical. Moreover, vines, the pleasantest adornments of a cottage wall, ivy and woodbine, with which nature seems to take possession of the works of our hands and tenderly take them to her bosom, cling without detriment to stone, while, attached to wood, they are the readiest agents of decay.

But, whatever material you use, remember the maxim, "Truthfulness in building." Let the treatment correspond with the substance with which you build. Do not carve stone details out of wood, nor, with false pride, attempt to make it resemble something else. Above all, do not try to hide the face of stonework with plaster, painted to appear as if dressed. One need never blush at any expression of truthfulness in his dwelling, however homely that expression may be; but falsehood and imitation give indisputable evidence of vulgarity of taste—*snobbishness* is the modern word.

Having selected the site and chosen the material, the next step is to procure a design best suited to the wants and conveniences of your family, improving the advantages of the finest exposures and views, protecting yourself from the inclement points in winter, and excluding from sight the objectionable portions of the grounds. And we cannot reiterate too often the injunction, that in external treatment the house should harmonize with the surrounding scenery. Can you furnish this design yourself? Decidedly not, unless you have spent years in study and practice. Or, possessing good ideas yourself, can a carpenter or mason carry them into a successful realization? We think not, for such men, however excellent their workmanship may be, cannot be supposed to sympathize with your more refined notions of domestic elegance and comfort. They must, to a certain extent, realize them, but they cannot understand the *sentiment* which should pervade a design, and are content to copy and imitate, instead of composing and adapting according to the necessities of the problem laid before them.

The planning of a country house is something so peculiar and intricate, and demands careful study of so many outlying considerations, that none but an architect can do it justice. In a city house, to produce a merely respectable work, perhaps less judgment is required, as the process of design must be more or less conventional, and a certain degree of sameness is unavoidable, the same laws and requirements holding good, to a large extent, in all cases. Each house must stand on a fixed street line, and the general shape and arrangement must be somewhat similar. For the most part, it seems that the only room for the architect to display his originality is in elaborating his façade; and the restrictions of his street line, his twenty-five feet front, the city ordinances, and the conventionality of his plan, must act as a great check upon liberty of design. The only way in which he can vary the external appearance of his house from that of his neighbor, is in height of walls and stories, in material, and the detailed treatment of the uniform requirements. And even this variety must be restricted by the necessity of so harmonizing the façade with those in its neighborhood, as to prevent lines of one character, though good in themselves, from being nullified or injured by lines of another character, equally good, which may exist in proximity.

We do not mean to assert that all the buildings in a block should be uniform in all particulars, for irregularity is one of the chief beauties of architecture; but we do mean to say that one building should not be erected without some regard to harmony with those in the neighborhood, any more than a country house should be built in a style at variance with the character of surrounding scenery. To illustrate this idea with respect to harmonious city architecture, we would refer the reader to Design No. 30.

In the country, however, we are not restrained by any of these laws, but the field for design is as boundless as the variety of nature; and so is it not in bad taste to build in the country, on some choice, picturesque, or beautiful spot, a house thoroughly adapted to the city in all its details? Yet this is the most popular mode of country building. The vignette on Design No. 18, shows somewhat of this tendency, except that the roofs are usually flat, and that there are five windows in front. The interior corresponds exactly with that of a city house; having one large room with sliding doors, and two windows at either end. These, with the door, quite overload the front, and give to it an unpleasant aspect of formality. There is an obvious necessity for two windows in a city house, there being no other access for light; but here, where side windows are always added, giving twice the light that is obtained in a city drawing room, the rooms become crowded with useless windows, which give ready access to an overplus of cold in winter and heat in summer; and, as if to render the whole thing more absurd, many of these unnecessary openings are covered all the year round with blinds. No good reasons can be assigned for such concessions to fashion, and nothing can justify the conversion of a quiet rural retreat into a formal town-house. That others have done so, and continue to do so, is no excuse. From their folly let us learn wisdom.

The designs contained in this work are not intended for model houses, to be copied for all localities, but simply to show how important it is to have an original design adapted to the peculiarities of site, and how entirely erroneous it is to stereotype houses, all over the country, as has been the custom. Having selected your architect, let him visit the proposed site, that with careful study he may discover all its natural advantages, its exposures, its views, its facilities for drainage, &c., as also the disadvantages with which he must contend. Make him acquainted with your general wants, the height of your ceilings, the size and number of your rooms, and what other little details you may wish to have carried out; but the main arrangement, both inside and out, you will do well to leave wholly to him. This done, he will make you a sketch, embodying an architectural interpretation or modification of your ideas, and submit it for your approval and examination. Then, all further alterations and details of plan which may be desired being thoroughly understood by both parties, the proper working drawings will be made, subject to all the conditions of the amended design, careful specifications and contracts will be drawn up, and the whole submitted to the competition of several contractors, all of whom are known to be responsible. Thus the cheapest, readiest, and most effectual means of putting your intentions into execution will be obtained. During the progress of the work, in addition to these working drawings, consisting of the floor plans and elevations, the architect will furnish enlarged detail drawings, showing sections of external mouldings, &c., together with the internal members not seen on the other working drawings, and what other constructive explanations may be needed. That the true intent and meaning of the design may be carried out, it is essential that the architect should superintend the construction. He should visit the building during its erection, and explain the designs, and render the contractor all necessary architectural information.

Paul Schulze del.

DESIGN Nº 1.

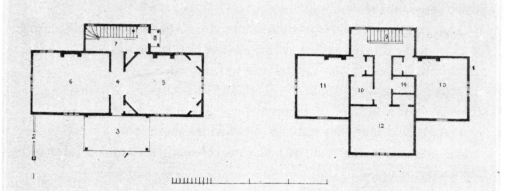

DESIGN No. 1.

THIS design may serve the double purpose of a Gate Lodge and Farm House, though the drawing was rather intended for the former, and to represent an entrance to grounds on which we propose to erect a mansion.

The architecture is of simple character, suitable for the adjunct of a neat and spacious villa, yet sufficiently pretentious to prepare us for yet greater elegance as we proceed.

There are but two rooms on the first floor—the one a kitchen, and the other a sitting room or parlor. These two rooms, being opposite each other, are entered by folding doors, which when open communicate through the hall, thus throwing the entire floor into one suite.

The stairs, it will be observed, are located in such a manner as to leave the main hall unobstructed, thus removing the thoroughfare from the body of the house ; which object is also facilitated by a rear entrance on first floor and basement.

The second floor is very spacious, being much larger than the first on account of its projection over the entrance porch. By this means we have an additional chamber, making three in all each provided with a closet. On the right is a large linen closet, while on the left is placed what may be deemed an unusual and perhaps unnecessary convenience for a gate lodge—a bath room. Certainly there is the truest and most humane economy in providing servants and all those under our protection with the means of enjoying the great blessing of cleanliness, which is the first advance to civilization, refinement, and self-respect.

The windows of this second story are somewhat elevated, but are so placed to avoid cutting through the wall plate, or horizontal beam on which the roof rests, thereby weakening the building and increasing the expense.

With reference to Gate Lodges it may be remarked, that for places of moderate size such an appendage is pretentious and inappropriate. Too frequently we meet with an ostentatious lodge standing but a few paces from a modest dwelling, displaying a singular disregard of the obvious proprieties of life, without the excuse of usefulness. When the domain is extensive, and the residence properly located at a distance from the highway, an entrance lodge is highly appropriate and necessary, not only as a home for the gardener or farmer, where one of the family may always be in readiness to open and close the gates on the arrival of carriages, but as a protection to the place from the trespass of improper persons. Lodges may not be considered objectionable features when attached to places situated near the road, if the grounds are so planned and planted as to afford a proper amount of retirement from observation, and through the contrivance of the landscape gardening are made to appear more ample than they are. It is proposed to presently treat this subject of artificial perspective more at large.

Gate Lodges, as well as all other outbuildings, should, in their architectural treatment, partake somewhat of the style of the dwellings to which they are subordinate, but should in all cases be of a much simpler and perhaps of a more rustic character, as is befitting their modest office in the duties of household hospitality.

Estimate.—A Gate Lodge of this character could be built, under favorable circumstances, for from $800 to $1,000.*

* The following estimates include simply the mason's and carpenter's contracts.

Paul Schulze del.

DESIGN Nº 2.

DESIGN No. 2.

THE architect, in the discharge of his duties, is called upon to perform many severe tasks, but none more arduous than that of remodelling a country house, where he has to contend with the blunders and conventional distortions of " carpenters' architecture," to develop harmony out of discord, beauty out of ugliness, elegance out of the commonplace. Consider, reader, how you would appal an artist of recognised ability by applying to him to finish a picture commenced by one who had no more exalted idea of art than what might be acquired in the æsthetic meditations of house and sign painting; how you would shock a Hosmer or Powers by presenting for the finishing touches of their delicate chisels some rude sculpture attempted by an ordinary stonecutter. Would not the enthusiastic devotee of art wonder at your applying to such a source at the first, and still more when you would have him remodel and give to the ill-used marble character and expression ? Would he not, with all the eloquence inspired by his profession, remonstrate against your course in employing at the outset so inferior an artist, and earnestly set forth the difficulty of overcoming the many radical errors of the inexperienced tyro ? Would he not justly fear the injury he might do his own reputation by undertaking it at all ? Yet every day do we see men of wealth, and sometimes of intelligence, applying to ignorant builders, self-styled architects, to furnish designs for cottages, villas, or even mansions of great pretension.

For in that very worthy class of mechanics, some one may be found in every town, whose ambition or conceit has so led him astray from his true path, that we find him rushing in where artists might fear to tread, and leaving such traces of his folly as render the whole neighborhood hideous with the whims of his untutored imagination. He may "draught a plan" which on paper will deceive the eye of the client, and actually persuade him into the delusion that, as it is the composition of a "practical man," it will appear well when erected. For many have thus unfortunately built in haste, and repented at leisure.

The usual resort in such cases, after the building is spoiled, is to apply to an architect of recognized ability to remodel the work. With perplexed brain the professional man sets about his expensive and difficult task of correcting that which, had it in the outset been properly done, would have saved both himself and the owner much vexation and annoyance.

Design No. 2 represents a cottage which the author remodelled for Dr. C. W. Ballard, at Noroton Darien, Conn. The original structure, which is shown in the vignette at the left, was purchased by its present owner of a farmer, and is a good specimen of the small farm houses or cottages of Connecticut. Devoid of beauty, grace, or expression, pinched and contracted in all its features, placed usually in the most unattractive spot, directly on the road, with a formal avenue of cherry trees leading up to the door. These structures are indefinitely multiplied in the rural districts, and are the natural homes of a thrifty and enterprising, but unimaginative, tasteless, and perhaps overworked people.

The ceilings are low, and the rooms small, crooked, and without ventilation; green wooden shutters *adorn* the windows, and the outer walls, if painted at all, are sure to be of a staring white or a brilliant red; yet within the shadow of the humblest of these cottages have been born and reared some of the most distinguished men of our history. Perhaps there still exist, under such unpromising shelter, many "hands which the rod of empire might have swayed." Let it be our task to surround them with such refining influences as will render them better fitted for the higher and nobler life, and will smooth for them the upward path. Let us, in short, give them *homes* which may refine and elevate as well as shelter.

Yet, when a man of true taste and refinement comes in possession of so unpromising a subject as this, our drawing, we think, proves that with no considerable expense, effects of a striking and elegant nature may be produced, and the wholly unprepossessing building, under proper hands, be made comparatively a model of beauty no less than of convenience.

The vignette on the right represents an ornamental well curb, and shows how that appendage, ordinarily so awkward and ungainly, may be made a pleasing feature of the grounds, and an earnest of the elegant hospitality of the residence to which it is attached. The well, ever grateful in its associations with memories of dripping coolness, in the parched summer time, of mid-day repose, and of many an office of friendship in the presenting of the cup of cold water to the weary traveller, should always be adorned with the most affectionate fancies at our command.

Paul Schulze, del.

DESIGN No 3.

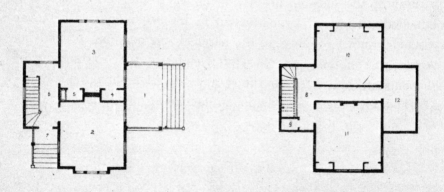

0   20

DESIGN No. 3.

It is often imagined by those who desire to build economically, that beauty is an extravagance in which they cannot indulge, and therefore that a cheap cottage can necessarily have no pretensions to elegance, and barely suffice for the comfort and shelter of its occupants: no higher aim is attempted. This error arises from the false but prevalent idea that beauty and grace are entirely extraneous considerations, rather matters of ornament than proportion and symmetry of parts. For this reason many small houses, whose owners wish to render them objects of taste, are loaded down with unmeaning and expensive decorations, or so frittered away with cheap and ready expedients of boards sawn, cut, planed, and otherwise tortured into utter uselessness and absurdity, that the entire building becomes subordinate to its appendages, and the arrangement of its important masses is entirely lost sight of.

When the architect is called upon to design a very cheap building, he must be content to express his art in the fitness and proportion of all its parts; he must combine beauty with the strictest utility. Thus in this design, which was prepared for a gentleman in Connecticut, we have availed ourselves of the necessity of providing an artificial shade by simply projecting the eaves; this at once gives to the cottage a pleasant expression of shelter. The windows naturally require more protection from the sun and rain than the walls, and, therefore, over these the eaves are extended one foot more than elsewhere, and in consequence of this extra projection require brackets for support.

The veranda in our climate has become a national feature, and is certainly a most useful as well as ornamental appendage to a house. In this particular instance its introduction adds much to the beauty and comfort of the cottage. An ornamental rail protects its sides, while strong timber brackets assist in supporting the superincumbent weight.

The bay window, always a charming feature, blends harmoniously with the design, and, by its intervention, breaks up a formal regularity of wall, both outside and in. Though of small dimensions, it not only materially enlarges the *actual* size of the room to which it is attached, but apparently, through the perspective effect always produced by an outward break of this kind, opens a much larger space within than it really does.

These then, it will be observed, are matters of practical utility in protection, construction, and comfort, and the only feature that seems superfluous is the ornament on the roof. This, it is granted, according to strict rules of economy, might be omitted, for there can be no other than an æsthetical use attributed to it,

especially as the chimney, from its central position, has the effect
of relieving the roof and sustaining the soaring tendency of the
lines; still, to project a pattern like this against the sky on any
ridge, certainly gives a very desirable and emphatic quality of
crispiness to the design.

The first floor is arranged with sitting and dining rooms; the
latter having two closets, one for china, and the other containing a
dumb waiter which communicates with the kitchen below. The
second floor comprises three good bedrooms and a linen closet.
This story, for purposes of economy, is low, the side walls being
six feet high to the roof, whence the ceiling starts at an angle,
somewhat less than that of the roof, making the ceiling flatter
and forming an air space between it and the roof, which protects the rooms from external changes of atmosphere. This object is also facilitated by the ceiling being deafened, thus making
these rooms as comfortable as if they had an entire story over
them.

It will be seen by this that we contrive to obviate that great
objection commonly entertained against houses of a story and a
half in height, that the bedrooms are like ovens in summer, and
like refrigerators at other seasons. We would take advantage of
this opportunity strongly to recommend the use of deafening in all
floors; as it is not only serviceable in preventing the passage of
sound from one room to another, but in binding the floors together
and rendering them stiffer and more solid. Little expenditures
like these, judiciously made, will never be regretted when the
house is finished, since they soon pay for themselves in a saving of
fuel, to say nothing of the protection they give from dampness,
heat, and cold.

Estimate.—This design, though on a somewhat larger scale,
was built for John W. Shedden, Esq., on the Morris and Essex
Railroad, about one mile beyond South Orange, N. J. With
an arrangement as shown, it would cost from $800 to $1,000,
being of about the same dimensions as design No. 1.

DESIGN № 4.

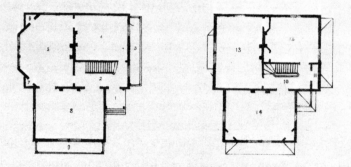

DESIGN No. 4.

THIS design is for a cheap cottage, with commodious accommodations, and of pleasing external appearance, uniting economy and convenience. It was intended for a village lot in Stamford, Conn., of 75 feet frontage, of which the principal facade of the house was to occupy 25 feet, giving an equal space on either side. The house is of two stories, with a basement and attic, affording a spacious drawing room, library, and dining room on the first floor, with six large chambers on the second and in the attic. The bedrooms for servants, with kitchen and store cellars, are in the basement. The kitchen communicates with the dining room by a dumb waiter, through one of the closets in the latter apartment. The opposite closet in this room is intended for china and table linen A large linen closet is shown on the second story. Instead of verandas we have adopted terraces with canopy roofs over them, supported by brackets, which are much more economical than posts or columns, though perhaps not as commodious. The entrance porch, which is at the side, has a balcony over it, with access from the second story hall.

One peculiarity of this design is the truncated or "gambrel" roof, used to give space to the upper rooms, and to lessen the apparent height of the structure, which, if composed of three entire stories, would be too lofty for the amount of ground it occupies. This expedient also gives a pleasing variety to the lines of the roof, a feature usually so bare of interest. This differs from the common "gambrel" roof of New England farm houses and homesteads, in the projection of the eaves, and in the truncation of the gable ends, which makes a hipped roof of the upper slope, giving to the general outline a pleasant resemblance to the rustic hayrick, and affording a more immediate shelter to the gable windows from the sun and rain. The decorated barge boards at the eaves produce shadows, relieve the walls, and serve as a protection to the sides of the house, thus forming a useful and ornamental appendage, often cheaper than brackets. The ballustrades of perforated plank, around the balconies and terraces, partake of the style of the house, corresponding with the barge boards, and contributing to the harmony of the design.

One great advantage architects possess in this country is the strong contrast of light and shade produced by our clear atmosphere, which assists materially in producing good effects in building. The introduction of irregularities, such as projections of roofs, canopies, verandas, and bay windows, together with the intersections of gables, dormers, and the height of chimneys, serve to break up the bare formality of the usual barn-like outline, and to obtain the ever varying sentiment and expression which the *great Architect* never fails to give to all his rocks and hills. Light and shade are the happiest instruments of design, and most easily procured in our climate, and are ever ready to give new life and spirit to forms properly managed for their play. The repetition of the perforated barge boards in shadow against the walls, ever making new interpretaions of its patterns, shows how tenderly and delicately nature assists the sympathetic architect.

In cities, where the great value of land almost precludes the designer from availing himself of opposing masses of light and shade, which can be produced in emphasis only by costly irregularities of plan, and large reëntering angles of outer walls, it seems necessary to resort to some other expedient where delicacy of line is not considered a sufficient substitute for the more massive effects of *chiaro-oscuro*. The luxurious and sensuous Mahometans, not content with the more serious and sober habits of the North in design, not only were in the habit of breaking their sky lines with pierced parapets and lily patterns, with swelling domes, with endless pinnacles and fantastic minarets, to a degree never thought of elsewhere, but availed themselves of strong and vivid contrasts of bright colors. It would be well for us to take a lesson from the Eastern nations in this respect, and while we repudiate perhaps, as undignified, any complete adaptation of their endless fancies of form, to study their picturesque use of external colors, and let the walls of our cities assume new life and meaning by contrasting tints of various bricks and stones, and the introduction of brilliant tiles and slates of different quarries. This source of design, if used with discretion in our Metropolitan structures, would effect the happiest results, and preserve their architecture from inanity and insipidity. But in the country, where growth of shapes and forms is unchecked by any considerations of economy of space, it seems almost superfluous to use decorative external color to any very great extent, certainly, we think, never for its own sake, as in the town; but so far as it may serve to protect wooden surfaces, to assist in giving expression to form, and to harmonize masses with the nature around, its employment is of great value. It is, then, important to know by what rule we are to be governed in the use of colors under these circumstances. It is evident that the general tint covering the plain surface of a small house surrounded by trees, should be light and cheerful, warm in its tone, and of a neutral rather than positive character, as the latter very readily harmonizes with nature. But do not fall into the opposite extreme, and paint your house white, which is no color at all, always cold and glaring, and makes an ugly *spot* in any landscape; we find nothing there to warrant so forcible an intrusion. A white building might not be so objectionable in the city, where we have no nature to assimilate to and work with; but in the country nothing but snow and chalk cliffs are white, and these put out the eyes by their intensity. Choose, then, any of the hundred soft, neutral tints which may afford to your house the cheerfulness or dignity it may require. These are to be determined especially by its location and size. A house of large and commanding proportions, occupying a conspicuous position in the scenery, would present a ludicrous appearance if painted a light color; while one of smaller size, subordinate to its natural surroundings, and well shaded by trees, would, if painted dark, give an impression of gloom.

Having selected the general tint, the trimmings should be of a darker shade of the same, or a deeper color, to give them prominence, and assist in bringing out the design. The roof, when not covered with slate, should resemble it somewhat in color, and the window blinds, when used at all, should be darker even than the window dressings, and should assimilate in color to the general tone of the house.

It is always advisable to consult the architect as to his views in this matter of color, since an improper application of paint might quite nullify the effect of his design, and render that ridiculous which was intended to be dignified, small which was intended to appear large, and obtrusive which was intended to be modest and retiring.

By a judicious subordination of various tints, many errors and incongruities of style may be lessened or quite concealed, and the good points of design be properly emphasized and made to assume a worthy prominence in the composition.

Estimate.—This design would cost, under favorable circumstances, about $3,000.

Paul Schulze, del.

DESIGN Nº 5.

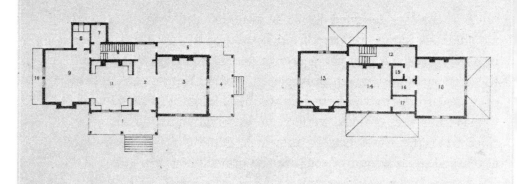

0   20   20

DESIGN No. 5.

FIRST FLOOR PLAN.

1. Veranda.
2. Main Hall, 9 × 18.
3. Drawing Room, 18 × 20.
4. Veranda.
5. Balcony.
6. Staircase Hall.
7. Store Room.
8. Butler's Pantry.
9. Dining Room, 16 × 18.
10. Balcony.
11. Library, 15 × 18.

SECOND FLOOR PLAN.

12. Hall.
13. Bedroom, 16 × 18.
14. Do. 15 × 18.
15. Linen Closets.
16. Closets.
17. Do.
18. Bedroom, 18 × 20.

THIS cottage, designed for some secluded valley in a wild and mountainous region, is irregular in its plan and very much broken in its sky lines, in order the nearer to assimilate to the character of the scenery amidst which it is placed, and to form a natural part of it, according to the principle we have already touched upon. Considering these things, we have instinctively adopted some motives from the Swiss Chalet, in which galleries, very projecting eaves, and great extent of roof are the prevailing features.

A gentleman, by frequent communications with his architect, necessarily to a very great extent imprints his own character upon his house, and this is one of the most important æsthetic ends of the art, and proves how possible it is to express in a manner even the most delicate idiosyncracies of human character. It is the duty of the architect, studying the desires and needs of his client, carefully to manage the design in all its parts, so as to fit into and harmonize with the lives to be spent under its roof.

Thus a house of this kind, we think, will at once impress the beholder with the conviction that it is the habitation of a gentleman of small family and limited means, yet possessing education and refinement, and an appreciation so delicate for the scenery amidst which he lives that he would have his very dwelling-place sympathize with it, and be a fit companion for its rocky undulations and its forests of pine and hemlock.

The library, occupying the central portion of the house, shows that this is his favorite room, from which he can easily approach his drawing room on the one side or his dining room on the other. Evidently he is rather a man of nice literary taste than a close student, for this apartment is too liable to intrusion and household noise to serve the purposes of a study, strictly so considered. The size of his drawing room indicates his fondness for society, and the arrangement of the folding doors, by which the entire first floor may be thrown into one apartment, gives evidence of generous hospitality and large social qualities.

The dining room opens into a spacious butler's pantry, containing a dresser for table linen and china, also a sink with hot and cold water, and a dumb waiter communicating with a similar pantry below, connected with the kitchen. Over this pantry, in the second story, a bath room might be made; but none is here introduced on account of the expense. The dining room and kitchen chimney is placed partly outside to give more room within, at the same time relieving the external plainness and forming one of the architectural features of the house.

The balcony from the dining room window forms a shelter over the kitchen door, which, on account of the descent of the grade in this direction, is entirely above ground, making a fine, light, and dry kitchen, connecting with the store cellars and servants' apartments, also on this floor.

A kitchen arranged in this manner is better than one on the same level with the dining room, as in the latter case the erection of an additional building is necessary, increasing the expense, and being inconvenient by reason of the distance to the store cellars. By this arrangement also, the servants have apartments so removed that they are not brought into immediate contact with the family; and if the floor is deafened the noise and disagreeable odors from the kitchen are more effectually excluded from the main house. The admirable plan now generally in use, for dumb waiters, renders them noiseless, and obviates entirely the necessity of passing up and down stairs for each article required. When possible, it is well to have the dumb waiter communicating between the chamber floors and kitchen, or laundry, to carry clean or soiled linen, &c.; this arrangement renders back or servants' staircases almost unnecessary.

The bedrooms on the second story have each a closet (with another in the hall for linen), and fireplaces, with a studied arrangement for the furniture, a matter too often neglected in planning a house. Nothing is more common than to see sleeping apartments so constructed that no place is left for a bed without interfering with a door, window or fireplace, no place in the dining room for a sideboard, no place in the drawing room for a piano or sofa, no place in the library for bookcases, and no place in the dressing room for a toilet table.

This also proves the danger of altering an architect's design without his consent, since there are always certain meanings and intentions for every detail, however trifling, obvious to none but the originator. To change a door or window, therefore, is very apt to interfere with some internal or external feature of the design. If the architect is consulted, he can usually devise a way to carry out any alteration without interfering with the arrangements of the general plan.

Estimate.—A building like this could be erected for about $2,500.

DESIGN No. 6.

WE recommend this design, not only for the agreeable and elegant effects of its exterior, but also for its economical and simple yet commodious arrangements within. The entrance porch, which is apparently distinct, acts as an enlargement of the veranda, of which it is a part. The hall serves as a large sitting room, and communicates with the drawing room by folding doors, while the stairs, which ascend through the tower, from basement to attic, are so secluded, as to obviate the necessity of a private staircase.

It must be admitted that to enter at once into a large hall, treated somewhat like one of the living rooms of the house, and perhaps with a wood fire blazing cheerfully on one side in a wide open chimney, gives to the stranger the impression of generous hospitality and cordial greeting, as if the house itself at once had received him into its arms. This is frequent in England.

The dining room has a bay window, and communicates with the library by folding doors. The second story has a linen closet and four good bedrooms, and the attic has similar rooms. The windows throughout have deep embrasures and broad sills, which are 15 inches from the floor. With cushions, these form convenient and pleasant seats, and assist in furnishing the room.

The veranda, it will be observed, is rather limited, yet as a greater portion is on the east side of the house, it is in the shade the most of the day. It should always be remembered that where there is but one veranda it should be placed on the shady side of the house. Great mistakes are often made in painting the veranda roof a light color, for the purpose of coolness. But actually the effect is directly the reverse, the light tones reflecting the heat into the chamber windows. It is true that the roof is thus left cool, but it is no advantage, since if the rooms within are hot we care little how cool the veranda roof may be. The roof here, as over all parts of the house, is of dark slate, a material especially harmonious with brick or stone houses. When slate is used, however, sufficient steepness should be obtained to shed the water, while flat roofs should be covered with metal. The main roof here has, on account of its steepness, no gutter at the cornice, as the water is nearly all collected from the flat on top, in gutters at the curb of the roof. The objection often holds good, against towers arranged like the one in our design, that the snow will lodge between it and the main roof, and cause leakage. But by reference to the plan it will be seen that, in order to give entrance to the attic, this space must be filled up by a passage, the roof of which, not shown in this perspective, prevents such a lodging place. Expedients of this kind should always be resorted to in our climate, since picturesque vallies or internal angles of this kind are apt to leak.

We would take advantage of this opportunity to advise the application of some distinctive name to every detached country house, however small, since it cannot be distinguished by a number, as in town. The name should, of course, be suggestive of some fact connected with the house, its owner, or its location, and should be original, or at least not copied from any in the vicinity.

We would offer, as names not yet become common among us, the following taken from country seats in England, which may serve as suggestions :

Arborfield,	Brook Cottage,	Elmwood,	Highmont,
Ashhill,	Brookvale,	Fern Hill,	Ivy Cottage,
Ashfield,	Brookfield,	Fern Cottage,	Ivy Hill,
Ashridge,	Brook Hill,	Forest Hill,	Laurel Cottage,
Ashdale,	Brookwood,	Glen Villa,	Lawn Cottage,
Bayfield,	Blithefield,	Glenfield,	Longwood,
Bayswater,	Chestnut Cottage,	Glen Cottage,	Mayfield,
Baythorne,	Claremont,	Greenhill,	Myrtle Cottage,
Beach Cottage,	Cliff Hall,	Grove Cottage,	Melrose,
Beach Hill,	Cliff Cottage,	Grove Park,	Moss Side,
Beachside,	Crow's Nest,	Harewood,	Moss Cottage,
Beech Hill,	Cedars,	Haselwood,	Oak Bank,
Beech Land,	Clifton,	Hawthorne,	Oak Hall,
Beechwood,	Dale Park,	Hawkswood,	Oak Cottage,
Beltwood,	Daisy Bank,	Hayfield,	Oak Hill,
Berry Hill,	Doveridge,	Highwood,	Oakfield,
Birchwood,	Eaglehurst,	Highlands,	Oakwood,
Bloomfield,	Edgehill,	Holly Cottage,	Oaklands,
The Briars,	Elm Cottage,	Holly Grove,	Oatlands,
Broadlands,	Elm Grove,	Holly Hill,	Oldbrook,
Broadfield,	Elmstead,	Homewood,	Oldfield,

Oriel Cottage,	Sedgebrook,	Summerfield,	Westfield,
Raven Hill,	Sedgefield,	Sunning Hill,	Westwood,
Ravensdale,	Shelbrook,	Thorne Hill,	Willow Cottage,
Ridge Cottage,	Shoreham,	Thorne Grove,	Winfield,
Ridgwood,	Shrubhill,	Undercliff,	Woodbines,
Ringwood,	Spring Cottage,	Vine Cottage,	Woodcote,
Rosedale,	Spring Grove,	Walnut Springs,	Woodfield,
Roseland,	Spring Hill,	Walnut Grove,	Woodhill,
Roseberry,	Springwood,	Waterside,	Woodford,
Rushbrook,	Strawberry,	Wedgewood,	Woodlands,
Rockingham,	Summer Hill,	Westbrook,	Woodside,

Estimate.—This design, if built of stone, would cost about $4,500.

Paul Schulze del.

DESIGN No. 6.

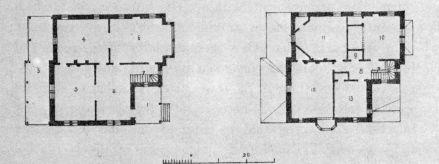

DESIGN № 7.

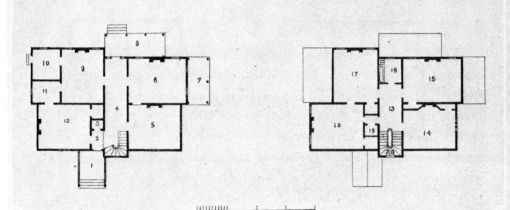

DESIGN No. 7.

FIRST FLOOR PLAN.

1. Entrance Porch, 9 × 10.
2. Vestibule.
3. Coat Closet.
4. Main Hall.
5. Library, 15 × 18.
6. Drawing Room, 15 × 20.
7. Veranda.
8.   Do.
9. Kitchen, 15 × 17.
10. Sink Room, 10 × 10.
11. Butler's Pantry, 7 × 10.
12. Dining Room, 15 × 18.

SECOND STORY PLAN.

13. Hall.
14. Chamber, 13 × 18.
15.   Do.   15 × 20.
16. Bath Room, 8 × 8.
17. Chamber, 15 × 17.
18.   Do.   15 × 18.
19. Linen Closet.
20. Tower Staircase.

THERE seem to be two classes of people who delight in an occasional retirement to the wildest, most picturesque, and unfrequented spots; who find it necessary, at certain intervals, to approach nature, when she abandons herself to her most fantastic and savage moods; to hear her great heart beating in the midst of her grandest solitudes, and to partake of the rude fare of the abounding wilderness. The man of letters and high culture yields to this impulse with the strong desire of recuperating his intellect at the very fountains of knowledge, of freeing himself from the dust of books, and of catching new emotions and intelligible ideas from the secret spirit whispers of the "forest primeval." The man of the world, on the other hand, seeks the same scenery, weary of his routine of dissipation, to obtain a new zest for his life amidst the bounteous freshness of nature, in the fish of her wandering mountain brooks and lovely lakes, and in the wild game of the endless woodland. Mount Desert, Moosehead Lake, the Adirondacks, and the Saguenay have all in turn been the savage Meccas of pale pilgrims who have followed the adventurous trail of the Indian, the hunter, the backwoodsman, and the artist, and sought with them refreshment, consolation, health, and the pleasures of delightful novelty.

In all these places—in the wildest and most picturesque of them—we find these pilgrims, not content with a brief, homeless tarrying there, building their huts and hunting lodges, and shooting boxes, for more convenient and easier sojourn in the summer. The philosophers of Cambridge and the sportsmen of Gotham have not only, like Cowper, longed

> " for a lodge in some vast wilderness,
> Some boundless contiguity of shade,"

but have made a prophecy of their desires and set up their rude household gods in the bosom of the Adirondacks, and by the forest borders of Lake George. Sunnysides and Idlewilds and Clovernooks are arising in abundance far from the trodden paths of travel; peaceful vine-clad fortresses for protection against the raids of *enemies*, and of all the world's follies, gaities, and dissipations— strongholds of homely, hearty hospitality, where the prodigal son may go back to the bosom of nature and find her affections unchanged, and her kind indulgence the same as in the pleasant associations of his childhood.

To meet requirements of this kind, we have prepared the accompanying design, adapted equally well for a hermitage or shooting lodge. The style adopted is that usually termed the "half timber;" in which the framing is allowed to appear externally and form the prominent decorative characteristic of the structure, while between the timbers there is a filling in of brick nogging or rough cast. The effect of this method of construction is highly pleasing, the wall surface being constantly relieved by this expression of wood construction, which is not merely suggestive of strength, but actually increases the firmness of the building. Examples of this style are constantly found in England and on the Continent; it is universal; many of them date back to quite a remote antiquity. Their stability is only exceeded by their picturesqueness and venerable beauty. The traveller will remember with what quaint freaks of form and color they hang over the narrow streets of Chester and Rouen.

The chimneys in this design are carried up to an unusual height, which, with the tower and the gables rising one above the other, strongly partakes of the character of the wooded mountain scenery around, while the broad spread and irregular contour of the roofs are in sympathy with the undulating sweep of valleys and prairie lands.

As we approach this house, the first feature that attracts our attention is the porch leading to the front door. This is quite spacious, admitting the gathering of family groups under its shelter, thus taking the place of a formal veranda, and with the strength of its crossing and supporting timbers bearing its harmonious part in the general sentiment of the design. We enter the vestibule, which is separated from the main hall by an arch. This hall begins at the tower and runs to the rear of the house. The main stairs, commencing at the vestibule and ascending through the tower, afford a landing on each story up to the observatory. The dining room, which is on the left, has a china closet, and communicates with the kitchen through a large butler's pantry, which also serves as a store room. The kitchen is provided with a spacious sink room.

The second story contains four bedrooms, a bath room and linen closet.

In arranging the rooms on the principal story, we have had constant consideration of the fact that they were intended not for any such formal hospitalities as balls or *fêtes*, but rather for that internal domestic comfort, that *dolce far niente* and *abandon* which the occupant came into the wilderness to find. Here the broadcloth coat or silk dress becomes a myth, and the bachelor's cigar knows no housekeeper's tyrannical limitations.

Estimate.—This design, if built plainly, would cost about $3,000.

DESIGN No. 8.

The accompanying cottage, which is the residence of John R. Kearney, Esq., at Rye, N. Y., was originally as shown in the vignette at the left, but was enlarged and altered to its present appearance from plans submitted by the author. The great defects of the old house were a want of relief from monotony and absence of shadows. In order to obtain these results in the altered design, the roofs were extended, and the projecting gable thrown up at the long unbroken side, while the little one-story addition served to create an irregularity upon the ground. The ornament upon the eaves was removed and placed upon the ridge, the chimney altered in design, and the gables surmounted by finials.

The site it occupies is quite picturesque, and rocks and wild-wood form the principal features of the scenery. In order to create a harmonious design, rustic work was introduced for the verandas, balconies, and supports of gables.

The vignette at the right represents a stable belonging to John Howland, Esq., at Belle Point, Darien, Conn., which was altered from an ordinary farm barn to its present appearance.

The stable itself is in the basement; the first floor is occupied by carriage house, tool house, grain and store rooms, with an apartment for a servant, and above these is the hay loft.

The feed is received in the basement through "shoots" which

are convenient to the horses. This stable is provided with two loose boxes and four stalls. These are paved with brick, the rest of the floor being of stone. There are two ventilators connecting with the lantern on the roof.

With regard to harness rooms, we would suggest that they be made larger than they usually are, and with some means of heating them to prevent the cracking of the harness by cold. Here, too, is a smoking room for gentlemen in the morning, and which may also serve as a pleasant resort for male servants in the evening.

Paul Schulze del.

DESIGN N° 8.

Paul Schulze, del.

DESIGN Nº 9.

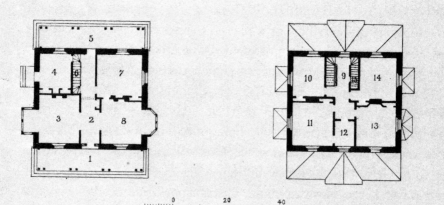

0   20   40

DESIGN No. 9.

THIS design, which is alluded to in Chapter II., was executed at Rye, N. Y., for Dr. J. H. T. Cockey. It is charmingly located, overlooking the windings of a pleasant stream through a beautiful bit of country. The grounds comprise about twenty acres, and in the centre is a natural mound, on which the house was built.

On excavating for the cellar, it was found that a few feet from the surface was a solid ledge of rock. Here was an obstacle not easily overcome, the only resort being a tedious process of blasting. The rock, however, proved of such excellent quality for building, as to obviate the necessity of quarrying elsewhere, and the sand and water being close at hand, no transportation of material was requisite. The rock foundation, also, it will be readily perceived, was far from objectionable, adding much to the stability of the walls.   Hence the house is known as Rock Cottage.

In building square houses, the chimneys are usually four in number, and placed at the sides; in this design, however, the reader will notice that there are but two, and these built inside the house, in the place generally occupied by folding doors.   The expense is, of course, thus decreased, and by the situation of these chimneys much of the heat is retained which would otherwise be wasted upon outside walls.   Instead of the two rooms on one side, communicating with each other by folding doors, according to the usual arrangement, here, apartments on opposite sides of the hall are placed *en suite* by double doors, thus including the hall itself. These doors and the opposite bay windows have arches over their openings, so that standing in the bays we may see a succession of four of these in vista, affording thus an imposing feature to the rooms.

The dining room is slightly enlarged by being extended somewhat into the hall, while the library is made smaller to give space for removing the stairs from the passage, thus obviating the necessity of a private staircase.   The second story has five good chambers, and there are also three bedrooms in the attic.

We have already had occasion to remark that regularity or formal balance of parts in strictly rural architecture is not generally desirable.   But in scenery of rather a mildly beautiful than wild or picturesque character, the more symmetrical designs are often admissible and sometimes singularly appropriate, the formal and stately seats, so common among the residences of the English gentry, most abound along the broad and easy slopes of the country side, by placid lakes and quiet streams, among gently undulating grassy lawns and parks, adorned with detached clumps of elms or oaks. Though we would scarcely wish to see repeated to any extent the quaint formalities of an old-fashioned Elizabethan garden, with its thick yew-tree hedges clipped into arcades and all sorts of strange fantasies of form, with its straight alleys and long artificial vistas, yet some sort of formality is often desirable in the midst of such park-like scenery as we have described, and we are justified in borrowing the terraces, fountains, and ballustrades of the Italian villa, and the nicely trimmed hedges, neat gravel walks and strictly kept boundaries of the English country seat. With such surroundings a purely symmetrical design is often most appropriate, especially when the house is very spacious. An American village, too, with its rectangular lots on the street, seems to suggest sometimes a similar formality of treatment on a smaller scale.

But let us change the location and imagine one more picturesque. Though the simple and inexpensive internal arrangement of the square cottage may be retained, we shall readily perceive that a strictly symmetrical external treatment would appear misplaced. It is usually supposed that in order to render a design picturesque, the plan must of necessity be irregular. This is a very common error; and in selecting a certain fixed plan, it is generally considered that the elevation attached to it must be adhered to under all circumstances. As an evidence that the adoption of such a plan does not necessarily involve a disregard of exterior agreeing with the surrounding scene, we would refer the reader to Design No. 15. This certainly has the appearance of an entirely different arrangement. But, on close examination, it will be found that not only the general disposition of rooms, but every door and window, with the single exception of an alteration of the bay, corresponds precisely in plan with the present design; whereas the exterior only is altered to suit a more picturesque style of country, by simply breaking the lines of the roof, and by certain contrivances of detail, giving the whole an entirely different aspect, and adapting it thoroughly to its new condition of site.

Estimate.—This design was built by contract for $4,500.

Paul Schulze, del.

DESIGN, N° 10.

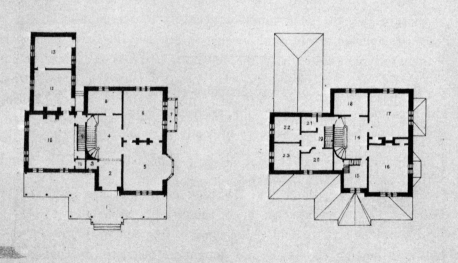

DESIGN No. 10.

Such picturesqueness and diversity of feature, as characterize the treatment of this little villa, are well adapted for association with the wild, romantic scenery of many parts of our country, especially on those abrupt and rugged slopes so common along the banks of the Hudson.

This structure, which was designed as a residence for J. D. Bedford, Esq., is situated on one of these slopes, at Nyack.

Its style is strictly Tudor, the same so frequent in those choice localities among the lakes and mountain districts of England.

The variety of its skylines, obtained by a careful composition of
clustered chimneys, gabled roofs and pointed finials, is in harmony
with the rugged character of the scenery around it; while its
broad veranda, bay window, and greenhouse serve to assist its
irregularity of outline on the ground, and to relieve the monotony
of formal and unsympathizing walls. The little gable at the right
breaks up and relieves the long extent of cornice on that façade,
and the chimney produces the same effect upon the ridge. The
pyramidal form of the group is effected by the towering of the
observatory in its central position, and the whole produces in the
general picture some resemblance to the peculiar features of the
landscape itself. The design is chiefly commendable for its convenience and its proper conformity with its immediate surroundings.

Another composition of equal merit, yet wholly different in
architectural character, may be found in Design No. 29. Here
may be seen an example of the horizontal tendency of those classic
structures whose representations awaken so many pleasing memories in the mind of one who has traversed the sunny plains of
Italy; but agreeable as they may be in a level region, a due attention to fitness admonishes us that an edifice designed after their
manner, would be quite inappropriate in the more rugged portions
of our country. And why is this? We reply that an article of
apparel, which is highly becoming to one person, proves frequently
quite the reverse to another, and thus, in order to be tastefully
attired, one must take into consideration form, complexion, and
features, and then select garments of a corresponding color and
shape. This, though a homely comparison, is precisely analogous
to the immediate question; a building, therefore, to be an object
of art, should conform in shape, color, and feature with the country
around. Thus the level, unbroken lines of the Italian villa, so
decidedly in harmony with the smooth, placid character of its

native land, would be as greatly out of place amid the wild, imposing grandeur of the Catskills, as would the rude beauty of the Gothic on the fair plains of Italy.

The interior of this building is more unique than extensive. The entrance, which is in the tower, opens into a spacious vestibule, provided with a coat closet, and is separated from the main hall by an arch, where folding doors may be placed in winter. The hall is also of good size, the staircase being in an alcove at the side, under which a sofa may be properly placed. The first apartment at the right is the drawing room, which has a bay window, and connects with the library by doors on either side of the fireplace: sliding doors might be introduced and the rooms thrown together at pleasure. The library has sufficient space for books, and is connected with a small greenhouse on the south side, which may be heated in winter by simply opening the glass doors by which it communicates with the library. It is protected from external cold by double glazed sashes: the floor and ceiling being deafened and the panels backed with brick. At the end of the hall is a small room, which may serve as a sewing or smoking room, or private office. The dining room and kitchen occupy the wing, which has its ceiling lower than the main part of the house; an arrangement peculiar, perhaps, but according with the taste of the owner. The upper portion of this wing is occupied by two bedrooms, a linen closet, and bath room, while there are four good chambers in the main house.

The main hall is lighted from above, and the observatory stairs, commencing at the second floor, ascend to the third and fourth stories of the tower, from whence is obtained a fine view in all directions.

Estimate.—We believe the estimates on this design were $3,500.

Paul Schulze del.

DESIGN No. 11.

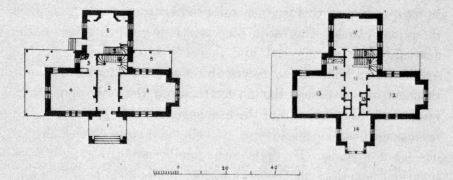

DESIGN No. 11.

NOTWITHSTANDING the general prosperity of our country and the rapidity and ease of acquiring wealth, yet in the midst of the fluctuations of commercial life, there is a constant liability to serious loss, if not entire reverses of fortune. It is sad to think that our own firesides, though far removed from the immediate bustle and keen anxieties of the exchange, are ever sensitive to the mismanagements or misfortunes of a single venture on the dangerous ocean of trade. By these, many families are driven from their luxurious mansions in the town to less pretending homes in the country. These families, thus prostrated by the changes of a day, reared in the midst of the refinements of luxurious ease, and surrounded by the golden opportunities of wealth, have, perhaps, under these impulses, so shaped their minds and manners as to have become ornaments in the circles where they were known. Such people are, of all others, equal to an emergency of this kind. They often find that adversity is not without its sweet uses. Knowing that they must, if they remain in the town, assume an inferior position, and one beneath their merits, they will turn to the country as affording a congenial home. Here, with true taste and sound judgment, they will build a cottage, which, though small in dimensions, will be complete in all its parts. In such a home, with the qualifications in themselves for making it happy, they will find, probably, a calm content unknown in the giddy turmoil of fashion, and a consolation full of gentleness and peace. Other associations, dear as those of old, will cluster around them, and they will find, as in the touching description of "the wife" in Irving's Sketch Book, that they have no desire to return to the noise and bustle, the whirl and excitement of a life in town.

Everything about such a house must be truly refined and chaste, with every convenience that comfort demands, and without any superfluities. The interior must be suggestive of the refinement of the occupants, not necessarily ornamental or showy, but in every respect tasteful and elegant. It is with such views that we have prepared the accompanying design.

The entrance porch is in character with the rest of the house, strong and substantial, and is embowered with ivy, which climbs up its columns and crowns its arches. The main stairs are at the end of the hall, which is thus left wide and unobstructed, and ready for all those uses of household pleasure which such a feature is sure to possess. The library has a bay window, and the dining room communicates with the kitchen by a butler's pantry. The kitchen has a private stairway and large closets. In the second story are four bedrooms, bath room, and linen closet, and in the attic, rooms for servants.

It is not uncommon to find in country houses one or more rooms from which the family are excluded save on rare occasions, and which are kept only for the entertainment of guests.

We have here supposed a residence for a family of refinement; and whatever is equal to its wants should certainly suffice for those of its guests. It will, then, be borne in mind that genuine hospitality does not consist in the provision, for guests, of luxuries denied ourselves. We have, therefore, omitted from this design everything superfluous. The drawing room proper is the first apartment we discard, it being one which always occupies a larger amount of space than is balanced by its actual usefulness in the household.

The ordinary objection to using a dining room for the purposes of family gatherings, is that it must necessarily be occupied by the servants after meals, for removing the service and "tidying up" generally. Much of this, however, may be obviated by the provision of a butler's pantry, and thus the dining room and hall may be used as sitting rooms, while the library remains for literary purposes.

The great want of small houses at moderate rents, and in respectable quarters of our cities, obliges many of limited means to seek homes in the country. If the custom of living on flats or floors were introduced in our country, this rural desire would be subdued, as in France; but while the old English maxim remains true of us, "every man's house is his castle," flats must be associated only with the lowest class of tenement houses. With the Anglo-Saxon, home and the family fireside are sacred, and in no small degree it is to this influence we owe our love of truth and virtue. Domestic qualities are almost unknown in France, and as a natural consequence the virtues we so much admire are held in low esteem.

It is not too much to say that every man owes it to himself, no less than his family, to provide a home; a spot around which he may gather his dear ones for counsel and instruction. Such a home is incomplete without one apartment, too often little regarded, which is a library. We would enlarge on this subject, which we deem so important, but consider it advisable rather to quote the language of a distinguished writer of the day, with which we close this chapter.

"We form judgments of men from little things about their house, of which the owner, perhaps, never thinks. In earlier years, when travelling in the West, where taverns were either scarce or, in some places, unknown, and every settler's house was a house of 'Entertainment,' it was a matter of some importance and some experience to select wisely where you would put up. And we always looked for flowers. If there were no trees for shade, no patch of flowers in the yard, we were suspicious of the place. But, no matter how rude the cabin, or rough the surroundings, if we saw that the window held a little trough for flowers, and that some vines twined about strings let down from the eaves, we were confident that there was some taste and carefulness in the log cabin. In a new country, where people have to tug for a living, no one will take the trouble to rear flowers, unless the love of them is pretty strong; and this taste blossoming out of plain and uncultivated people is, itself, like a clump of harebells growing out of the seams of a rock. We were seldom misled. A patch of flowers came to signify kind people, clean beds, and good bread.

"But, other signs are more significant in other states of society. Flowers about a rich man's house may signify only that he has a good gardener, or that he has refined neighbors and does what he sees them do.

"But men are not accustomed to buy *books* unless they want

them. If, on visiting the dwelling of a man of slender means, I find the reason why he has cheap carpets, and very plain furniture, to be that he may purchase books, he rises at once in my esteem. Books are not made for furniture, but there is nothing else that so beautifully furnishes a house. The plainest row of books that cloth or paper ever covered is more significant of refinement than the most elaborately carved *étagère*, or sideboard.

" Give me a house furnished with books rather than furniture! Both, if you can, but books at any rate! To spend several days in a friend's house, and hunger for something to read, while you are treading on costly carpets, and sitting upon luxurious chairs, and sleeping upon down, is as if one were bribing your body for the sake of cheating your mind.

" Is it not pitiable to see a man growing rich, and beginning to augment the comforts of home, and lavishing money on ostentatious upholstery, upon the table, upon everything but what the soul needs ?

" We know of many and many a rich man's house where it would not be safe to ask for the commonest English classics. A few garish annuals on the table, a few pictorial monstrosities, together with the stock religious books of his " persuasion," and that is all! No range of poets, no essayists, no selection of historians, no travels or biographies, no select fictions, or curious legendary lore; but, then, the walls have paper on which cost three dollars a roll, and the floors have carpets that cost four dollars a yard! Books are the windows through which the soul looks out. A house without books is like a room without windows. No man has a right to bring up his children without surrounding them with books, if he has the means to buy them. It is a wrong to his family. He cheats them! Children learn to read by being in the presence of books. The love of knowledge comes with reading and grows upon it. And the love of knowledge, in a young mind, is almost a warrant against the inferior excitement of passions and vices.

"Let us pity these poor rich men who live barrenly in great, bookless houses! Let us congratulate the poor that, in our day, books are so cheap that a man may every year add a hundred volumes to his library for the price of what his tobacco and his beer would cost him. Among the earliest ambitions to be excited in clerks, workmen, journeymen, and, indeed, among all that are struggling up in life from nothing to something, is that of owning, and constantly adding to, a library of good books. A little library growing larger every year is an honorable part of a young man's history. It is a man's duty to have books. A library is not a luxury, but one of the necessaries of life."

Estimate.—This design was estimated to cost in stone, $4,000.

DESIGN No. 12.

HAVING shown in the preceding chapter how a small cottage or country seat, complete in itself, may contain as many elements of artistic beauty, and in every respect be quite as respectable as a more extensive mansion, we would now endeavor to explain how such a cottage may be built with reference to capacities for future enlargement and more ambitious proportions.

Though people sometimes make the apparent mistake of building too large for their present uses, much more frequently they commit the greater error of building without reference to any possible or probable increase of means and necessities. In time it often becomes essential to enlarge household accommodations, and then occur all those difficulties of alteration so often alluded to in this work, unless the dwelling was originally designed with reference to such probable alterations. Now, in order to prove that architecture can accommodate itself gracefully and easily to such changing conditions of life, provided the necessity for such accommodation is understood at the outset, we propose to arrange a plan which shall be such as to necessitate the immediate execution of only a part, but that part complete in itself, both inside and out.

By referring to the plan, it will be observed that, though extensive, only the dark portion is included in our perspective view, which comprises a house about equal, in capacity and accommodation, to the preceding design. The entrance hall, which is large enough to serve as a sitting room for the cottage, becomes a fitting appliance for the more stately extent of the future mansion.*

Now this is a complete cottage in itself, without the present necessity of any additions or alterations. But should the owner, at any future time, desire to enlarge, he can readily add the light portion of the plan, without interfering with the present structure. For a view of its external appearance, when enlarged, we refer the reader to Design No. 20, where it will be observed the additions blend and harmonize with the group, so that our simple country seat has grown naturally into nobler state, and assumed the air and dignity of a mansion. All of which shows the advantages of careful bringing up in young cottages.

There is no more frequent remark made by those who have built country houses, that "It has cost me much more than I intended expending." This tends to dissuade people from building, and they take refuge in the proverb: "Fools build houses and

* For further description of the interior, see Design No. 20.

wise men live in them." Why is it that so many shrewd business men are deceived in building? Why is it that a man having estimated an expenditure of $7,000, finds his completed residence to have cost $10,000, or even more? A satisfactory answer to this question may seem an arduous task, but we are confident it can be explained so as to be comprehended by all. When a man has an intention of building, he begins to "count the cost," and decides how much he will expend: he then sketches his idea of the general arrangement and the amount of accommodation necessary for his family, and he settles himself down to the belief that these ideas must be carried out at his original suppositions regarding the expense. In his calculation he relies, perhaps, on the "judgment" of a friend who has built, or on rude comparison with a neighbor's house, but undertakes to make no detailed estimate of the necessary number of feet of lumber, of the squares of roofing, yards of plastering, or the number of doors, windows, stairs, mantles, grates, or closets, none of the amount of stone and brick work, none of the painting, carting, grading, draining; he has thought nothing of the number of days' labor that will be necessary, of the price per day, of the outbuildings, wells, and cisterns, or of the task of preparing the grounds on which to build: of the actual expense of all these he has not the least idea, and the only wonder is that in his "rough guess" he has not been even more mistaken. With these mature ideas he goes to his builder as to an expert, to see what all will really cost, when, to his astonishment, he discovers that even a builder cannot supply him with the desired figures until complete plans and specifications have been prepared and thorough estimates made on them. He, perhaps, then leaves the builder in disgust, and has final recourse to the architect, who he finds unwilling to commit himself to any statement of amounts until drawings and estimates are made in a proper manner. The necessary papers are consequently ordered, and, when returned, he is surprised that the estimates exceed very considerably his proposed expenditure. When time and labor have thus been thrown away, he appeals, at last, to his architect to suit the plan to the price; and then he has a melancholy vision of the slow departure, under those unsparing hands, of many a little household comfort or luxury which he had permitted himself to cherish in his imagination, when laboring under his melancholy delusion of costs.

An intelligent understanding established in the outset between his mea. and his desires would have spared him much disappointment.

There is a simple rule which sometimes enables one to approximate the cost of the house he intends to build. It is to find a house of the general character and finish of that proposed; to calculate the number of cubic feet it contains from the basement floor to the top of the roof; to divide the cost of the building by the number of feet it contains, which, of course, gives the cost per foot. Reduce your proposed house to cubic feet, and multiply by the same price per foot. This will give you about the cost of your house, unless you should decide on a greater expense in finish. This rule, however, is a very uncertain one; it should be applied cautiously, and not too much confidence placed in its revelations.

Estimate.—This design would cost, in stone, about $5,500, and the additions about $3,500.

DESIGN N° 12.

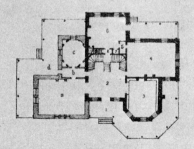

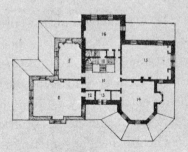

0   20   40

Paul Schulze del.

DESIGN Nº 13.

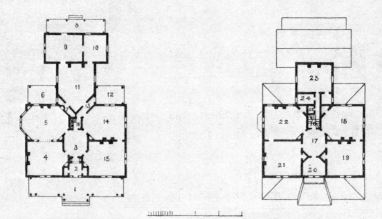

DESIGN No. 13.

THIS design represents another square building, containing all the advantages claimed for that form, yet so peculiarly arranged as to give, both within and without, a marked novelty and individuality of expression. The veranda-roof, over the front door-steps, projects so as to break the great length of cornice, and might be made to combine utility with ornament, by allowing the steps to recede, which would afford ample shelter in alighting from carriages.

The tesselated vestibule is well lighted by stained glass sashes on either side the door. This vestibule contains two spacious closets for hats, coats, umbrellas, &c. The side opposite the entrance is spanned by an arch separating the outer from an inner vestibule, adorned with niches for statues on both sides. From this an ornamental ground-glass door gives access to a rotunda of large dimensions, occupying the centre of the house, and extending to the roof, where a stained glass skylight admits a pleasant, modulated light, more grateful in such an apartment than the white light of noon.

In this octagonal hall there are six doors symmetrically arranged, each of which opens into a separate room. Turning to the left, we enter by one of these doors a bay, occupying the centre of one side of a small parlor. Within this bay the door is balanced by a small statuary niche. The parlor opens into a large drawing room, through an arch supported by columns, affording a cheerful vista, closed by a fireplace which is studied so as to form one composition with two small flanking windows.

The form of the drawing room is octagonal, one side of which is occupied by a large bay window. In the four corners of this room are shown small niches for statues.

This room, like the small parlor, communicates directly with the rotunda, and by the two doors on the opposite side of the rotunda we may enter the library and dining room; the former of which has a similar arrangement in plan to the parlor, except that the chimney occupies the place of the arch. The dining room nearly corresponds in shape and disposition to the drawing room opposite, with the same exception in regard to the fireplace, and with the omission of the bay window. This room communicates with the kitchen through a rear entry, which also serves the purpose of a butler's pantry, and prevents the smells from the kitchen pervading the rest of the house. Another pantry will be observed, connected with the kitchen and corresponding with this entry. On the opposite side, the kitchen has a store or milk room, and a spacious laundry. In this arrangement there is no provision for back or private stairs; but the principal staircase is so shut off from the main body of the house, and communicates so directly with the apartments of the family and of the domestics, as to be equally accessible to both, without trespass on either hand.

Ascending the stairs, before we arrive at the top, we reach a landing affording access to a linen closet, bath and bedroom, the latter of which is provided with a commodious and well-lighted dressing room. Continuing the ascent, we come to the main portion of the second floor, and again enter the rotunda by a gallery (accidentally omitted in the drawing), which passes around it, communicating by doors with the five surrounding bedrooms. These bedrooms are amply supplied with closets and fireplaces, and are well lighted. This main stairway ascends to the attic, and is provided with a skylight. By the peculiar construction of the roof, good apartments are secured in the attic, for which light is obtained from gable and dormer windows. The facilities for ventilation in this design are worthy of remark, as through the well of the staircase, and especially through the rotunda, a constant circulation of air is produced throughout all the rooms. The main portion of the house may be heated from a register placed in the centre of the rotunda floor, under which stands the furnace.

From the number of niches shown throughout the house, we are induced to give a short extract from Wightwick's "Palace of Architecture," which may serve to show what appropriate parts

statuary and other works of art may be made to play in the duties
of hospitality and entertainment.

" The portico receives you with a readiness symbolized in the
statues of Invitation and Greeting, which occupy the niches on
each side of the door.

" In the two arched recesses, on either side the entrance-lobby,
are figures typifying Welcome and Hospitality; while the vestibule
is dignified by the presence of others, representing the Seasons, to
indicate that we keep open house the whole year, and shall, at all
times, be happy to see you.

" On the landing of the staircase are the statues of Fidelity and
Protection, to intimate that you may confide in our truth and
sleep in safety.

" The breakfast room is hung with a series of drawings by our
eminent water-color artist, bright, fresh, and crisp, as the morning
of Youth.

" From above the book cases, around our library, look down
the intelligent countenances of the literary great,—either beaming
with poetic thought, or grave with philosophic reflection,—and indicating the character of the works respectively ranged beneath
them. The sculptured group at the end of the room represents a
boy rising from his completed studies, unconsciously to experience
those pure emotions of the heart, which form the Episode betwixt
youth and manhood.

" In one of the chambers of the tower is the only antique
treasure we possess, a sequel to the group last mentioned,—that
statue, unimprovable, which ' enchants the world,'—the *Venus de
Medicis.*

" The commingled pursuits of the drawing room are represented
by the poetry of History, the harmony of Landscape, the eloquence of gentle Portrait, and the charming varieties of Art repre

senting Art, as in the architectural pictures of Claude and Cana-letti. The picture over the fireplace illustrates the beauty of Noon and the matured graces of Manhood.

" Upon the walls of the dining room glow the symbols of Fes-tivity, and the rich tints of the fruit-piece, with its crystal vessels, and the citron wreathing its golden coil around the goblet's silver stem. The principal picture represents Age, in its decline, enjoy-ing, with cheerful gratitude, the bread of its early industry.

" Connected with the dining room is the Conservatory, redolent with softest fragrance, and radiant with perfect beauty—an asylum for the gentler of Nature's offspring—yielding a corrective to the Sensual, who would deem purity insipid, and gently re-proving the Sanctimonious, who would regard external splendor as unholy. From indulging in the charms of nature's *loveliness*, you will next turn to the adoration of nature's GOD in our Chapel, where, over the altar, is seen the ' Man of Sorrows,' the ECCE HOMO of Guercino! The marble group of *Praise, Thanksgiving*, and *Prayer*, and the statue of *St. Paul*, are evidences of the skill and exalted feeling of the modern British Sculptor : and we shall here anticipate your surprise, at finding in our mansion only one specimen of the *Antique*, and so few works by the ' old masters.' Pardon us, then, for refusing to employ our private suite of apart-ments as a Museum of Miscellaneous Art. It has been our aim to make Painting and Sculpture coöperate with Architecture in the completion of a perfect whole, expressive of that character and of those affections which we desire to cultivate ; and as involving an uncompromising esteem for *fitness*, with an especial sympathy for *contemporary* good and beauty."

Estimate.—This design could be built for about $6,000.

Paul Schulze, del.

DESIGN, No 14.

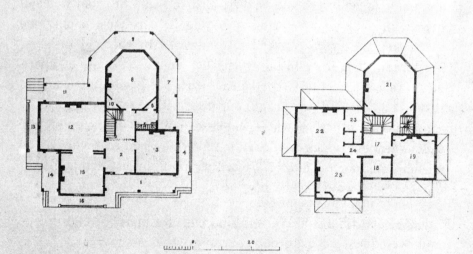

DESIGN No. 14.

FIRST FLOOR PLAN.

1. Veranda.
2. Hall.
3. Library, 15 × 15.
4. Balcony or Terrace.
5. Servants' Staircase.
6. Butler's Pantry.
7. Veranda.
8. Dining Room, 17 × 19.
9. Veranda.
10. Closet.
11. Veranda.
12. Drawing Room, 16 × 22.
13. Balcony.
14. Veranda.
15. Parlor, 14 × 15.
16. Balcony.

SECOND FLOOR PLAN.

17. Hall.
18. Chamber, 7 × 10.
19. Do. 15 × 15.
20. Servants' Staircase.
21. Chamber, 17 × 19.
22. Do. 16 × 16.
23. Dressing Room.
24. Passage.
25. Chamber, 14 × 15.

OCCASIONALLY we find·sites where the views in every direction are so pleasing that we desire to make them play their part in our household enjoyments, and be a continual blessing in our most frequented apartments. We would lose no feature of the landscape, and consequently must occupy our entire first floor with the family and reception rooms, while the kitchen and its offices must necessarily be placed below. The four sides of our house, then, must be taken up with parlor, dining room, drawing room, and library; and, in order that we may enjoy the views more openly and extensively, an ample disposition of veranda, balcony, and observatory seems especially appropriate.

At first sight it would appear that these considerations would be satisfied by the ordinary and vulgar arrangement of a square house, with a hall through the middle, a veranda all around, and an observatory on top. This is the pure and simple expression of what is called *sound judgment* in the matter, and as such it is entitled to respect. We only regret that this respect is accorded to such an extent that our country is filled with houses after this pattern, only varying in some minor point of detail, according to the whim of the builder. We propose, however, to prove that *good taste*, while according with sound judgment, meets the exigencies we have described more fully than this conventional pattern does, and obtains besides a work of beauty and grace. In short, we have here an emphatic repetition of the old and honorable architectural truth, that beauty and utility are never necessarily in discord one with the other. Let the reader judge for himself how far this is accomplished in the accompanying design.

It will be readily seen from the elevation, instead of proposing a square habitable box, we have indulged in some irregularity of outline and picturesqueness of feature, in our design. The practical advantage arising from this irregularity is, that each room commands a prospect in three distinct directions, without the aid of bays; all the windows open to the floor and give access to an outer platform, which, instead of being treated as a veranda, surrounding the house in the usual way, thereby darkening the rooms and disturbing the grand outlines, so that the house itself becomes secondary to its adjuncts, is managed as part balcony or terrace, protected by a bracketed canopy, and part veranda or porch, with the customary posts. This arrangement gives pleasing variety to the design, admits much more light into the principal apartments, and allows the outlines of the house to be prominently visible, from foundation to roof, at the corners.

The interior of this house is simple and convenient. The drawing room, which is of good size, connects with a less ambitious parlor by sliding doors. Directly opposite the drawing room is the library. This is in the most retired part of the house, adjoining no other room, and being central yet quiet. The dining room has an entrance from the main hall for family use, and also communicates with the private entry, where are the back stairs, which lead from basement to attic for the servants' accommodation. The form of this room is octagonal, one end being occupied by a three-sided bay, and the other made to correspond by cutting off the angles, thus producing a private passage, a pantry, and a china closet.

It may be asked where are the places for furniture, and more especially for a sideboard in this apartment? The window at the end opposite the entrance door is elevated above the rest, giving room for a sideboard to be placed under it, and is of an oval form composed of one sheet of plate glass like a mirror. The upper part of this sideboard should be made to form a frame for this window, so that the window will appear to be a part of the sideboard, and that a part of the room.

The peculiar arrangement of a window over the chimney-piece in the small parlor will be observed. This, though novel in our country, is quite common in Europe, and is often introduced with a happy effect. The mantlepiece, as usual, surmounts the fireplace, and the window frame above is gilt or otherwise treated like the frame of a looking glass, and is filled with a single sheet of plate glass. Such a contrivance produces an agreeable surprise, and enables persons sitting at the hearth to command a view of the scenery without, as if painted in a landscape by more than human art. But even this is attended by some objections unless guarded by another contrivance of equal ingenuity. It is objectionable when the sun is in such a quarter as to shine through it upon a person reading at the fire. This difficulty may be obviated by furnishing the window with a sliding shutter, which will answer the double purpose of security against burglars and a protection from an excess of light. Let the inside of this shutter be occupied by a landscape: then when closed it will have precisely the appearance of a finely framed picture hung over the mantlepiece. A mirror is sometimes used to play the same part. The flues of the chimney of course pass on either side the window, and operate quite as effectually as under the usual circumstances.

But let us turn from these pleasing fancies to the more practical subject of halls and bedrooms. The entrance hall, which is of good width, has placed in it, for the sake of economy, the main stairway, but it may be separated from the hall, if deemed desirable, by glass doors, thus obtaining a large, square, unoccupied vestibule. The chambers above are large and commodious; one having a dressing room, with two closets, where might be placed a bath room. Each of the other bedrooms is well supplied with closets, and the places for furniture are carefully studied.

A tower might be run up, with advantage, over the back stairs, but, anxious to show the reader how an observatory may be placed in the middle of the roof with good effect, the design has been arranged as shown.

Estimate.—This design, in wood, may be built for $6,000.

DESIGN No. 15.

THIS design, which has an interior arrangement similar to that of No. 9, in the candor and simplicity with which it expresses the plan on which it is built, in the picturesque breaking of its sky-lines, with gables, hips, crests, and chimneys, its fair acknowledgment of all constructive obligations, and in its freedom from the cockney frippery of pretence, may serve as a fair illustration of the progress which American rural architecture has made since its days of Puritan plainness. But few specimens are now left of the real Puritan architecture of " the good old Colony times " in New England, or of the old stone revolutionary Dutch farm houses on the Hudson, or of the plantation houses of Maryland and Virginia, built by the first settlers with imported bricks. There is an old-world expression about these venerable buildings which recommend them to our interest as historical reminiscences. And it must be confessed that there is a truth and solidity about their construction which we look for in vain in the architecture of a later day. Undoubtedly they fairly express the solid energy, determination, and great-heartedness of the founders of a new empire in the wilderness. The straightforward respectability and honorable pride of the old Governors, are strongly imprinted upon their mansions. These are reproductions of the contemporary architecture of the mother country, England or Holland, so far as the limited

resources of a new country could reproduce it. The prosperity of
the next generation, however, was too great and too rapid to preserve inviolate this marked self-respect and simplicity in architecture, and soon pretentious display, without the refinement of education, became the aim, finally settling into an era of domesticated
Greek temples and immense classic porticos in wood. The true
refinement of the colonial aristocracy, the hearty hospitality of the
gentleman of the old school, seem to have been overwhelmed by
the pretentious show and glitter of a society whose "new-crowned
stamp of honor was scarce current," and which naturally in architecture developed a fever for base imitation, which it is one of the
special objects of this work to reprehend and criticise. Apropos
to this, our readers will, perhaps, remember that in Coleridge's
narrative of the "Devil's Walk" it is related how

> " He saw a cottage with a double coach-house,
>   A cottage of gentility;
> And the devil did grin, for his darling sin
>   Is pride that apes humility."

The possession of wealth by the ignorant does not generally
bring with it an immediate, refining influence. The plain, honest
man, who by integrity and enterprise has won for himself and
family a respectable name and an ample fortune, has, in the pursuit
of these ends, also acquired certain habits of thought and life more
honest and practical, than refined and elegant. He leans rather
toward the useful than the beautiful, as is natural with those who
have had a hard struggle with the world. In the latter part of
the last century and early part of the present, when our country
was yet young, were the *working days* of our people, and, so far as
regards art, therefore, it was truly *an iron age*. The associations
of wealth, with less occupation of actual labor and more attention
to the amenities of life, necessarily lead to advanced ideas of edu-

cation and personal accomplishments, and thus the children are by one degree near to the refinement of the highest civilization. But early education and the force of early habits cannot be quite forgotten. Blood cannot be purified so soon. Yet a desire for knowledge, an ambition for improvement, has sprung up, and this stage of our part we may (to continue our figure) call the *silver age*. And so in the third age, the *golden*, we may expect to discover a higher tone, a more polished state of society; a culture observable, not only in manners and habits, but in the surroundings of life, in its elegancies no less than comforts, and in the nearer and more effectual union of the useful with the beautiful, the perfection of which is the acme of true refinement.

We may fairly suppose that our people are entering this new degree of civilization, and that their minds are beginning to cherish a national taste, made up of all the good points of the ruder eras of their history, combining the practical common sense and utility of the first with the ambition of the second, and the whole softened by the refinement of the third. Therefore, it is fitting for us to ascertain whether we are taking our proper position, nationally, in the world as lovers of art; whether we are assuming the insignia of progress; whether, for instance, government is founding national galleries of statuary and painting, collecting objects of art from the old world, and encouraging our own artists at home.

All this is not so foreign to our subject as may at first be thought. No one art can be entirely separated from the others, as the same æsthetic principles run through all. He who has cultivated a love for one branch of art, must have some sympathy for, and appreciation of, every other. No man can be a true lover of painting or sculpture, and not find pleasure in beholding the triumph of the sister art of architecture. Taking this as an index of popular artistic culture, we think we have reason to congratulate our readers on the happy prospects before us, as certainly of late years there has been evinced an increasing interest in architecture, both publicly and privately. During the last ten years our advance has been rapid and certain, and full of promise. Our public buildings at the National Capital compare favorably with similar buildings in other countries: our State Capitols, many of them, are well worthy of the important position they occupy; and generally our religious, municipal, and, indeed, all our public buildings, show that a great degree of interest in this subject has been aroused. And this interest bears its inevitable fruits.

With reference to rural architecture, the question may be asked, Why, especially in the vicinity of Boston, rural tastes seem more highly developed than in the suburbs of New York, or why in England are the people so universally chaste and elegant in this particular? Is it not on account of the examples furnished in beautifying certain available portions of public grounds, in making parks and commons? Does not this lead people to love rural culture and elegance, and induce them to enrich the appearance of their own homes in the surrounding country?

It has been observed, in reference to the Central Park of New York, that, when finished, wealthy persons will be content to live in town, finding there the pleasures which they have been in the habit of seeking in the country. We think, on the contrary, the effect will be to educate a rural taste, and to create a passion where it never before existed, for an out-of-town life. We believe that, from such impulses, in a few years the suburbs of New York will vie with those of any other city in the world.

The vignettes represent a rustic summer house and gateway, the former of which was built in New Jersey by A. Gerster.

Estimate.—This design, on account of its irregularity, would cost a trifle more than Design No. 9.

Paul Schulze, del.

DESIGN Nº 15.

Print by H. Lawrence, 83, William St. N.Y.

Paul Schulze, del.

DESIGN Nº 16.

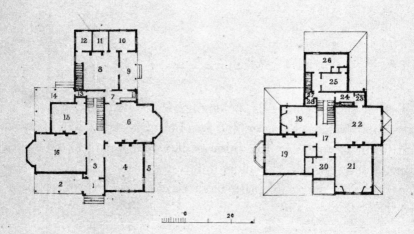

DESIGN No. 16.

THE accompanying villa, belonging to O. Benedict, Esq., is of an irregular Italian character, and was built in Bethel, one of those beautiful little towns in the interior of Connecticut, where manufacturing has become the chief interest of the inhabitants, and where industry and enterprise have received their proverbial reward.

At present there are but few trees on the place, and, therefore, verandas and canopies are resorted to for shade. The house is built of wood, the principal timbers being of pine, while the sills are made of chestnut. The frame is filled in with brick, and sheathed on the outside with rough hemlock boards, before the clapboards are put on. Generally one of these precautions is considered sufficient protection against the weather, but in exposed situations, where the wind has much power, the bricks serve to make the frame more solid, while the sheathing binds the building together, and effectually protects the house from inclemency of the weather. In using rough, external boarding, it is always well to have it placed diagonally, as it thus serves the purpose of bridging and strengthening the frame.

The interior of this house is arranged on a liberal scale. The main hall, which is spacious, contains the stairs, which are placed at the end to afford more room. The dining room has a niche for the sideboard, and communicates with the kitchen through a butler's pantry. This kitchen is provided with store, milk, and wash rooms. The ceilings of these are lower than those of the main house, making the rooms above, which are for servants, on a level with the landing of the main stairs. The rest of the chambers, provided on the second floor, are furnished with closets and places for furniture. Good bedrooms are constructed in the attic. Hot and cold water are carried throughout the house, which is heated by a furnace.

The owner has made provision for gas in all the rooms, this being supplied from private works upon his place; such works are now readily constructed at very moderate cost, and occupy but little room, while their arrangement is so simple and effective as to require but an hour's labor, of an ordinary workman, to obtain a fortnight's supply.

We would not ordinarily recommend the use of gas in a country house, unless a supply may be had from some public works; as too much machinery in a house of this kind, being liable to get out of order and need repairs, frequently causes great annoyance, in consequence of difficulties arising from the absence of mechanics. For the same reason we would not recommend the use of steam furnaces, extensive plumbing and similar works, unless it can be ascertained that the means for repairing are at hand. Gas, too, is not so indispensable an article as many of our countrymen might suppose. In the large cities of Europe it is excluded, in a great measure, from private houses, and in the palaces and dwellings of the nobility it is never introduced except for inferior purposes. During the visit of the Prince of Wales to this country it was the express stipulation of the Queen that no gas should be used in any of his apartments. At fashionable parties in our cities it is often superseded by wax candles.

The reasons for this prejudice are various. It is said, in the first place, to have an injurious effect upon the hair, eyes, and complexion; secondly, it is deemed plebeian in Paris, as there it is more or less associated with cafés and places of public amusement. A final and more potential reason is, that its intensity has not a favorable effect upon the delicate colors and shades of ladies' dresses, and we would say, confidentially, of course, that the injurious effect produced on the expression of their eyes, by the contraction of the pupil, may be avoided, without resort to belladonna, by shunning gaslight, and using some gentler means of obtaining artificial illuminations.

Estimate.—The estimates on this building were $7,000.

Paul Schulze del.

DESIGN Nº 17.

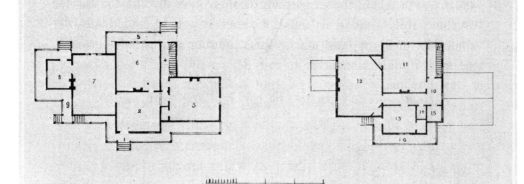

DESIGN No. 17.

FIRST FLOOR PLAN.

1. Terrace.
2. Hall, 13 × 15.
3. Dining Room, 14 × 17.
4. Staircase Hall.
5. Terrace.
6. Library, 15 × 15.
7. Drawing Room, 15 × 20.
8. Cabinet, 8 × 9.
9. Balcony.

SECOND FLOOR PLAN.

10. Hall.
11. Chamber, 15 × 15.
12. Do. 15 × 20.
13. Do. 9 × 11.
14. Linen Closet.
15. Bath Room.
16. Balcony.

THERE are several marked features about this design, which, we think, should recommend it to the attention of our readers. It possesses, in the first place, the advantage of a decidedly picturesque and irregular outline, without the usual complicated and expensive roofs which are generally considered essential to obtain the same result, and which, if not properly constructed, are liable to need frequent repairs, and to form lodging places for snow and ice—a very material objection, considering the length and severity of our northern winters. It is not meant by this that irregular roofs are necessarily subject to such inconveniences, but simply that roofs of this description have not generally sufficient attention given them in design to avoid these dangers. Irregular roofs are often taken from foreign examples, which are not exposed to the same contingencies of weather, and so not unfrequently indulge in valleys and reëntering angles, which, reproduced in our climate, are fatal to the tightness of the roof. Yet, if properly managed, irregular roofs may act better to shed the heavy falls of snow, than many of the more flat examples, which are perfectly plain and regular.

Another feature in this design is a saving of the expense of verandas by the adoption of balconies and terraces in their stead. These extend around the principal rooms both on the first and second stories, those in the latter position serving as a protection for the terraces below, and are themselves sheltered by the projection of the main roof of the building. The expense of a finished underpinning is also avoided by heaping the earth around the house, in the manner of a terrace, up to the first-story beams, leaving openings for window views, and keeping the cellar warm and dry. By this contrivance the house has what most buildings seem to lack, a base or firm footing upon the ground. It seems to afford a closer connection between the earth and the building, giving the architecture more the appearance of growing out of nature and being its offspring, than of being the handiwork of man, and placed by him formally upon its lap.

This house may be used as a *cottage orné*. The entrance is approached by steps, forming a part of the terrace. We enter at once the main hall, which, unobstructed by stairs, may be occupied as a spacious sitting room. The dining room is entered on the right of this hall, through an arched alcove. The position of the windows, doors, and fireplace in this room, is carefully studied to give symmetry. Access is obtained directly from the dining room into the staircase hall, which may be approached with equal facility from the rear of the building and from the entrance hall. The stairway thus treated has its several advantages: from its privacy it obviates the necessity of a servants' staircase, and is in direct communication with the basement, kitchen, dining room, outside entrance, second story, and attic. The library is a large room with broad, unbroken walls on either side for books, a fireplace in front and one large window in the rear, thus preventing cross light and giving the occupant, when seated before the fire, the light upon his book rather than in his eyes. The drawing room, which is on the left, has a small cabinet attached. The chamber-floor is divided into commodious rooms provided with closets, a bath room, and linen closet.

But this design, with some slight alterations, would more appropriately serve the purpose of a *double lodge*, accompanying a mansion, the first floor being occupied by the farmer, or, perhaps, the lodge keeper, and the second by the gardener, who would approach his apartments by the balcony staircase. Should the gardener reside elsewhere on the place, this second story might be fitted up as a billiard room, the floor being well deafened to prevent disturbing the family below.

These internal arrangements are susceptible of easy alteration to suit such fancies, and any clever architect can readily adapt the building to serve any of these purposes.

Estimate.—This house, if plainly built, would cost about $3,500.

Paul Schulze, del.

DESIGN Nº 18.

DESIGN No. 18.

It is usual with persons about purchasing a country residence, to desire to find a place where "improvements," as they are called, have already been made, where the outbuildings have been erected, and the trees have attained a considerable size. The house may not be exactly equal to their requirements, and it is vainly imagined that by adding a wing here and a bay window there, with some alteration of doors, the patching of a few leaks, and the aid of new paint and paper, it may be made to answer all the purposes required. The alterations are hardly begun before the owner finds that, instead of a few patches in the roof, it is so far gone as to demand an entirely new one. In remodelling the rooms, the old work does not at all correspond with the new, and some of it is so far decayed as to be actually unworthy the house. The style of the house, too, is out of keeping, and so many and constant are the suggested alterations, that an entire renovation is needed. After repeated attempts to make the old work match the new, the building is, with protracted difficulties, completed, though in a most unsatisfactory manner. The house, even as renovated, contains so many disadvantages that we are reminded of the proverbial impropriety of putting new wine in old bottles; and when it is too late, the owner begins the old story of wishing he had followed the advice of his architect and abandoned at the

outset the idea of altering, since, with the same expense, he might
have had an entirely new house, and one completely satisfactory.
In the grounds, too, perhaps, from which he had anticipated so
much pleasure, he often finds himself disappointed, as, after some
experience, he discovers that they in no part accord with modern
taste in landscape gardening. The land has been cleared of its
natural growth of oak and chestnut, which so nobly adorned it, to
make room for formal rows of fruit trees.

The vignette at the left will serve as an example of the abor-
tions we so often find disfiguring the most beautiful sites throughout our land. It was built as a public boarding house, and is
situated on one of those charming points, so much admired, on the
north side of Long Island Sound, just east of the village of Stamford, Conn., and notwithstanding its unattractive appearance, its
delightful location made it a favorite summer resort for families
from town.

It has recently been purchased by John Howland, Esq., of
New York. It was a matter of some doubt, in the mind of this
gentleman, what disposition to make of the building, as it was too
large for a farm house and inferior as a dwelling. It was finally
determined to attempt to convert it into a respectable country
seat, and the accompanying design was prepared for that purpose,
with what success the reader must decide for himself.

The ceilings were much too low. This difficulty we were enabled to overcome, on the first story, by proposing to raise the
house bodily above the foundations, leaving the floor in its present
position and filling up below. The attic beams were raised to give
greater height to the second story. The rooms were too small,
and the main stairs obstructed the hall, but by altering some partitions the rooms were readily enlarged, and the stairs were removed to an alcove in the hall. The design, on completion, was

submitted to the owner, who, though he confessed himself satisfied at the result, rather than alter at so great an expense, wisely concluded to convert the structure into a farm house, with few alterations, and to build a new residence on a choice site, which should, in every particular, accord with his own ideas and wants.

The vignette at the right represents a summer house and ice house combined. It was designed for Mr. Howland, in accordance with the following suggestions of Mr. B. S. Carpenter, in "The Rural New Yorker:"

"The perfect success which I met in keeping ice last summer, I think, is owing largely to a new principle involved in the building; therefore I speak of the plan for the consideration of those who are about to build for that purpose. Instead of one hollow wall for a non-conductor of heat, as in ordinary ice houses, I have two, with a space between them for confined air. The site is on a gravel slope. The foundation, for convenience in storing ice, is dug two feet below the surface of the ground. The outside wall for non-conducting material is six inches in the clear. The inside walls are four inches, with space for confined air of four inches. The doors for entrance correspond perfectly with the hollow walls in thickness, and are filled in the same manner—being shaped to shut with a bevel edge, like the doors to safes used by merchants and bankers. At the lower side of the plates is a ceiling, upon which I put spent tan one foot thick, which tan is in direct connection with the side walls, so that any settling in the walls may be supplied from overhead. From the under side of the ceiling runs a ventilator, with a hole of one and a half inch bore, up through the roof, and is finished with an ornamental cap.

"The room for ice is eight by ten feet in the clear, and eight feet high. Without a more minute description, I think the building will be understood. If not, inquire further, any who wish to do so. About all the waste of ice that I observed during the summer was at the bottom; and this was so slow that we used the ice without regard to economy, for a large family, and in a dairy of thirty-five cows, besides giving freely to our neighbors.

"I put sticks four inches thick at the bottom to put ice on, and also some straw about the sides as well as underneath the ice."

DESIGN No. 19.

THIS suburban villa was designed for Mrs. T. D. Wheeler, and executed in Prospect street, New Haven. It is pleasantly situated opposite the beautiful grounds belonging to the Hillhouse family. The exterior bears an English character, bordering somewhat upon the Tudor, but slightly Americanized by the addition of verandas. Perhaps the English Tudor or late Gothic cottage is more readily adapted to our houses here in America than almost any other, as it had its growth in very nearly the same domestic exigencies which hold good with us, and its great *pliability* of style renders it applicable to dwellings of almost any extent or peculiarity of plan. The readiness with which its steep roofs shed the frequent rains and snows of our climate is another cogent reason for its more general adoption.

This house is built of brick, with hollow walls, stuccoed on the outside, and colored a neutral tint. This mode is somewhat confined to this locality, where it is practised with considerable success. The roof is covered with slate, from the Vermont quarries, with the exception of a small flat or deck on top, which is covered with tin, and used for the purpose of collecting water for the tank in the attic. By reference to the first floor plan, the reader will perceive that the accommodations are of a liberal character. The main hall is entered through a spacious vestibule; this is paved with encaustic tile, and well lighted by a window at the side. Folding doors of plate glass give entrance into the hall. This hall is nine feet wide by thirty-eight feet in length, and entirely unobstructed, the stairs being placed at the side. Halls of this kind are usually objectionable, from presenting a long and naked appearance, and being dark in the centre. These objections are, however, here, in a great measure, remedied; the monotonous extent of the hall being broken by two arches, as indicated by dotted lines, and additional light being obtained from the stairway at the side. There is another exit from this hall without going to the extreme end, which is at the left, under the main stairs, where sufficient headway is obtained to admit a good-sized door. This, then, renders that portion of the main hall beyond the staircase superfluous, if great economy of room is desirable, and it might be included in the study, making this room equal in size to the library. The present arrangement is, however, considered far preferable for considerations of free ventilation, for a promenade in bad weather, and for the generous effects of ample space obtained on entering the house.

The two principal rooms, viz., drawing room and library, are large, and provided with spacious bay windows. The doors entering these rooms are opposite each other, and might be made double, thus, as occasion required, throwing the suite into one grand apartment, including the hall. The dining room is of good size, and is connected with a large butler's pantry, which is provided with a sink, dresser, and dumb waiter, communicating with a similar pantry below, opening into the kitchen. A very convenient addition to a dwelling of this kind is a gentleman's wash closet on the first floor; such an one is provided here, connecting with the main hall, and also serving as a passage to the butler's pantry. The grand feature of this house, next to the hall, is, undoubtedly, the stairway, which occupies a large space at the left, and is well lighted by a stained glass window. Too often, in allowing the stairs to ascend through the hall, both features are spoiled, the hall being cut up and its continuity destroyed, and the stairs themselves made tiresome by their long, straight, unbroken rise to the floor above, no landing intervening as a happy resting place in the ascent.

The study is, perhaps, the most agreeable and attractive feature of the house. Its chimney, it will be observed, is placed diagonally in one corner of the room, while the other three are filled with corresponding diagonal book cases. The mantel is of richly carved black walnut, and the book cases, wainscoting, ceiling, and doors of the room are also elaborately designed and executed in hard wood, the whole oiled and polished. The brick flue from the fireplace recedes above the opening, giving space for a cabinet over the mantel, which well balances the book cases. These all extend to the ceiling, and their heavy oaken cornices and bases skirt the entire room. The furniture of the room is appropriately of carved oak. The owner has recently enclosed with glass a portion of the south veranda, opposite the study windows, for a greenhouse on a moderate scale.

The chambers are all commodiously arranged; two of them communicating with the bath room, and having separate dressing rooms. All the rooms have closets, while linen and cedar closets are separately provided.

The plumbing is economically arranged, as, the tank, bath room, butler's pantry, and kitchen being directly over each other, long lines of horizontal piping are avoided. These are, however, unfortunately, on the north side of the house, where they might be affected by frosts; but this is guarded against by their being packed in sawdust and coming in contact with the kitchen chimney. The drains are purposely made small, as by this means the liquids run through with greater rapidity, and act effectually to keep the drain pipes free from obstructions.

Estimate.—The estimates on this house were $13,000.

DESIGN Nº 19.

Paul Schulze del.

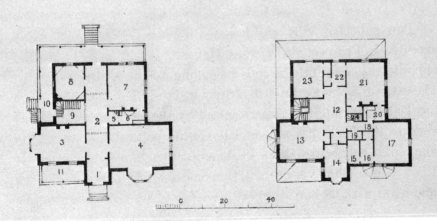

0   20   40

Paul Schulze, del.

DESIGN N⁰ 20.

DESIGN No. 20.

THIS design, which is an enlargement of No. 12, and whose plan is shown on that plate, we shall now attempt to describe in detail.

The entrance hall, as before stated, is large, and well worthy the extent of the mansion. Its floor is composed of narrow, hard wood boards, with a border of a different color, and a mosaic centre around the register. The walls are wainscoted with black walnut, and the doors and trimmings are of the same. The staircase, which is the principal feature, is also composed wholly of this material, and occupies the entire rear of the hall; it ascends, as we noticed, in two flights from the right and left to the landing, and continues thence in a single flight to the floor above. The ceiling of this staircase is supported by carved wood ribs, which continue across the hall and intersect with the mouldings of the front door; these ribs are repeated elsewhere across the ceiling, forming panels, which are ceiled with narrow oak boards, unless, for economy, plaster should be preferred, in which case a delicate sky-blue tint might be used with good effect. The library, which is finished in the same appropriately grave but rich manner, has walnut book cases extending to the ceiling, the cornices of which run around the room. This apartment communicates with the hall by folding doors, and, the drawing room opposite having a similar communication, the whole range of apartments may be thrown into one suite when occasion requires. The drawing room is of large dimensions, but, instead of being finished in natural wood, has its floor carpeted for the sake of the warmth, comfort, and color so essential in an apartment which is the social centre and abiding place of the household. Its ceiling and walls are painted with brilliant tones of vermilion, cobalt, and gold, on a ground of some delicate tint. The mantel is of Italian marble, while those in the library and dining room are of carved walnut and oak. The latter room, though receiving a similar finish to the hall, should be of oak instead of walnut. In all these rooms the furniture must of course correspond with their respective styles of architectural treatment, the furniture of the dining room being of carved oak, and that of the hall and library of walnut. These woods should in no case be varnished, but oiled and polished, while the hard wood floors should be waxed. Carpets for these floors would be entirely out of place, but mats and rugs may be used with elegant effect. In the drawing room, rosewood furniture, with the richest carpets and gilded mirrors, are highly appropriate. The hall has a side external entrance, at the entry B, which connects with the boudoir and drawing room. The boudoir has a fireplace located diagonally in one corner, the flue of which opens into the kitchen chimney. The other corners are similarly occupied by cabinets. This is the private room of the mistress of the house, and is in direct communication with both the family and domestic portions of the establishment. By a slight alteration of the private stairway, a door might be arranged connecting this room with the kitchen, through a closet.

The kitchen, which is large, connects with the dining room through a butler's pantry, and is also conveniently placed with reference to the hall, which, when desired, is large enough to be used as a breakfast or tea room. The second story contains five chambers, a bath room, and linen closet, and in the attic are good bedrooms.

The vignette at the left illustrates a bit of rock work with a rustic bridge over a brook, as executed at Central Park by A. Gerster, showing how picturesque the simplest natural feature may be made. That on the right represents a boat and bathing house, placed some distance from the shore, to secure deep water, and approached by a bridge. The whole is ornamentally designed, but sufficiently strong to withstand any storm.

Paul Schulze del.

DESIGN № 21.

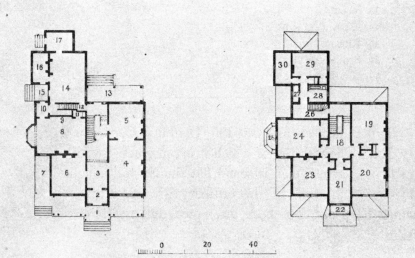

0   20   40

DESIGN No. 21.

THIS building was erected at Danbury, Conn., for A. E. Tweedy, Esq. The material of which it is constructed is unbaked brick, made of concrete, and is somewhat similar to, though much more durable than, that of the ordinary gravel or rough-cast walls, which have so often been attempted, and nearly as often proved failures.

In the interior of the country, where stone may not be readily obtained, and brick and lumber can be transported only at great expense, this material will be found of great advantage, as it can be manufactured on the spot, from the loose gravel that comes from the excavation of the cellar, provided the gravel is sharp, and free from loam or clay. The material is then mixed in the proper proportion with lime or cement, placed in moulds, and subjected to great pressure. The bricks thus formed are carefully placed on boards, where they remain until the mortar is set. They are then perfectly hard and ready for use. The size of these bricks is ten inches long, by five inches wide and four inches deep, with a hollow space in the centre, which prevents dampness passing through. This latter object is also aided by the manner in which the walls are laid, the joints being "*broken*," as it is called. The hollow space in the outside brick just covering the solid portion of the brick behind, it is impossible for dampness to penetrate.

The manner in which these bricks are made renders them perfectly smooth and square. They are of a neutral gray tint, which could not be improved as a color for the house. They require no paint, but only an occasional coat of boiled oil, for the purpose of better resisting the weather.

It is particularly necessary, however, that persons building with this material should employ the most experienced workmen for making it, since, if the proportions and method of manufacture are not exactly understood, this brick is apt to be weak and porous, and consequently to prove unsafe ; but if proper precautions are taken, actual experience has proved that it is among the cheapest and best materials for building. Mr. Tweedy's house has the interior plaster laid directly upon the brick, so that the important items of lathing and furring are avoided in the bill of expenses, and he assures the author that he has never discovered any dampness upon the inside walls. The woodwork of the house is nailed directly on the brick, so that there is no occasion for introducing the usual wooden blocks, which are liable to shrink and decay, and thereby weaken the walls. The following letter from Mr. Tweedy may prove interesting, as it gives his opinion in this mat. ter, and somewhat of the history of his house:

" DANBURY, *May* 2, 1859.

" HENRY HUDSON HOLLY, ESQ.:

" DEAR SIR: I have neglected till now writing you in answer to yours of 18th April, in relation to what is called the Foster brick, from which my house is built. I have the fullest confidence in them, if they are made of the right material, and properly manufactured. Ten parts of clean grit or coarse sand to one part of lime is the mixture used for the blocks for the outside course of my house. About five per cent. of cement was added to the above mixture. My house is about 40 feet square, main body, two stories and attic; walls 28 feet in height, 10 inches in thickness. The L or kitchen part, two stories, about 20 by 24 feet. I began building two years since, laid the walls 21 feet high, to attic floor timbers; stopped the latter part of October; covered the tops of the walls with boards, and left the building open and exposed during the Winter and Spring of 1857 and 1858, and found the walls all sound and solid. In May last, carried up the walls, and completed the outside and partition walls during last Summer and Fall; and now the building is as strong and solid as any brick can be. Although my house may be considered an experiment here, for one of the size—three or four smaller ones having been built of the same material in the mean time—I should have the fullest confidence in putting up a building of any size, with the experience now had in making the bricks.

"My inside plastering is put on without furring and lathing, on the outside walls, and is perfectly dry and solid. It is my opinion, with suitable arrangements for making the blocks, the saving over ordinary clay burnt bricks will be 25 or 30 per cent. per cubic foot in the walls. Any information in regard to the material and building will be cheerfully given by

"Yours, respectfully,

(Signed.)   " A. E. TWEEDY."

Estimate.—The estimates on this house were $12,500.

DESIGN No. 22.

This building was designed and executed for William R. Fosdicke, Esq., of Stamford, Conn., and stands on the summit of a rising ground north of the village, called Strawberry Hill, from which is obtained one of the finest views of the Sound and the surrounding country that may be had in that vicinity.

The principal object in the arrangement of this house was to bring all the rooms into such a position that each might have the advantage of the view which is on the veranda side, toward the south. The disposition of apartments on the ground floor, accordingly, is such that but one of them is without this advantage. This happens to be the dining room, which is seldom occupied for any other than its legitimate purpose; therefore, exterior views are of comparatively small consideration. This room might have been made to exchange places with the kitchen, and thereby have received the same advantage; but this would have brought the latter into too close proximity with the family apartments, and the dining room would not have been so pleasantly situated. The owner was also anxious to have it connect with the drawing room, by sliding doors. For these reasons the plan resolves itself into the present arrangement. These sliding doors, it will be remarked, are placed on the broad side of the room instead of at the end, which is the usual mode. By this plan the doors may be made much wider, and the two broad sides of each room being thus joined give more the appearance of a single large apartment.

The symmetrical arrangement of these rooms adds very much to their beauty. Exactly opposite the fireplaces in each are windows; the bay window in the dining room is crowned with a Gothic arch, corresponding to similar ones over the sideboard niche and sliding doors. The windows and doorheads throughout this floor terminate in a similar manner, and the whole house, both outside and in, has a decidedly Gothic sentiment, partaking principally of the characteristics of the Tudor period.

The grand external feature of this house is the veranda, which extends across the entire southern portion. This, though running along the side of the kitchen, has no connection with it, as the servants are provided with a spacious porch at their entrance door. The laundry and milk room are placed in the basement, under the kitchen, which communicates with an area under the veranda, making them, in fact, rooms above ground.

The furnace is placed in the centre of the cellar, and under the main hall. This cellar is provided with a coal slide and several bins, convenient to the furnace, for the different kinds of coal. The milk-room door is constructed with panels, which may be opened to obtain a draft from the opposite window—an essential requisite in a room of this kind.

The cellar walls are built of twenty-inch stonework, the bottom being composed of large flags projecting six inches on either side, and laid in concrete. This footing course serves a double purpose: as a base for the stonework, preventing the building from settling, and also as a safeguard from rats. It is the nature of this animal, in getting into a house, to burrow down by the side of the foundation walls, but, when coming in contact with a stone or other impediment, to return and start anew rather than go around the obstacle. This six-inch projection acts, therefore, as a formidable barrier against the entrance of vermin. The several floors, also, are deafened, thus not only preventing the communication of sound, but leaves no space between ceiling and floor for rats to occupy.

In a building of this kind, outside blinds are not only out of place, but impracticable, as the moulded lables or drips above the windows would prevent them from swinging around. Inside sliding or folding blinds must therefore be substituted. These are much more convenient, as they may be opened or closed without raising the windows, which in cold and stormy weather is objectionable, and in a house with thick walls there is always sufficient room in the window jambs for a box to receive these blinds. The windows opening on the veranda are peculiar, being a combination of French and sliding sash. The difficulty of these has generally been that they cannot be made sufficiently tight to exclude the rain and cold of our northern winters, while the latter cannot be easily made to slide up high enough to give proper headway for passing in and out. These combine the two advantages of security and providing ample headway, the first by sliding, the second by swinging, in the ordinary manner, when raised above the weather sill. Another advantage possessed by these over common swinging sashes, is that they may be opened, to admit air, without interfering with curtains or inside blinds.

Estimate.—The estimates on this house were $10,000.

Paul Schulze, del.

DESIGN Nº 22.

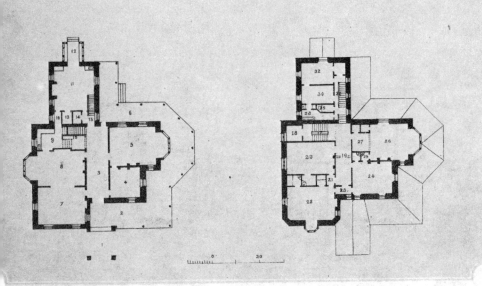

DESIGN Nº 23.

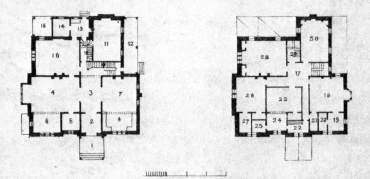

DESIGN No. 23.

THE irregularity and diversity of outline in this building are intended to accord with a picturesque locality, or, by the variety of its skylines, as seen above surrounding trees, to offer a pleasing indication from afar of domestic comfort and hospitality, and of an extensive household. The plan, with the exception of the projection of the kitchen, approaches a square, thus obtaining economy in walls, although the general effect of the structure affords the impression of an irregular plan.

The entrance, which should always be the most prominent external object, is here placed in the tower itself, and rendered still more conspicuous by the large, hospitable porch, which seems to extend a welcome even before we enter. This porch furnishes a sort of footing for the tower, and the veranda and buttress serve as a base for the house itself, and overcome the abruptness of formal walls springing directly from the ground. The interior of the building is arranged for comfort, combining utility with ornamental design. The vestibule is large, and might have a closet for coats taken off the cabinet on the left. It is separated from the main hall by folding doors of plate glass. The first thing that attracts the eye, on entering this hall, is the beginning of the stairs, starting up into a sort of L, which conceals the most of the staircase from view, exhibiting only the newel and a small part of the rail; these, if properly treated, may be made highly ornamental, giving to the entire hall a marked character and expression. These stairs are somewhat cut off from the main hall by an arch, represented on the plan by dotted lines. Between this arch and vestibule are broad sliding doors opening into the drawing room on one side and the library on the other, thus obtaining a fine vista through the house.

The drawing room has opening from it a small cabinet, which is often a very pretty addition. It may be used as a private office or small reception room, and have a door opening into the vestibule. At the left of this is a large music alcove or bay, separated from the drawing room simply by an arch. The library has a similar alcove, used for books, thus leaving the main portion unobstructed for a sitting room. By the introduction of curtains, this alcove might be converted into a place for reading. The dining room is symmetrical, and has a niche for a sideboard opposite the fireplace. Its connection with the kitchen is through a spacious entry, also used as a butler's pantry, and containing a sink, dresser, &c. This entry also communicates with a back staircase and store room, and has an external entrance for servants. The rear entrance for the family is at the end of the main hall, under the staircase, where sufficient headway is obtained for a full-sized door.

The second floor is provided with a bath and five spacious bed rooms, all with studied places for furniture and large closets. Two have dressing rooms, and a third is provided with an alcove similar to that in the drawing room, from which we may enter, on one side, the bath, on the other, a dressing room. Both staircases extend to the attic, where are servants' rooms, spare chambers, and billiard room. Here, too, the observatory stairs begin. The front of this house commands but a limited view, for which reason the best rooms and verandas are placed in other parts of the building.

Estimate.—This building, in stone, would cost about $12,000.

Paul Schulze del.

DESIGN Nº 24.

0   20

DESIGN No. 24.

THIS house is designed with particular reference to durability and facilities for warming and ventilating. No perishable material is used in its construction. The walls are built of stone; the partitions, where the proper support is obtained, are of brick, and elsewhere of galvanized lath; the window frames are of iron, and all the floors of cement, with a strip at the side for securing carpets. The roof is of slate, while the stairs and inside trimmings are entirely of metal or composition. Thus the building is rendered secure from the ravages of fire and from decay.

Much has already been said on the importance of ventilation, yet there is danger of doing too much as well as too little in this matter. The subject has become almost a monomania with some, and it is imagined that, unless there are top and bottom injecting and ejecting flues, arranged on scientific principles, and so complicated as to keep both mind and body continually in action in the management of them, the air must be poisonous.

Again, we see the same wild schemes in regard to heating. The idea prevails, to a certain extent, that a hot-air furnace is, of all things, most injurious; that the heat generated by it consumes instantly and effectually the vital properties of the atmosphere. Therefore, hot-air furnaces are condemned *in toto*, and steam, hot water, and other complicated and expensive contrivances are resorted to.

The fact is, that the fault is often more in the owner than in the furnace. A man purchasing a furnace for the purpose of heating his house frequently contents himself with one of the smallest possible size to save expense, knowing that, although the amount of air passing through it will be small, yet, by heating that small amount red hot, it will warm his house. Undoubtedly this object will be effected, but no less surely will the oxygen of the air be burnt out with such violent heat, and the lungs, habitually inhaling this parched and vitiated atmosphere, be much injured thereby. Were he to expend a trifle more for a furnace which would introduce a larger volume of air, moderately heated, he would find that air as soft and pleasant as that radiated from steam or hot water, and at the same time he would procure a saving in fuel, and perhaps still more in doctors' bills.

The only advantage we perceive in the steam and water furnaces over those constructed for hot air, is the impossibility of producing by their agency more than a certain degree of heat. Therefore, in order to have a sufficient amount, the radiating surface must be increased in proportion to the extent of space to be warmed; while the superiority of the hot-air furnace must be evident from its greater simplicity of construction and its costing but about one third.

"Modern improvements" are excellent things until used in excess, and they then become more troublesome than useful. This is especially true of ventilation; for, however complicated an arrangement may be requisite in a public building for this purpose, yet, in a dwelling, the more simple the method, the more effectually it will act. It is perhaps difficult to say which, among so many, is the best system, but we would suggest the following as simple and effective.

We will suppose our house to be heated with, say, one of Boynton's hot-air furnaces of large dimensions, so that the fresh air flows from it throughout the building in no way diminished in purity, but merely changed by having the chill taken off and rendered mild and delightful. Warm air, as we are all aware, has a tendency to rise; hence, if we place our ventilator at the ceiling, the flow of air will be in a direct line from the register to it, and thus only that portion of the room which lies between these points will be either warmed or ventilated. Where, then, shall the opening for ventilation be? Placing it at the bottom of the room, the warm air rises, as before, to the ceiling, but, finding no escape there, it must seek a downward channel; and if now the opening be on the opposite side from the register, all the air in the room must be kept in motion. We thus obtain an atmosphere pure, and, at all seasons, as agreeable as that of summer. It remains to describe the construction of the ventilating flue. Every room in our house, of course, has a fireplace, though we have obviated, in a great measure, the necessity of fires. Here is unquestionably the place for the ventilator, and the whole complicated mystery of successful heating and good ventilation is solved by a large hot-air furnace in the cellar and a fireplace in every room. We would also advise, as a material assistance in the work of ventilation, a little fire in the grate, securing, by this, a better draught, and requiring less heat in the furnace. The old style of anthracite grates has almost fallen into disuse, and the English soft-coal grates are taking their place. Soft coal is not only more cheerful, reminding us of the good old days of wood fires, but its effect is not so drying upon the air.

If wood or bituminous coal is used, however, the chimney flues should be built larger, as they otherwise are apt to become obstructed by soot. Finally, we would recommend the use of double sashes in winter, by which a great deal of cold air is excluded.

Estimate.—This building, in stone, would cost about $11,500.

DESIGN No. 25.

A BUILDING like this, which is of the feudal or castellated style, should be adopted only with the greatest caution, as the contrast between modern and feudal life is so great that, without a nice adaptation of circumstances, it may appear ridiculous to build, and much more ridiculous to occupy, such an establishment. This style, referred to in Chap. I., is similar to that which existed prior to the union of the Houses of York and Lancaster, after which event there no longer existed any necessity for private fortifications.

The following extract from an English writer will give the reader some idea of an edifice of this kind :

" The situation of castles of the Anglo-Norman kings and barons was most commonly on an eminence and near a river—a situation eligible on several accounts. The whole site of the castle (which was frequently of great extent and irregular figure) was surrounded by a deep and broad ditch, sometimes filled with water, and sometimes dry. Before the great gate was an outwork called a barbican, which was a strong and high wall, with turrets upon it, for the defence of the gate and drawbridge. On the inside of the ditch stood the wall of the castle, about ten feet thick and twenty feet high, with battlements on top ; on this wall, at proper distances, high, square towers were built, which served for lodging some of the principal officers, and on the outside were erected, lodgings for the common servants or retainers, granaries, store houses, and other necessary offices, and on the flat roofs of these buildings stood the defenders of the castle, when it was besieged, and from thence discharged arrows, darts, and stones on the besiegers. The great gate of the castle stood in the course of this wall, and was strongly fortified with a tower on each side, and rooms over the passage, which was closed with folding doors of oak, often plated with iron, and with an iron portcullis, or gate, let down from above. Within this outward wall was an open space, or court, in which stood frequently a church or chapel. Here, also, was another ditch, wall, gate, and tower, enclosing the inner court, within which the chief tower, or keep, was built, which was the residence of the baron. Underground were dismal, dark vaults, for the confinement of prisoners, called the dungeon. In this building, also, was the great hall, in which the owner displayed his hospitality, by entertaining his numerous friends and followers. At one end of the great hall was a place raised a little above the rest of the floor, called the *dais*, where the chief table stood, at which persons of the highest rank dined. Though there were unquestionably great variations in the structure of castles and palaces in this period, yet the most perfect and magnificent of them seem to have been constructed on the above plan. Such, to give an example, was the famous castle at Bedford, as appears from the following account of the manner in which it was taken by Henry III., A. D. 1224 : 'The castle was taken by four assaults. In the first was taken the barbican ; in the second the outer ballia, or court ; at the third attack, the wall by the old tower was thrown down by the miners, when, with great danger, they possessed themselves of the inner ballia, through a chink ; at the fourth assault, the miners set fire to the tower, so that the smoke burst out, and the tower itself was cloven to that degree, as to show visibly some broad chinks, whereupon the enemy surrendered.' "

After the age of Edward I., we find another kind of castle introduced, approaching nearer to the idea of modern palaces. The first was that of Windsor, built by Edward III. This convenient and enlarged style of building was soon imitated on a lesser scale by the nobles of the realm, and two remarkable instances, wherein convenience and magnificence were singularly blended at this period, may be found in the castles of Harewood and Spofford, in Yorkshire. The improvements at Kenilworth afford another instance of the great enlargement which the English castles received during this age. Of course, a full description of these feudal residences need not be entered into here, especially as this has already been done by other and abler writers. For descriptions of this kind, the reader is referred to the works of Sir Walter Scott, and more particularly Kenilworth and Ivanhoe.

Shortly after this period gunpowder was invented, which, instead of bringing war and bloodshed into the world, proved the

most effectual means of preventing them. The people of England,
instead of requiring castellated residences, now put their trust in
their "wooden walls," and their fighting was done far away from
their native shores. Their private strongholds were soon in ruins,
dismantled by shot and shell; and with the dissolution of feudal-
ism, the mind of the nation soon broke the cords which had bound
it for so many centuries; a ray of light dawned, and the "dark
ages" dated among the things that were. From this time until
Tudor architecture was fully established in England, a style between the castellated and that described in No. 27 was generally
adopted for domestic dwellings, of which the accompanying design
is an attempted imitation. It will be observed that all the old
contrivances to obtain strength and seclusion are here omitted, and
comfort and convenience are substituted. The walls, for example,
are no thicker than ordinary walls, and the windows, instead of
being mere warlike loopholes, are of ample, peaceful dimensions,
and are filled with glass. Here, too, we have committed the ana-
chronism of introducing chimneys and bay windows, with, what is
still more unusual in castles, a porch without a portcullis, and a
veranda. All these, however foreign to the requirements of a castle, are yet of use to us, and whatever style we may adopt, we do
not hesitate to add to it, to the best of our ability, any improvement which convenience or necessity may require. Yet all such
additions must be treated with the greatest care, lest we violate
some of the characteristics of the style.

Our site, then, for an edifice like this, must be somewhat formidable, and have at least the appearance of being able to resist a
siege. The interior we find provided with modern improvements,
and generally convenient. A door gives entrance to the vestibule
from the porch, and this conducts us to the hall. The first door at
the right opens into a coat closet; the next communicates with the

Paul Schulze del.

DESIGN Nº 25.

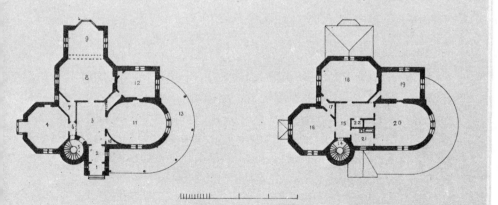

drawing room. This is elliptical in plan. The boudoir is a cozy apartment, quite retired, and is furnished with a closet. The dining room is of spacious dimensions, and has a large alcove somewhat after the fashion of the Dais, above mentioned, separated from the main apartment by an arch, from which curtains may be hung, thus rendering this Dais or bay sufficiently private for a sitting or music room. This, too, would be an admirable arrangement for tableaux or private theatricals, or, in case of an entertainment, as a practical enlargement of the dining room. The butler's pantry is of good size, communicating by a dumb waiter with the kitchen below. The library is octagonal, having four sides for books, while the others are occupied by doors, windows, and fireplace. There is but one stairway in this house, which extends from the basement to the top of the tower, but so retired that other stairs are deemed unnecessary. The second story contains four large bedrooms, a linen closet and bath room, while the servants' and store rooms are in the attic.

Estimate.—This building, in stone, would cost about $9,500.

DESIGN Nº 26

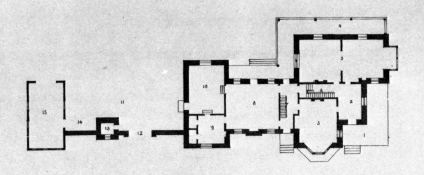

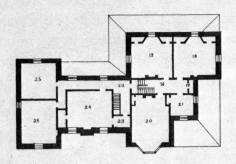

DESIGN Nº 26.

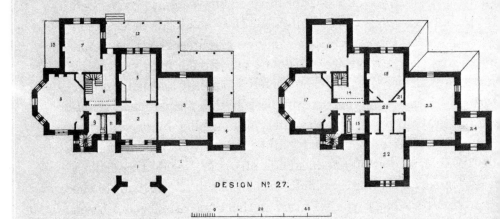

DESIGN Nº 27.

0   20   40

DESIGN No. 26.

THERE is a passion prevalent in our cities, and the rural districts are not wholly exempt from it, for producing the greatest possible show with the least amount of expense. We are well aware that this tendency is generally considered vulgar, and when developed to any great degree, is doubtless open to this imputation; yet in moderation it is but the expression of a considerable self-respect. In building, we think a just amount of this feeling is eminently laudable.

As an illustration, let us suppose a small domain of some two or three acres to have been selected, on which we propose to establish a dwelling, and all the appendages of a small country place. With limited means, we desire to make our place as imposing in appearance as possible, the house itself to be of moderate size, having three rooms and a kitchen on the first floor. Now, instead of scattering about the grounds the necessary out-buildings, let us group them in such a manner that, taken in connection with the house, they shall each have a value in the *tout ensemble*, and appear of the grand design. We thus have our wood house, shed, carriage house, &c., together, with an enclosed yard for domestic purposes, all apparently forming an extension of the dwelling, and giving our humble house a very desirable degree of dignity and importance, while the position of these subordinate appendages is most convenient. But should we stop here, we defeat our object; for nothing can be more unbecoming or pretentious than so imposing an array of buildings in so small a domain. We require at least the appearance of a tract of forty or fifty acres, to correspond with the proportions of the building. How shall this be effected? Shall we make the glass of our windows magnifiers? This would do if we were always within doors, but would hardly give the same result from without. The remedy is an easy and natural one. Instead of enclosing your narrow park with a formal fence, standing out in bold relief, and absolutely diminishing by one half the apparent extent of your land, build a stone wall of barely sufficient height to prevent the incursion of cattle; inside this make a bank of earth, sloping gradually from the top of this wall to the ground. This bank you will turf in the same manner as a lawn. Thus the wall is entirely removed from sight, and the adjoining land blends with your own, and appears as much a part and parcel of the whole as if you owned for miles around.

Let us now proceed to a detailed description of the building itself.

As we approach the main entrance, we pass a wide veranda, which communicates with the principal rooms of the ground floor. The main hall is spacious and well lighted, and, being unobstructed by the stairs, might serve the purpose of a sitting room. The drawing rooms are separated by sliding doors, so that one might be used as a library. The dining room has a niche for a sideboard, and a bay window, surrounded outside by a balcony. This room communicates with the kitchen offices by a private entry, which contains a stairway, dresser, butler's sink, &c., and has an exit front and rear. The kitchen is of large proportions, well lighted, and connecting with the wood house and laundry, the latter of which is provided with large pantries and a fireplace. The woodhouse floor is lower than that of the main building, and on a level with the yard, to give greater height for accommodation of stores. The yard before spoken of, is for drying clothes and other domestic purposes, and is concealed by a high wall, provided with a wide gateway, and broken by a lofty, picturesque aviary.

The stable and carriage house, with a room for a man servant in hay loft above, are at the extremity of the group. The advantage of having these appendages thus remote from the house is obvious.

The shed, at No. 14, we would always recommend as an appendage to every country house; for it not only acts as a store place and refuge for fowls, but serves the hospitable purpose of sheltering both horse and carriage of your transient guest.

The chamber accommodations of this house are ample, as it contains seven bed rooms, a bath room and linen closet, while ser-

vants' and store rooms may be had in the attic. The kitchen
chimney is built on the outside of the house, thus serving to relieve the bareness of the walls, by a pleasing external feature,
affording more room for the first and second stories, and excluding
the heat in summer.

An objection was raised in Design No. 3 to the finials and
ridge ornaments, as serving merely an æsthetical purpose, but here
this objection does not obtain, since they are of practical utility.
They are of iron, and, bristling with a decorated design, form
points for the lightning, and are connected with an ornamental con-
ductor, leading to the ground.

Estimate.—This building, in stone, would cost about $10,500.

DESIGN No. 27.

THE reader is now presented with a design, which may be regarded as approaching that of an old English seat, built on a liberal scale. The style adopted is that described in Chap. I., called the Tudor, which was in vogue in England between the reigns of Henry VII. and Elizabeth. This may be considered as the first real development of domestic architecture in England, since, previous to the union of the Houses of York and Lancaster, through the marriage of Henry VII., the fortified castle was the only safe place of residence for either royalty or nobility. When, after years of internal broils and civil discord, permanent peace was restored to the nation, the entire mode of life was radically changed, and instead of fortified dwellings, the nobility and gentry began to build mansions more in accordance with the modern idea of domestic comfort and elegance. Formidable barriers of rock were no longer considered the most eligible building sites, but the shady grove, the gentle slope of lawns and parks, the hill and river side, became the chosen abodes of the wealth and culture of the nation. The portcullis and drawbridge were no longer required, the massive walls were not an imperative necessity; the loopholes gave place to windows and bays; ornaments of convenience and utility made their appearance, clustering chimneys towered up to the skies; porches and oriels adorned the walls, and the roofs were combinations of battlement and gable; in short, the Tudor style was a union of all that was beautiful in both castle and abbey.

The main entrance of this design has rather an ecclesiastical character. The pointed roof and window of the second story is of the style of the thirteenth century, while the flat arch of the carriage porch and the buttresses which stregthen the piers are of the fifteenth. The battlemented towers and parapets which here and there show themselves, partake strongly of the castellated feeling, and the bay windows, chimneys, &c., may be regarded as new features, peculiar to the Tudor.

As we drive under the porch, which is under a portion of the second story, we enter a broad and spacious hall, which communicates by folding doors with the library in the rear. This library is lighted by a triplet Gothic window, facing the folding doors. The light coming from but one direction in rooms of this character, is an advantage of which we have had frequent occasion to speak. The drawing room is of good size, and connects with a little cabinet used for the purpose of containing curiosities, but which may be converted into a private music room. The staircase hall is apart, and communicates with the dining room and bedroom, and has an exit on the rear veranda. The dining room is somewhat octagonal in form, but the fireplace and opposite window recede, so as to give a greater length in this direction. The butler's pantry, which connects with the private staircase, tower, and main stairs, contains a sink, dresser, and dumb waiter, which communicates with the kitchen. A kitchen might be arranged on the first floor, in lieu of the bedroom, communicating with the dining room through its present closet. A kitchen on both floors, in a house of this size, is frequently advisable. The private stairs, above alluded to, extend from the basement, winding through the tower, to the various stories above, and so to the top, which is protected, as will be seen, by the battlement. This roof is of such a height that the views from it, even on ordinary sites, must be very extensive. After ascending the main stairs to the second story hall, we are struck with the spacious apartments so numerous upon this floor.

The bath room and water closet communicate with the hall, and the plumbing of the various stories, which are supplied with water from a tank in the attic, is economized by the exact superimposition of the apartments in which it is used. The billiard room and spare chambers are arranged in the attic, where sufficient height of ceiling is obtained, without infringing on a large space between the ceiling and roof, which is designed to prevent the direct action of the weather, and to give good air for the rooms below, whose ventilating shafts terminate in this space, and all pass through an " Emerson ventilator " above the roof.

The view given of this house is taken from a point in front, where the verandas, which are all in the rear, are not seen. The reason of this is, the exposure and view from the front are not particularly desirable, while in the rear they are peculiarly so.

The material of this house would naturally be stone; yet if that is not of convenient access, brick or stucco would not be objectionable; but wood is not in any case adapted to this style of architecture, as its details are designed only for masonry.

Ivy or other vines are always appropriate for the ornamenting of the Gothic, and add much to its picturesqueness. As the English ivy is not a hardy plant in our country, the Virginia creeper is often substituted with good effect. Its only disadvantage is that it is not an evergreen; yet it leaves out early in the Spring, and is in constant verdure until late in Autumn, when it is changed by frost into the most gorgeous tints imaginable. The English ivy in some localities has, even in our coldest exposures, been made to thrive and grow vigorously, as at the residence of the late Washington Irving, where the ivy literally covers one side of the house.

It will be found advantageous, in cultivating this vine, to plant it on the north side of the house, where, after it has been touched by frost, it is not immediately exposed to the sun, which is often the greater enemy of the two. It needs but little heat, and considerable humidity of atmosphere, as in England.

Estimate.—This building, in stone, would cost about $28,000.

Paul Schulze del.

Print by H. Lawrence, 83, William St. N. Y.

DESIGN, Nº 27.

DESIGN No. 28.

ALTERATIONS of old buildings, when extensive, are not usually considered advisable, as the cost of much alteration is nearly, if not quite, equal to that of an entirely new edifice. Another serious objection is the embarrassment usually attending the fixed lines of the original structure, which limit the architect to a narrow field for the display of whatever ability he may possess. Yet it frequently happens that a family have already on their land a decent dwelling, endeared by many associations, whose total destruction would seem almost sacrilegious, as well as wanton waste of property. Either a new field must be sought for the desired improvements, or we must alter the present mansion; and the latter is the usual and perhaps more natural course.

This is no easy task for the architect, who, when a double labor has been expended, and but a partial effect produced, may well shrink from that paternal responsibility which otherwise he would readily have assumed, and deprecate the criticism which, under other circumstances, he would gladly have invited.

The accompanying design will somewhat illustrate how far we have been successful in the alteration of a moderately sized dwelling, which was the residence of Geo. A. Hoyt, Esq., of Stamford, Conn. The original building, which may be seen in the vignette at the right of the ground plan, was finely situated within an enclosure of some half dozen acres, shaded by deciduous trees. The building was of stone, and of so substantial a character and so well arranged, that the owner wisely concluded that alteration would be better than tearing down and building anew. In the plan of the first story, the dark portion represents the old house, and the lighter the additions.

The original arrangement was preserved so far as was practicable. The drawing room, which was added, being much larger than the other rooms, it was thought should have a greater height of ceiling than the rest of the house, and this caused a discrepancy of some four feet between the roofs. Some difficulty was anticipated in the management of this room to obtain sufficient size, as we were unable to extend it more than twenty feet from the house, and the rear wall was fixed by the position of the dining room windows. Not wishing to cut off the light, it was decided to extend the addition ten feet in front, and thus, by the aid of a large bay window, sufficient room was obtained. Again, the library and chamber above were too small. How else could we enlarge them than by extending them in the same manner? We cannot have a bay window in the library, as it would project into the road leading to the carriage porch; but this room is now large enough, and the trouble is with the bedroom above. This must be increased in size; but how shall it be effected? The idea suggests itself that a bay window may be placed in the second story, not extending to the ground, but supported by brackets, forming what may be called an oriel. Now that we have an interior of sufficient size, how shall we treat these awkward projections without? It occurs to us that we require an observatory, as no extended view can be had from the lower rooms, and the view in the distance is fine. We will therefore run the library projection above the roof and form a tower. This we will furnish with a railing, that we may mount to the very summit. Thus we relieve the discrepancy in height of the drawing room roof, which made the house look one-sided and unsymmetrical. Now we have obtained a balance of parts; and the irregularity of the roof gives the whole design a distinctive and decided character, and a broken and picturesque skyline.

The French chateau roof, which we have adopted, gives ample space for servants' apartments and other necessary rooms in the attic, and, by the flat on top, furnishes a means of collecting water for the tank, and provides a place on which we may walk, surrounded, as it is, with an iron railing for protection. We have provided, also, that the projections of the drawing room and library shall be just sufficient to receive the veranda, which extends along the front and sides of the house, and fills up the vacancy between. We now discover that the veranda around the saloon excludes the light from the kitchen, which is directly beneath it. Here is an unforeseen difficulty. We must have this veranda, and the location of the kitchen cannot be changed. We have seen in the city large blocks of glass let into the floor, that the light from a skylight above may pass through to the story below. This idea we adopt. That part of the veranda floor directly over each window in the kitchen we make of this thick glass, and are gratified to find that our experiment is entirely successful.

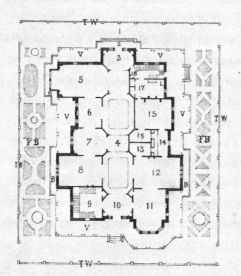

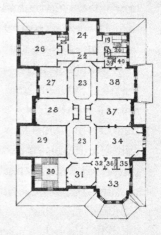

DESIGN N.º 29.

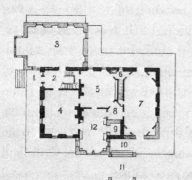

DESIGN N.º 28.

DESIGN No. 29.

THIS villa was designed for a wealthy gentleman, who has recently purchased one of the most charming sites on the shores of
the Sound. The grounds are of some years' standing, and were
laid out by one of the best landscape gardeners in the country.
They are covered with the choicest kinds of evergreen and deciduous trees, so arranged as to enhance the natural beauties of the
place. The estate has lately been much improved by the introduction of artificial waters in fountains, lakes, and streams, with
the usual concomitants of aquatic birds and plants, arbors, bridges,
and pleasure boats. The roads are well made, and wind gracefully
among groves and lawns, and by the water side, in such a manner
as to deceive the eye, and cause the small park of fifty acres to
seem double that size.

It is pleasant to note this growing disposition among our
wealthy citizens to cultivate the refinements of rural beauties. In
our cities we often find sums lavished on palatial residences, sufficient to build a host of villas in the country, and yet the effect
of such lavish expenditure is comparatively lost amid so much tedious repetition of design. It seems to us a marked indication
of wisdom and good taste, instead of expending a princely amount
on a narrow plot of ground in some aristocratic quarter of the
city, to establish an elegant and independent country seat, at a less
actual outlay, with gardens and pleasure grounds, and all those
elegant appliances of a luxurious rural home, which, while they
delight and give occupation to the mind, do not, like the dissipations of the city, debauch the body and undermine the health. To
be " monarch of all he surveys," in the midst of the fine repose and
healthy ease of an estate in the country, is the unfailing desire of
every man who has resources within himself against *ennui*, and
large capacities to develop in the paths of elegant culture. It may
be said that such a home as we have pictured is a luxury too ex-

pensive to be dreamed of save by few. Such is not the case to the extent generally supposed. The difference in taxes alone between town and country would defray the extra expense of maintaining the grounds, and the many economical advantages of a country life have been too often dwelt upon to need recapitulation here.

The exterior of this house, which is strictly Italian, and in harmony with the scenery amid which it is placed, is intended to convey the sentiments of refined household comfort and repose, and of a large and noble hospitality. The architecture being rather of a grave and formal character, it seems necessary to separate it somewhat from the easy slopes and natural grace of the lawns and banks around, by a broad terrace, which acts as a base to the building, and prepares the mind for the comparative severity of its lines. By referring to the ground plan, it will be observed that on two sides of the house the carriage road occupies the space between the terrace wall and the house, while on the other sides this space is occupied by flower beds, statuary, and fountains. The introduction of these latter features upon the lawn would produce an incongruous effect, they being too precise and formal for such a position. But this objection does not attach to their present location, where the object is to establish a connection between the severity of architecture and the easy, natural grace of nature. While the advantage of such artificial ornaments, as seen from the windows and balconies, is obvious, yet they form but a foreground to the wider extent of the park and woodland beyond.

The carriage porch is unusually large, being long enough to shelter both carriage and horses. The veranda and balconies, which are very wide, extend quite around the house, forming a walk of several hundred feet. The ceilings of the first story are twenty feet high, and the extreme width of the main hall is the same. This hall has two large openings (23, 23) in the ceiling, extending through the second story to the roof, where there are domes surrounded by skylights.

The drawing room, boudoir, music, and billiard rooms supply a vista through the house by the opening of folding doors, while the dining room, hall, and billiard room may be connected in the same manner. The billiard room, also used as a picture gallery, extends up to the roof, and has a railed balcony between the openings (23, 29). This room is lighted from above, and also at the side, by a high triplet window, which may be regulated by shades.

The dining room communicates with the kitchen by a large butler's pantry, the laundry with the linen closet on the second story, and the drying room in the attic by a dumb waiter. The second story contains nine sleeping apartments, all large, and most of them connected with bath and dressing rooms. The grand staircase occupies the entire tower, and extends to the observatory, while, at the other end of the hall, are other stairs of less pretensions, extending to the attic, which is divided into good apartments for servants' and store rooms.

Estimate.—This building, in brick, would cost about $45,000.

Paul Schulze del.

Print by M. Lawrence 83 William St. N.Y.

DESIGN Nº 29.

DESIGN № 30.

Paul Schulze del.

Print by H. Lawrence, 83. William St. N.Y.

DESIGN. No. 30.

Of city architecture but little has been said, because it is not strictly within the province of this work. There is, however, one phase of this architecture which recommends itself to our notice, as embodying many of those principles which we have repeatedly enumerated with reference to rural architecture, such as a more careful distribution of masses and a nicer study of extensive skylines with reference to block designs as seen from a distance. In building on open spaces or parks, a proper observance of these principles is essential to elegance and artistic effect.

Though our streets are lined for miles of their extent with expensive buildings, their general perspective effect is so unsatisfactory that the stranger, for the first time in New York, is puzzled and embarrassed to find out the system on which we build. Probably there is no city in the world having streets as extensive as our Broadway and Fifth Avenue, adorned with the same amount of pretentious and costly architecture; but still the result is less pleasing than that in some streets of European towns, whose buildings are of a much plainer character. The reason of this is our total disregard of harmony. Our designs are often elaborate, and sometimes beautiful, yet, as they rarely have an opportunity for fully expressing themselves, but are usually confined to one or two city lots, and as they are likely to be elbowed by uncongenial buildings on either side, the character of whose lines may materially obviate or entirely cancel that of our own, the general result is like the *disjecta membra poetæ*, chaotic, disconnected, and discordant.

These are defects which can scarcely be remedied where they already exist, but which should be avoided in future erections. Especially should they be regarded in the construction of those buildings which are to spring up around our parks. Occupying sites so conspicuous, these blocks should be carefully studied in masses and outline, so that each house may not be entirely independent and individual as now, but a responsible part of a general design. This can only be effected by an agreement of all the parties proposing to build in the block, or by care being taken that each successive house, as it is erected, may form an harmonious union with those which have preceded it. It is not meant that all should build alike—far from it ; since irregularity, with a due attention to harmony, is an important source of beauty in architecture. One roof may tower above another, neighboring houses may vary in height of stories or size or fashion of apertures, without being necessarily discordant one with another. It is only essential that these differences should be so managed as to combine with mutual advantage, so that no part of a block may seem to be accidental or intrusive.

Houses around parks may be viewed from a distance, where details are not visible, and their beauty must therefore in great part consist in a judicious grouping of the several buildings in the block to produce some general design. What would be the appearance from the middle of a park of a block composed of eight separate and distinct styles of architecture, bearing no relation to each other—one tall, another short, one wide, another narrow, one with horizontal lines predominating, another with perpendicular lines predominating, one ornate, another bare, and so on ? Would it not remind one of the marshalling of the army of Falstaff?

In a narrow street, where we can do little more than examine from a near point the details of each façade, the general design of a whole block is not of so much importance ; but in blocks fronting on an open square, it is not sufficient that each component house should be irreproachable as regards detail, but it should so harmonize with its neighbors that the whole would be a case of *E pluribus-unum*, from which secession would be equivalent to dissolution.

What would be the result were the grand Park, which is to be the pride not only of our city, but of the entire country, a field for the disconnected operations of fifty different architects, each following his own design, without reference to the others ? Each might have merit in his invention, yet, without a proper mutual understanding, the entire effect would be absurd, and a result attained inferior to what the most unworthy among them might have accomplished, if left to himself.

Extensive property holders or speculators, who build an entire block, may carry throughout, of course, any design they prefer. It is to be regretted that they make use of this privilege not to create a *unity* of design, but rather a *uniformity*—a weary and monotonous repetition of general features and details, the whole having the appearance of cheap contract work turned out with a machine, and the unfortunate purchaser, in the middle of such a block, can only recognize his own house by his name on the doorplate, or by the color of his curtains.

The design we offer is an attempt to prove that houses of different heights and of different degrees of finish and costliness, may be put together so as to produce a harmonious whole. Obviously, it is the duty of architects, when, as is usually the case, they are called upon to *sandwich* a house from between obstinate and stiff-necked neighbors, with windows of different heights, built of different materials, and with discordant lines, to act as a peacemaker, and do all he can with his own design to reconcile all these painful differences. The task is a difficult one, and the architect's skill is scarcely recognized by the public. But the problem is given, and it is for architects to solve it as best they can.

Other governments have seen fit to legislate upon the subject of street architecture with the happiest results, and though certainly sumptuary laws of this kind are not with us advisable, yet we have sometimes dreamed that architectural harmony might be encouraged by offering certain privileges, as a temporary reduction of taxes, to those who will submit their plans to the censorship of a public officer, chosen by architects, whose duty it shall be to observe certain approved æsthetic standards of design of generous and not tyrannical application, as well as to preside over the operations of the laws for protection against unsafe buildings.

DESIGN No. 31.

In our country, utility and ugliness seem to be almost synonymous terms. It is not understood that a useful object may be made beautiful, not only without destroying its utility, but even adding to it. For one of the great sources of beauty is fitness, and it has been observed that all those implements, whether of mechanism or husbandry, which are best suited for the purposes to which they are applied, are the most graceful and pleasing in form.

Perhaps no object suffers so much, from a total disregard to this principle, as the saw mills of our country. They always, from necessity, occupy the wildest and most picturesque localities, where the best water-power can be obtained, and so unworthy are they usually to associate with such scenes, that we are in the habit of considering them nuisances and desecrations. We have endeavored to show in our sketch that such buildings need not necessarily be an offensive intrusion into the wild scenery where they belong. It needs but a judicious emphasis of those necessary features which may add to its picturesqueness of outline, such as irregularity of roof, dormers and apertures of varying shapes, together with an artistic adjustment of great beams and foundation piers, so as to enter happily into the composition. Actually, such careful adjustment of parts need not add to the expense of the building, or in the slightest degree interfere with its usefulness.

But the rustic design which we present was scarcely intended to serve any legitimate purpose of practical utility. It is the proposed remodelling of an old dilapidated mill, which happened to stand within the grounds of an extensive estate belonging to a wealthy proprietor, and which, instead of being suffered to fall to decay, was thought worthy of applying to uses not contemplated in its original intentions.

With a slight outlay, such a structure may be converted to various purposes of pleasure, while it may be made to harmonize happily with the scenery amidst which it stands. The old bridge, with its shed, which in bygone days served for the protection of the farmer's load of corn, may now shelter the saddle horses of a pleasure party on a sultry day. The first floor may serve as a summer house, a noonday resort for the family. The second floor may be used as a billiard room. Even the wheels may be preserved, and, as the water privilege is as good as ever, it may be used to work the force pump connected with a reservoir, from which may be obtained the household supply of water, and which may furnish a head for the fountains in the garden. The reservoir tower, too, may form another agreeable feature in the landscape, and from its elevated position may serve also as an observatory. In an estate like this, of one or two hundred acres, abundant resources for every amusement are embraced. Rural sports of all kinds may be enjoyed without leaving the grounds, and here the family, after the winter campaign of city life, and perhaps a brief dissipation at the watering places, may live as quiet and independent as if nothing of the world's follies could ever enter within the gates.

Paul Schulze del.

Print. by H. Lawrence, 83, William St. N. Y.

DESIGN Nº 31.

Paul Schulze del.

Print. by H. Lawrence, 85. William St. N.Y.

DESIGN № 32.

DESIGN No. 32.

SOME of the most pleasing and poetic ideas of our literature have arisen from associations connected with unpretending rural churches. Every person capable of sympathizing with these sentiments will at once perceive the importance of allowing them to exercise a large influence over the construction of every such building. It is from a continual and systematic disregard of these poetic associations that have arisen that vacancy and coldness of sentiment which distinguish most of our parish chapels and " meeting houses."

On a Sabbath morning, after the toil and cares of the week, spent, perhaps, in the town, and quite worn out by fatigue and heat, we involuntarily find consolation and pleasant greeting in the sweet sounds of " the church-going bells." Gently the melodious strains fall from the modest spire and echo among the hills. Our steps are irresistibly drawn churchward. The village meeting house is nearer, and attended by a more fashionable audience, but we have seen enough of such worship, and long for a participation in that of a simpler and purer tone. So our first glance at the plain and almost severe architecture of this little church gives us a sensation of relief, and we feel that this indeed is "the house of God." We draw nearer by the winding roads, and at length reach the litch gate, that gives entrance into the churchyard. Here, shaded by noble trees, and among moss-covered gravestones, "the rude forefathers of the hamlet sleep."

> " Yet e'en these bones from insult to protect,
> Some frail memorial still erected nigh,
> With uncouth rhymes and shapeless sculpture decked,
> Implores the passing tribute of a sigh."

Hard by stands the church. The ivy has crept quite up its rugged walls, and, undisturbed and undirected, invested them with tokens of the tender sympathy of nature. As we enter, we instinctively and reverently bow. As without, so within, all is plain and, it may be, rude, yet so strictly appropriate that the very air seems holy.

Let us turn from this quiet picture, and compare with it that much more frequent one of the pretentious and formal place of worship, which doubtless is a characteristic of our country. It stands in a cramped and unattractive spot, given, probably, by some worldly-minded parishioner, who, as he gave, estimated the sure rise in his surrounding land. A lumber merchant, a carpenter, and a "solid man" constitute the building committee. The material selected is wood, of course, that it may be furnished by the lumber merchant, and the carpenter make a good profit on the contract, while the plan adopted is that most pleasing to our "solid man," from whom a liberal donation is expected. This is not an overdrawn picture, but only too truly indicates the manner in which many of our churches are built. Frequently, stone designs are built in wood, sanded, and blocked off most cunningly. The interior walls of plaster must also represent stone, and the really respectable furniture of wood must be painted in imitation of some more expensive material.

There can be no greater inconsistency than these continual expressions of falsehood, in a place which should, of all others, be devoted to truth. If compelled, from a scarcity of stone, or other cause, to employ wood, let your churches show a wood construction; if your interior walls are of plaster, so let them appear, appropriately ornamented, if you will, but never deceptive.

The interior of the design we present is bold but simple. The north entrance porch is balanced by a similar structure on the south, which is used for the organ and choir, thus carrying out the cruciform plan. The principal feature is the deep and spacious chancel, which not only always adds great effect to the design, but gives solemnity to the services of the church.

In regard to the bell, it may be necessary to state that the rope should pass through a pipe built in the wall and terminating in the vestry room, otherwise it would hang awkwardly before the chancel.

Estimate.—The above design would cost about $6,000. The author has recently furnished similar designs for a church at Wilton, Conn., to cost $4,500, with 350 sittings.

Paul Schulze del.

Print. by H. Lawrence, 83, William St. N.Y.

DESIGN No. 33.

WE have frequently been asked why Catholic places of worship, and especially those of the Church of England, generally present an appearance so much more pleasing than those of other denominations. What is the secret of that graceful gravity, that "beauty of holiness," which so distinguishes the churches and chapels of the Romish and the "Established" faiths? From the time of Constantine until the Reformation, the Christian architects, inspired by the idea of making a visible religion, of rendering the material church an exponent of the spiritual church, studied very deeply the æsthetical significance of form, and embodied the results of their researches in the most impressive series of buildings the world has ever seen. They seemed to amalgamate matter and spirit into a vast system of symbolism, which exercised a despotic sway over the art of architecture, not only in decorative details, but in the general plans and outlines. It was not unnatural, therefore, that the Lutheran Reformers should regard with great distrust a style of architecture which seemed to have arisen from

the Popish Ritual, and to be full of the emotional wiles and strat-
egies of the corrupt church.   After the Reformation, the feeling
became so strong against the abuses of Rome that, in the anxiety
to throw off all her evils, they discarded many good points, and
among these, her grand and beautiful symbolic architecture.

The Church of England, however, less radical than the other
branches of Protestantism, within the present century has discovered this error, repaired her dilapidated cathedrals, and revived in
her parish churches the pure styles of bygone ages.

The accompanying design, which was intended for a country
parish church, is of the style of the fourteenth century, as described
in Chap. I.   The plan is cruciform, and the chancel window looks
toward the East, thus preserving the two leading symbols of the
mediæval churches, and commemorating the birth and death of
our Saviour.   If we build for the worship of God, our building
should be worthy of its sacred object.   Doubtless, a lavish introduction of symbols, as such, without any practical advantage attached to them, would not be consistent with the prejudices of
many modern Christians; but we wish to show that many of these
emblems originally had a no less definite use than signification.
With respect to the cruciform plan, for instance, it is always necessary in public auditoriums to bring the audience as near as possible to the speaker.   Now, as, in the accompanying design, the
proportions of the roof limit the width of the nave, and the distance from the chancel limits its length, we are obliged to add
wings or transepts.   These, if placed near the chancel, with their
galleries, bring the greater part of the congregation near it.   We
have also in this design extended the nave laterally by the aid
of low aisles.

To give light and ventilation to the upper part of the church,
we introduce gablet windows, which supply the place of the more

costly clerestory windows, and a lantern ventilator upon the roof. All these, it will be noticed, also act as æsthetic features, serving to break up the bareness and length of the roof, and give piquancy to the general lines.

If a chimney is required in the church, we should not hesitate to show it, only the detailed treatment should be harmonious with the general design. Such an one we have endeavored to show on the right of this sketch.

Estimate.—The above design would cost about $15,000.

Paul Schulze del.

DESIGN Nº 34.

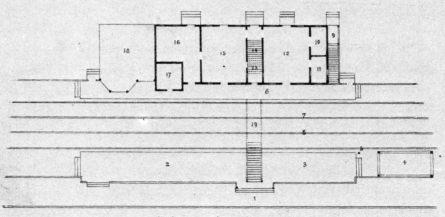

DESIGN No. 34.

It is now received as an axiom in modern political economy, that the construction of railways from large cities through the rural districts not only must increase the population and industry of such districts, but must act as most effective agents of social reform. The natural overflow of the city into the country necessarily carries with it an element of refinement and culture, so that we find society, in every village which is touched by a railroad, slowly and surely improving, as is plainly shown in the vanishing of old Puritan, Dutch, or Quaker prejudices

in the matter of architecture, before the healthy example of
the rusticating citizen, who builds his elegant villa or picturesque
cottage in their neighborhood.   It is certainly reasonable to suppose that railway companies themselves, being thus the great
modern *civilizing* instruments, would be foremost in setting examples of improved taste and culture before the people, by building
stations along their lines, which should be agreeable objects to look
upon, and stand as models of design.   Such seed, though sown by
the wayside, would not be entirely lost, but would surely bear its
fruits in the increased refinement of rural sentiment, and the greater demand for country places along the lines of railway routes.
Usually, however, these railway stations, even on our most prominent roads, are of the most uninviting or even ridiculous appearance.   When they are not beggarly, they are often absurdly pretentious.   We remember seeing a frequented railway station fash-
ioned somewhat after the manner of a hugh Egyptian temple, with
the fuel house near by imitated from the towering Pylon, *yet all
built most palpably and painfully of boards !* We are glad to note,
however, that in some individual instances an evidence of an improved taste and a more refined feeling for elegance or propriety
is shown.   We wish that the stranger, entering an American town
or village, were welcomed by something more inviting than those
rude sheds under which he shakes off the dust of travel.

Perhaps nothing more readily attracts the attention of the
American traveller than the beautiful little stations which, with
endless variety, are dotted along the railway web of Great Britain
and the continent.   There railway travelling is a luxury, not only
in the assurance of safety, and the splendid fitting of the carriages,
but in the tasteful little stations which not only charm the eye by
their agreeable exteriors, but comfort the weariness of journeying
by their convenient and perfect arrangement within. In our country

such a mode of conveyance involves somewhat of personal danger, as the lists of casualties assure us, and the eye is constantly offended by those unworthy structures which we dignify with the name of stations.

We by no means advocate extensive or expensive buildings for wayside stations, but, on the contrary, merely convenient and economical arrangements, with a large amount of that inexpensive commodity—*taste*. Considerations of safety, we think, should exercise more influence over the designing and placing of these structures, and the management of their surroundings. In no other country do we find the rails so exposed, so subject to the intrusion of cattle and other obstructions, with carriage roads crossing the track, unguarded by gates or bridges. Many valuable lives have been lost from the necessity of crossing the track to enter the station. Travellers from abroad look aghast at such wanton carelessness, while we, with our go-ahead propensities, think nothing of it, and take no measures to prevent such accidents.

In the present design we have endeavored to obviate some of the faults alluded to. Here, it will be observed, it is unnecessary for persons to cross the tracks, a bridge being provided, to enable travellers to cross from one side to the other of the rails without danger. Thus direct entrances are obtained into the station from both sides of the tracks. The rails are protected by an outside fence. The cross roads should either be bridged or protected by gates, which should be closed across the road when a train is expected, and at other times across the rails, to prevent the entrance of cattle.

THE END.

THE ENTRANCE.

MODERN DWELLINGS

IN

TOWN AND COUNTRY

ADAPTED TO AMERICAN WANTS AND CLIMATE

WITH A TREATISE ON

FURNITURE AND DECORATION

BY H. HUDSON HOLLY

WITH ONE HUNDRED ORIGINAL DESIGNS COMPRISING COTTAGES
VILLAS AND MANSIONS

NEW YORK

HARPER & BROTHERS, PUBLISHERS

FRANKLIN SQUARE

1878

PREFACE.

IN the spring of 1876, I prepared an article on Country-houses for *Harper's Magazine*, which was followed by a series of papers on interiors, containing a few suggestions on household art in general. It then occurred to me that the importance of the subject would justify its treatment in a more extended form. With this view, I began the preparation of the present work, which, although it might have been extended to several volumes without exhausting the subject, will, I trust, prove a practical and reliable guide for those persons who wish to build, furnish, and beautify their houses without an extravagant outlay of money.

In the following pages I have profited considerably by the writings of Eastlake and others. In some instances, I have quoted from *The American Architect* and London *Building News*, and also from a work of my own published in 1863, which has been for some years out of print.

In regard to the designs, I must acknowledge my indebtedness to Mr. H. F. Jelliffe, who rendered me great assistance in working them up, and to Mr. Charles Parsons, Superintendent of the Art Department at Harper & Brothers, who has added greatly to their attraction by the graceful introduction of suitable figures and scenery.

I feel some hesitation in giving the cost of the various dwellings described, as the fluctuations in prices are such that the expense of building a house in any one year might not be a guide at another time. The estimates I have given are based upon the value of labor and material in the year 1878.

H. HUDSON HOLLY.

111 *Broadway, N. Y.*

CONTENTS.

I.—CONSTRUCTION.

CHAPTER VII.

FRAMING.

CHAPTER VIII.

ROOFING.

CHAPTER IX.

GLASS.

CHAPTER X.

CHIMNEYS.

CHAPTER XI.

COST OF HOUSES.

CHAPTER XII.

ARCHITECTS' DUTIES AND CHARGES.

CHAPTER XIII.

PLUMBERS' BLUNDERS.

CHAPTER XIV.

HEATING AND VENTILATION.

CHAPTER XV.

STEAM HEATING.—ELECTRICITY.

CHAPTER XVI.

ALTERATIONS.

CHAPTER XVII.

LIBRARY.

CHAPTER XVIII.

KITCHEN.

CHAPTER XIX.

BILLIARD-ROOM.

CHAPTER XX.

BLINDS.

CHAPTER XXI.

CARE NECESSARY IN ADAPTING A ROOM TO FURNITURE.

CHAPTER XXII.

THE MANSION.

CHAPTER XXIII.

CITY ARCHITECTURE.

II.—FURNITURE AND DECORATION.

CHAPTER IX.

LEGITIMATE WOOD-WORK.

CHAPTER X.

FIREPLACES.

CHAPTER XI.

COLONIAL FASHIONS.

CHAPTER XII.

BOOKCASES AND PIANOS.

CHAPTER XIII.

PLANTS.

CHAPTER XIV.

BEDROOM FURNITURE.

CHAPTER XV.

METALS.

CHAPTER XVI.

HOME ART.

CHAPTER XVII.

ART-SCHOOLS FOR WOMEN.

MODERN DWELLINGS.

PART I.

CONSTRUCTION.

CHAPTER I.

THE QUEEN ANNE STYLE.

Gothic Revival.—Cottage Architecture.—Suburban Homes.—The Park System.

ARCHITECTURE is a comparatively new art in this country, and has had but little earnest and intelligent study; so we cannot be said to have any styles and systems peculiarly our own. In the absence of such, we have been too apt to use, inappropriately, the orders of foreign nations, which express the especial needs of those countries, and those alone. Yet out of our necessities there have grown certain idiosyncrasies of building which point toward an *American style*. Doubtless we may introduce from abroad methods of design which meet our requirements, but we must not hesitate to eliminate those portions for which we have no use, or to make such additions as our circumstances demand.

For instance, in our pure atmosphere, where odors are readily absorbed, it would be foolish, except in large establishments, to build the kitchen apart from the house to escape from its fumes, when a simple butler's pantry between it and the dining-room would effectually prevent their entrance. So, too, it would be the merest folly, in building an English cottage, not to have a veranda, simply because its prototypes in England have none. We evidently have need of this appliance in our dry and sunny climate. From such requirements a distinctive feature of American architecture must arise.

In this way we are doubtless building up an architecture of our own, profiting, as other founders of style have done, by precedents in older countries. Our materials, climate, and habits differ enough from those of Europe to demand a material change in their use and arrangement. For example, in European countries, wood, a most valuable building material, is rare and expensive, while in most sections of our own, it is very abundant. But instead of using this in accordance with its nature and capacities, we have stupidly employed it in copying, as exactly as we can, details of foreign architecture, which were designed with reference to the constructive capacities of brick and stone; hence we see rounded arches, keystones, and buttresses of wood; wood siding is sanded and blocked off to represent stone; and the prosperous American citizen, with a taste for feudal castles, like Horace Walpole, may live to see three sets of his own turrets decay. Fortunately our people are beginning to recognize the folly of such unmeaning shams; and when brick or stone is adopted, it is treated as such; and when wood is employed, we are properly commencing to show details adapted to its nature. Until, however, we come to possess a vernacular style, we must content ourselves with copying; and the question arises, Which of the innumerable systems is best suited to our requirements? We have tried the Egyptian, but nothing cheerful seems to have been the result, as our City Prison will testify. The Greek, as set forth by Stuart and Rivett, has had a more successful career; but while "counterfeit presentments" of the temples of the gods have mocked the eye with their exterior of wood and whitewash, so, within, we might sometimes find the Pythia with a wash-bench for a tripod, with the fumes of soapsuds representing the vapor of inspiration.

But the Gothic revival, started by the masterly hand of Pugin, glorified and made national by such men as Street and Ruskin, seemed to have decided the matter, and both England and America rested with unmolested satisfaction until within the last few years, when it was suddenly discovered that the Gothic, however well adapted for ecclesiastical purposes, was lacking in essential points for domestic uses; and Norman Shaw, J. J. Stevenson, and others have openly advocated this view. Their argument was that the Gothic meant the development of the arched construction in the pointed work, vaulted and traceried windows; and that while these features were suited to churches and great halls, they were unfitted for modern domestic structures, divided as they are into comparatively low stories; therefore, that even in the dwellings of the Middle Ages, when this style reached its highest perfection, its characteristic features could not be displayed. In fact, Gothic architecture was not originally intended to meet domestic wants.

There are some who are so carried away with the architecture that happens to be in vogue, that they consider it indispensable, regardless of its adaptability, like the quack doctor, who, finding that a certain medicine is efficacious in one disease, advertises its infallible power to cure "all the ills that flesh is heir to." This was displayed recently in a competition for furnishing plans for a town-hall in Paisley, England, in which a Gothic design was selected, resembling, not only in its general appearance, but in all its details, inside and out, a cathedral. So, too, in this country. An expensive villa near our city, built after a Gothic design, is so wedded to the style, that, notwithstanding the absence of natural shade, it has neither porch nor veranda to serve as a protection from the rays of our almost tropical sun. Common-sense should be at the base of all true art, as well as of all true living and thinking.

These writers exempt themselves from a slavish conformity to the Gothic, admirable as it may be in its proper sphere, on the ground that it is manifestly inadequate to meet all domestic requirements. One of the principles upon which the promoters of the Gothic revival insisted with energy and eloquence was "truth in architecture;" that the construction should not be hidden under some fair-seeming mask which had no affinity with it, and often represented something very different from it, but should be made apparent, and the basis of whatever adornment should be employed. But the new reformers say that truth is not the peculiar possession of Gothic architecture; and, indeed, *modern* Gothic has often found the temptations of an age that loves to be deceived too strong for it, and has fallen into the errors of the system it has attempted to replace. What, then, do they propose as a substitute for this in domestic architecture? They claim that in what is loosely called the "Queen Anne" style we find the most simple mode of honest English building, worked out in an artistic and natural form, fitting with the sash-windows and ordinary doorways which express real domestic needs (of which it is the outcome); and so, in our house-building, conserving truth far more effectively than can be done with the Gothic. One great advantage in adopting this and other styles of the "free classic" school is, that they are in their construction, and in the forms of the mouldings employed, the same as the common vernacular styles with which our workmen are familiar.

They are described by Mr. Ridge somewhat as follows: "The Queen Anne revival shows the influence of the group of styles known as the Elizabethan, Jacobite, and the style of Francis I., which are now indeed to be arranged under the general head of 'free classic;' but it has also been influenced by what is known as the 'cottage architecture' of that period."

These cottages, which were common in the home counties, are partly timbered, partly covered with tile hangings, and have tall and spacious chimneys of considerable merit. They have really nothing by which to fix their date. Their details partook strongly of the classic character, while the boldness of their outline bore striking resemblance to the picturesque and ever-varying Gothic. Nevertheless, they were very genuine and striking buildings, and have been taken freely as suggestions upon which to work by Mr. Norman Shaw, in Leyswood, Cragside, and a house at Harrow Weald, which are certainly some of the most beautiful and suitable specimens of modern cottage architecture in England; and those erected by the British Government at the Centennial Grounds at Philadelphia are adequate illustrations of this style.

I have frequently noticed that whereas formerly the introduction of any novelty excited a certain amount of adverse criticism, that it took some time to remove (such as "All Souls," in Fourth Avenue, which, though a good specimen of Italian Gothic, bore for years the sobriquet of the "Beefsteak Church"), the Queen Anne, from its thorough adaptability to the uses to which it was applied, seemed never to call forth any comment of this kind, and, as an evident exponent of domestic requirements, became popular at once, not only among the educated, but even among the rustic population.

Mr. J. J. Stevenson, one of the most celebrated architects in England, in his admirable article in the January number of *Harper's Magazine* (1876), after styling Gothic as the "artistic expression of an obsolete mode of construction," and proving most conclusively the inappropriateness of this style for domestic uses, concludes as follows: "As there is a common language which every one more or less understands, so there is a common architecture which arose with the growth of modern thought, and has been the architectural style of the country for the last three centuries, which every builder naturally follows, which every workman has been apprenticed to, and more or less understands. But while our language has been kept up to a reasonable mark of artistic excellence by a high standard of criticism and the constant effort of educated minds, our vernacular architecture is characterized by the vulgarity and commonplaceness of the men in whose hands it has been left. The interest of refined and educated minds for the last thirty years has been directed, not to improving the vernacular style, but to the hopeless attempt of supplanting it by another (the Gothic), which appeared at first to flourish, but has not taken root in the soil of the country."

Now, this vernacular style is precisely what this book is intended to advocate, it being none other than the free classic, or Queen Anne.

In America it is the privilege of nearly all classes to build for themselves homes in the country, where, for such rent as they would pay for a flat or tenement in town, they can secure an entire house with sufficient ground for a garden and ornamental lawn; and, if not immediately in a village, sufficient acres can be obtained to afford the luxury of a horse and cow, the products of the little farm going far toward the support of an extra man, and with good management may be made a source of profit also.

Railroads and steamboats have now become so numerous that all classes, from the humblest mechanic to the wealthy banker, can have their homes in the country, reaching them in about the same time and as cheaply—or nearly so—as the old omnibus ride from the City Hall to the upper part of the city. It is not an occasion of wonder, then, that there are so many ready to avail themselves of this rapid transit, and that we see studded along the lines of our railroads picturesque and cheerful homes, where the heads of families are not only recuperating from the deleterious effects of the confinement of city life, but are, with the aid of fresh air and wholesome food, laying the foundation for greater strength and increased happiness for their children.

The following is quoted from the *New York Herald* of April 19th, 1877: "New York is gradually, year by year, becoming the home of the very rich and very poor. The middle classes are surely, rapidly, and permanently removing to the neighboring localities; the ample railroad facilities to all places embracing a radius of twenty miles around the city, together with cheap rents, pure air, and freedom from infectious diseases caused by dirty streets and other causes prevailing in large cities, tending to make residences in such places more and more sought for every year by old New York residents."

In the selection of a site, of course, the sanitary considerations are paramount. Next should be the advantage of fine scenery. Our country abounds in beautiful ocean, river, and mountain views, equal to, if not surpassing, those of Europe. Yet how seldom is this considered in locating our homes! It is too often the case that an unattractive, barren spot is selected inland, apart from views, devoid of trees or other natural beauties. If a pretty pond or brook should enliven the scene, the former is probably filled up, or, at least, stoned around like a dock, and the brook is, as likely as not, turned into a sewer. Of course there are reasons why these beautiful sites cannot always be chosen. One is, they are apt to be lonely. Society is a consideration, and society, strange to say, will not bear you out in the love for the picturesque; so that your family must either possess superior resources within themselves, or have the means of entertaining largely in order to find contentment in the "Happy Valley."

Design No. 1.—Small Cottage, or Lodge.

There is a method adopted in England, however, by which fine scenery and agreeable company may not be incompatible. It is by a number of families clubbing together, and procuring an attractive spot, filled with shady nooks and pleasant streams, which, by mutual agreements and some slight restrictions, can be laid out in a picturesque manner for building.

The park system has been attempted in this country, but hitherto it has generally failed of success, for the reason that the projectors lacked the knowledge necessary to select the locations, to say nothing of laying out or conducting the parks when complete. Instead of employing an educated landscape-gardener, who would take advantage of its topography, and with care and judgment would accommodate the roads to the natural curves and best positions for building, they are satisfied if only an outline survey be made, the roads laid out on the checker-board pattern, and the lots numbered in the auctioneer's office. The proprietors then cause the place to be extensively advertised, and the lots sold to the highest bidder. The result is that the ground is seldom improved, because one does not know who his next-door neighbor may be, or what he may do; or if one has the temerity to build and settle, he finds the roads are left to grow up with weeds, and there are no funds to keep them in order; moreover, he discovers that none of the owners intends building, as each has bought only on speculation, and will not sell unless for extravagant prices. Like the dog in the manger, these speculative owners neither improve the land nor allow any one else to do so.

Now, as parks on this system have hitherto proved a failure, could not the community plan be adopted, combining real business and real taste, making judicious laws and restrictions simply with the view of facilitating improvements and keeping up the enterprise? Of course the value of this would not be solely of a social character; for if each one takes pains to keep up his own place and contributes to the care of the roads, he enjoys the advantages of cultivated surroundings as if the whole were his private estate. It has been objected that, by this method, they experience too much restraint; that all their ground is common lawn; that they cannot keep a horse or cow, etc. But there can be no objection to having each place enclosed, though pains should be taken to have a tasteful barrier. All kinds of fencing would not be suitable for a park. An inexpensive plain wire-work painted the color of the grass, so as to be as nearly invisible as possible, would be the most appropriate.

Perhaps as satisfactory a way of arranging these conditions would be to submit all plans of improvement to the censorship of a commission; but it would be wisest to have as little constraint as possible, for men of education and taste in our day seldom go very wide of the mark. No one is expected to grow potatoes on his lawn, or build a barn in front of his house.

DESIGN No. 1.

1. Porch; 2. Main hall; 3. Kitchen, 10 × 17; 4. Living-room, 10 × 12.—*Estimated cost*, $2200.

In this series of cottages, it would, perhaps, be appropriate to commence with the gate entrance, in connection with the porter's lodge, at the entrance of such a park as we have just described, in which we might expect to find, each on its appropriate site, the following designs.

The lodge should not be so large or conspicuous as to be mistaken for the mansion, but should be more simple in its architecture, although according sufficiently with it to show its relationship. For this reason we build the foundation only of brick, while the first story is of less pretentious material. Here the simple clapboard construction appears; and to give it variety and, at the same time, to show its connection with the mansion, the second story is covered with cut ornamental shingles, while the roof should be of slate. One of the most important requirements is that there should be an agreeable effect of color. Let, therefore, the clapboards on the first story be of French gray—a color harmonizing with the brick—the shingles buff, and, if the house be well shaded, the trimmings might be of Indian red with black chamfers. If there is not much shade, however, a kind of salmon color with Indian-red chamfers would appear well: the roof to be of dark or red slate. Red for roofs seems to be growing much in favor, and some of the quarries in Vermont are producing admirable slates for this purpose; but the introduction of various colors I consider objectionable, as it is apt to destroy the repose, and appears frivolous.

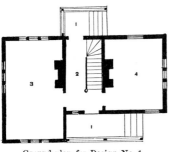

Ground-plan for Design No. 1.

The chimney, being of red brick, unpainted, might be relieved occasionally with brick of dark color, or even black.

As black bricks are difficult to procure in this country, the following recipe for producing them, by T. M. C., taken from the *American Architect*, may be valuable:

Black Bricks.—The black bricks used about Boston are colored by heating red-hot, and dipping the exposed surface into a pan containing half an inch or so of melted coaltar. Soft bricks are the best. Hard bricks or hard spots prevent the tar from penetrating the surface, as it should do, to a depth of one-sixteenth to one-eighth of an inch, and the coating peels off.

One great advantage architects possess in our clear atmosphere is the strong contrast of light and shade which assists materially in producing good effects in building. The introduction of irregularities, such as projections of roofs, canopies, verandas, and bay-windows, together with the intersections of gables, dormers, and the height of chimneys, serve to break up the bare formality of the usual barn-like outline, and to obtain the ever-varying sentiment and expression which the GREAT ARCHITECT never fails to give to all his rocks and hills. Light and shade are the happiest instruments of design, and most easily procured in our climate, and are ever ready to give new life and spirit to forms properly managed for their play. The repetition of the perforated barge boards in shadow against the walls, always making new interpretations of its patterns, shows how delicately and tenderly Nature assists the sympathetic architect.

In cities, where the great value of land almost precludes the designer from availing himself of these opposing masses, which can be produced in emphasis only by costly irregularities of plan, and large re-entering angles of outer walls, it seems necessary to resort to some other expedient, where delicacy of line is not considered a sufficient substitute for the more massive effects of *chiaro-oscuro*. The luxurious and sensuous peoples of the East, not content with the more serious and sober habits of design of the North, were accustomed to break their sky lines with pierced parapets and lily patterns, with swelling domes, with endless pinnacles and fantastic minarets, to a degree never thought of elsewhere, and availed themselves of strong and vivid contrasts of bright colors. It would be well for us to take a lesson from the Eastern nations in this respect, and, while repudiating, perhaps, as undignified any complete adaptation of their endless fancies of form, to study their picturesque use of external colors, and let the walls of our cities assume new life and meaning by contrasting tints of various bricks, stones, and brilliant tiles. This source of design, if used with discretion in our metropolitan structures, would effect the happiest results, and preserve their architecture from inanity and insipidity.

But in the country, where growth of shapes and forms is unchecked by any consideration of economy of space, it seems almost superfluous to use decorative external color to any great extent—certainly, we think, never for its own sake, as in the town; but so far as it may serve to protect wooden surfaces, to assist in giving expression to form, and to harmonize masses with the nature around, its employment is of great value. It is, then, important to know by what rule we are to be governed in the use of colors under these circumstances. It is evident that the general tint covering the plain surface of a small house, surrounded by trees, should be light and cheerful, warm in its tone, and of a neutral rather than positive character, as the former very readily harmonizes with nature. But do not fall into the opposite extreme, and paint your house white, which is no color at all, always cold and glaring, and making an ugly spot in the landscape: we find nothing to warrant so forcible an intrusion. A white building might not be so objectionable in the city, where we have no nature with which to assimilate and work; but in the country, nothing but snow and chalk cliffs are white, and these put out the eyes by their intensity. Choose, then, any of the hundred soft, neutral tints which may afford to your house the cheerfulness or dignity it may require. These are to be determined chiefly by its location and size. A house of large and commanding proportions, occupying a conspicuous place in the scenery, would present a ludicrous appearance if painted a light color; while one of smaller size, subordinate to its natural surroundings and well shaded by trees, would, if painted dark, give an impression of gloom.

Having selected the general tint, the trimmings should be of a darker shade of the same, or a deeper color, to give them prominence and assist in bringing out the design, though they should be rather in harmony than in violent contrast. As a general rule, any trimmings forming a frame to a panel should be darker than the background or body of the house; as also, the stiles of a door should be more emphasized than the panel.

I would not have it supposed that positive colors cannot be employed to advantage on the exteriors of country houses. For example, green as the color for the blinds not only has a cool and cheerful effect, but seems to be that chosen by Nature in which to clothe her natural bowers. Still, if neutral tints are used on the body of the house, green is apt to appear in too violent contrast unless a line of some other harmonizing color be interposed. If the general tone of the house is drab or olive, a line of Indian red between this and the blinds would produce a relief. But in coloring our houses it is certainly well to follow the architect's advice, since an improper application of paint might quite nullify the effect of his design, and render that ridiculous which was intended to be dignified; small, that which was to appear large; and obtrusive, that which was to appear modest and retiring.

By a judicious subordination of various tints, many errors and incongruities may be lessened or quite concealed, and the good points of design be properly emphasized and made to assume a worthy prominence in the composition.

It is well for the architect, in studying the colors for a house, to make a tinted drawing of one or two of the elevations, in order to give the painter an intelligible idea of what is required. The great difficulty is, however, in exactly matching these cólors, and the slightest variation often destroys the effect. I have been much assisted in this by using the sample card of some of our manufacturers, by which the painter is enabled to order the exact colors, mixed and ready for use, by simply sending the number of the sample. I lay particular stress on the architect's directing the arrangement of the colors, as so many buildings are utterly spoiled by this important branch being taken out of his hands and intrusted to the mercies of the painter. Many of them are color-blind; and if they are unable, from their own skill, to match the sample given them, how much less should they be trusted with the original selection!

In the course of conversation between a gentleman and a painter regarding the color of a house, the latter remarked, with the same authoritative air in which a *modiste* would lay down the fashion to her customer, "We don't trim as much as we did, sir," thus stupidly establishing a change of fashion, governed by no rule or reason, and tacitly acknowledging that if he were right at the present time, he must have been wrong last season. The fact is, the laws of color are such that they cannot be regulated by ignorant caprice. We may improve as the science of art advances, but to imagine that they can be changed by mere vulgar prejudice is beneath intelligent consideration.

Upon any portion of the house receding from the façade, such as an alcoved balcony or recessed door-way, when deeply sunken, positive colors would be in keeping, as they have the appearance of protection from the weather, and form brilliant contrasts with the neutral tints of the exterior, with fittings and decorations of soft and delicate hues. Thus, in Design No. 9 the exterior is of neutral buff, the sides of the embrasure are painted a deep ultramarine green; the trimmings of Indian red are relieved by lines of black, while the coved ceiling is of brilliant blue.

Some years ago it was quite customary to paint houses a sort of dirty yellow, which custom arose from the fact that Mr. Downing, in giving some figurative instructions as to the color employed, said: "Pluck from the ground the roots of the grass, and the color of the earth thereon will be the color of the house." Now, the gist of this was that the color of the house should be in harmony with the landscape; but some of his unimaginative followers failed to see that it was not to be taken literally, and hence arose a fashion which, we are glad to see, has gone by, of painting houses an offensive mud color.

Painters seem to have the idea that a leader-pipe should be disguised as much as possible, and so paint it the same color as its background; therefore, when it crosses the cornice it is dark, and when arriving at the body of the house, chameleon-like, it assumes the lighter hue.

It is a rule in all good architecture that whatever is necessary in the construction of a building should be accepted in the decoration, and be treated according to its importance in the general design; thus the leader, when viewed in this light, may become a *leading* feature. For this reason we place it conspicuously on the house, not necessarily following the trimmings, but running boldly down the facade wherever it is required. The top may be made ornamental; and instead of attempting to conceal the pipe, the color should be such as to give it due prominence, which need be neither that of the trimmings nor the body, as its material and use are of so different a character that a color denoting its purpose would be more appropriate. The tube, then, might be made to imitate galvanized iron, and the cap rendered more prominent by decoration.

CHAPTER II.

ECONOMY OF COUNTRY LIFE.

Fluctuations.—Blessings of Poverty.—Small Homes.

NOTWITHSTANDING the general prosperity of our country, and the rapidity and ease with which wealth is acquired, there is yet, in the fluctuations of commercial life, a constant liability to serious loss, if not entire reverse of fortune. It is sad to think that our firesides, though far removed from the bustle and keen anxieties of the exchange, are ever sensitive to the mismanagements or misfortunes of a single venture on the dangerous sea of trade. These fluctuations affect all classes of society, compelling them to retrench their expenses—the rich by giving up their carriage and reducing the number of their servants, and sometimes changing their luxurious abodes in town for less pretentious homes in the country; while the "well-to-do" must content themselves with a "flat," where they may be comfortable with one servant, or perhaps sufficiently independent to dispense with one altogether. A lady, in speaking of the blessings of poverty, remarked to me that in her zeal to assist her husband, after misfortune had befallen him, she had persuaded him to take a small house out of town, and that she and her daughter would, as long as they had their health, do the work themselves, stipulating only that the house should be provided with modern conveniences. Although at the time she considered this a great sacrifice, she found, after systematizing their work, that they experienced more comfort, had more cleanliness, and more time for reading and other occupations than when they kept a servant; and it certainly proved far more economical; for joints which were formerly sent from the table and never heard of again, now served for a variety of dishes for several days, and her husband declared that his dinners never tasted so good, nor were so well selected. His approval more than compensated for all their trouble, and they were no longer afraid to talk freely of their affairs on account of the girl's eavesdropping; and altogether her absence was an inexpressible relief. Such families, prostrated by the changes of a day, reared in the midst of refinement and

luxury, and surrounded by the golden opportunities of wealth, have, perhaps, under these influences, so shaped their minds and manners as to
have become ornaments in the circles in which they moved. They are
often, of all others, equal to an emergency of this kind. They find that
adversity is not without its sweetness. Knowing that if they remain in
town, they must assume a position inferior to their station or custom,
they will turn to the country as affording a congenial home. Here, with
true taste and sound judgment, they will build a cottage, which, though
small in dimensions, will be complete in all its parts. In such a home,
with the qualifications within themselves for making it happy, they will
probably find a calm content unknown in the giddy turmoil of fashion,

Design No. 2.

and a consolation full of gentleness and peace. Other associations, dear
as those of old, will cluster around them, and they will find, as in the
touching description of "the Wife" in Irving's "Sketch Book," that they
have no desire to return to the noise and bustle, the whirl and excitement, of a life in town.

Everything about such a house should be truly refined and chaste,
with all the conveniences that comfort demands, without superfluities.
The interior must be suggestive of the refinement of the occupants; not
necessarily ornamental or showy, but in every respect tasteful and elegant.

The great want of small houses at moderate rents, and in respectable
quarters of our cities, has obliged many of limited means to seek homes
in the country. But now the custom of living on flats has, in a great

measure, met this requirement, although these have their drawbacks, especially where children are in the question. The advantages of gardens and spacious lawns, where they may have pure air and room to exercise their lungs and muscles without disturbing the family, is a matter which should be considered. True, it may be argued that a flat could be closed during the summer, and the family visit the mountains or sea-shore, or even a summer cottage may be taken. But for the class where economical living has become a necessity, this double expense cannot be borne. Besides, we do not think the American people, as a general thing, take to flats. The old English proverb " Every man's house his castle " remains true of us, and the Anglo-Saxon home and family fireside are still sacred. It is to this influence, in no small degree, that we owe our love of truth and virtue.

DESIGN No. 2.

First-floor Plan.

1. Vestibule; 2. Parlor, 15 × 23; 3. Dining-hall, 14 × 18; 4. Dining-room closet; 5. Butler's pantry; 6. Kitchen, 14 × 16; 7. Main stairs; 8. Back stairs; 9. Kitchen closet; 10, 10, 10. Verandas.—*Estimated cost*, $4500.

This is a design for a small cottage of moderate cost. It was intended for an alteration of an ordinary square house, with a kitchen wing, the lines of the house and roof remaining the same, the interior materially changed.

The principal features added are the two bay-windows in front, the one on the right for the parlor, and that on the left accommodating the main staircase, each running the entire height of the building. The space between these windows is used as a hooded porch, with a recessed balcony

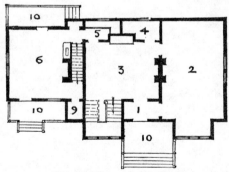

First-floor Plan of Design No. 2.

above, giving the whole a varied and somewhat original aspect. For motives of economy, the main staircase is placed in the dining-hall, the vestibule acting as an entrance to the dining-hall and parlor, so that guests may be introduced into the latter without disturbing the family while at meals.

The dining-room has a large china-closet and butler's pantry, with recess for sideboard. The kitchen contains a back staircase and two closets. The room over the kitchen is intended for servants, and is approached directly by the back stairs. The second story has three large bedrooms and bath; there is space for two rooms in the attic.

CHAPTER III.

SITE.

Cesspool remote from the House.—Earth Closets.—Ventilating Sewers.—Grading Cellar Floors.—Areas.—Foundations on Made Ground.—Terraces.—Side Hills.—Hydraulic Rams.—Cistern Filters.—Force-pump.—Windmills.

THE first thing to be considered in building a house should be the judicious selection of a site; and here good drainage is not only necessary for the health, but adds materially to the fertility of the soil. Latham says, "It is absolutely necessary, in order to render the soil capable of performing its functions of oxidizing or neutralizing the elements of decomposition which are brought into contact with it, that works of subdrainage should be prosecuted. It is now well known that the admission of air into the soil enables that soil to exert a most powerful chemical influence upon all organic compounds, so great, indeed, as to be capable of purifying the crudest sewage. The effect of drainage upon the soil is to promote porosity, and the effect of porosity is to make the soil drier, warmer, and less capable of conveying extremes of temperature. It is also well known that a soil perfectly saturated with water, which can only part with its water by evaporation, is rendered cold and unwholesome as a site for human dwellings; for all the impurities that enter the soil accumulate. Soils which are naturally porous, from which rain rapidly disappears, are known to be the healthiest for the sites of houses. In this case the action of the soil oxidizes all organic impurities, the resulting product is washed away by the rain, and the soil remains sweet and wholesome. The advantages of site appear to have been known from the earliest ages of antiquity. Vetruvius in his works lays down special instructions for selecting the sites for towns and hospitals; namely, regarding the quality of porosity and the perfection of drainage, the absence of a water-logged soil being looked upon as the best situation for the location of buildings."

In order to effect good drainage, high land is generally considered necessary; but much depends on its geological formation. There are often rock or clay basins not appearing upon the surface, which offer a barrier to the lateral flow of water, and the moisture thus prevented from escaping is retained in a stagnant pool. That low level ground is objectionable for drainage is apparent; yet this seems a favorite spot for building, and people wonder why the country is so unhealthy. In order, therefore, to find a safe location, good drainage must be secured. The centre of a knoll from which the water may run in every direction from the house, if possible to obtain, would be preferable. But if this cannot be, a side hill affords good drainage — one way, at least. The surface on the higher ground can be so graded as to turn the water aside and prevent its direct entrance into the cellar, although in wet weather, when the ground is saturated, it is apt to find its way there. This may be avoided by sinking drains below the foundation around the exposed sides of the house, made from two to three feet wide, and filled in with broken stone, into which the water coming from the higher ground may collect before reaching the cellar, and may be carried off, not to lower ground—where it would settle, and generate malarious gases— but connect, if possible, with the main sewer, and through that be conveyed to some outlet.

Of course, when the ground drainage empties into a small stream, a separate drain should be arranged for the sewage, which should terminate in a cesspool or vault underground, to avoid poisoning the water. And here it would be well to mention that one of the most important things in regard to drainage is, that when a leaching cesspool is used, to have it remote from the well; and when I say remote, fifty or seventy-five feet are not sufficient. A distinguished physician, speaking on this subject, stated that he had often heard of wells being affected by a cesspool a hundred feet distant, and would advise that they should never be less than a hundred and fifty feet apart, as the fluids percolating from the vault are sure to infect the water, making it not only disagreeable to the taste, but very liable to the poison to which the most dreaded diseases may be traced. It is, therefore, not alone essential that they themselves should be kept well apart, but that even the drains connected with the cesspool should be at a distance, as more or less of their noxious contents are apt to escape from their joints. It might be supposed that a cistern cemented and made water tight would not be exposed to this danger, but I have often known of the seeds of disease being carried into it. The impurity of rain-water in cisterns is a phenomenon which has often puzzled the minds of our sages, who never seem to consider the fact that two leaders in close proximity may absorb each other's contents.

Ordinary tile-pipe, from four to six inches, laid three or four feet beneath the surface, so as to be below the action of the frost, answers the purpose best. It is a mistaken idea that large pipes are less liable to foul than small ones; for, from the fact of the latter presenting less surface, the friction is diminished, and the flow of water is more rapid, whereas pipes of larger diameter are apt to clog in consequence of the more sluggish movement of the fluids. In case of main sewers or trunk drains, where the capacity must be large in order to carry off the extra flow from the freshets, it is well to make them smaller at the bottom, something of the shape of an egg, which will concentrate the water and cause it to flow rapidly in dry times, when the supply is naturally less.

In surface drainage, it is a mistake to cement the joints of these pipes, as we depend upon their openings to admit the water. So, in soil-pipes, the cement often forms an obstruction to the solid matter, which, collecting, eventually chokes the pipes. These, however, not being used for surface drainage, should have their joints cemented in order to avoid poisoning the ground; but before the cement is set, it is well to clear out these ridges, so that they may be free from obstruction.

In the country, if there be no outfall, and the sewage must consequently be confined to one's own estate, the simple system afforded by the use of earth closets for the management of solid matter is to be preferred. The fluids may then be carried to a water-tight tank or vault underneath the ground, as far distant from the house as possible, and may serve for irrigation.

The necessity for ventilating cesspools and sewers is of the utmost importance, as the gases from them are liable to create a back pressure and find their way into the house. The readiest way of preventing this seems to be by connecting a pipe with a ventilating flue arranged in the stable chimney, the top of which is provided with a cowl in order to prevent a downward draught. This, when of sufficient height, seems to obviate the difficulty by discharging the poisonous gases beyond the reach of harm, provided always that there be an inlet to supply the vacuum. If, however, a vent of this kind be impracticable, a galvanized iron pipe may be carried to the top of a high tree; and I have known instances where a ventilation pipe was returned and discharged into the smoke flue of the kitchen chimney, which, being always heated, insures a thorough draught, which causes the gases to escape at a safe elevation. The old idea that sewer gases may be kept from the house by means of traps seems to have generally exploded, as it is well understood that as these gases generate they are apt to force their way into the house through the traps. Of course, a sewer thoroughly ventilated will, in a measure, prevent this; but even then, in certain winds, a back pressure is produced, so that the only safe method is to ventilate all traps and soil-pipes as well, by extending them above the roof, and capping them in such a manner as to prevent a downward current.

The danger of these foul emanations, carrying the germs of typhoid and diphtheria, cannot be too forcibly impressed upon the public; and since of late numerous cases of disease directly traceable to this miasma have been prominently brought to notice, it is time that some active measures should be taken to prevent their entrance.

A physician told me that he had never known a case of diphtheria which was not produced by these causes; even those in the country, he says, are directly traceable to the influence of some foul vault, which is sufficiently near the well to poison the water, or so near the house as to allow the gases admittance.

There are, however, cases in which it seems impossible to ventilate, when fumigation or disinfectants may answer the purpose. Common salt, and nitric acid, and chloride of lime have been recommended, and are frequently used, as absorbents of noxious gases; but nothing has proved so efficacious as charcoal, which, placed in an apartment where sewer gases or other foul odors arise, will absorb and effectually destroy their malarial qualities. Professor Voelcker says of charcoal: "It possesses the power of absorbing certain smelling-gases, also destroying the gases thus absorbed. The evil effects of sewer gas upon public health were known in the ages of antiquity, for it appears from 'Justinian's Digest,' which was completed in the year 555, that, quoting Ulpian, 'The prætor took care that all sewers should be cleansed and repaired for the health of the citizen, because unclean or unrepaired sewers threaten a pestilential atmosphere, and are dangerous.' The Romans, too, displayed a clear knowledge of the necessity of underground conduits, as may be seen in the provisions for the construction of their aqueducts whenever they passed below the level of the ground."

Leaching cesspools, as a general thing, should be avoided, as their poisonous contents, being absorbed by the earth, in time not only emit malaria into the atmosphere, but are liable to infect our own and our neighbors' wells. This danger may, in a measure, be obviated by vegetation. Sometimes the roots of trees, when located near, are attracted to their vicinity and absorb a large amount of their contents. I know of a case in which a cesspool has been in constant use for twenty years without requiring to be cleansed, which I am convinced is attributable to a large willow-tree that grows beside it, and has sent into it such a mass of fibrous roots that the contents have been absorbed as fast as they accumulated.

A cesspool or vault made water-tight, which can be cleansed at pleasure, is less objectionable. If possible, this should be situated near the garden, where, with the aid of a force-pump and hose, the contents may be conducted to any point where its fertilizing qualities are required. Colonel Waring, one of our leading sanitary engineers, in the *American Agriculturist* of October, 1877, describes a flush tank invented by Mr. Rogers Field, which, at slight expense, may be placed just outside of the walls, and receive the waste of the house; this, when filled, is automatically emptied on the principle of a siphon, its contents being discharged into open drains, placed in the ground ten or twelve inches deep. The matter is then absorbed by the earth, and, being near the surface, is again taken up by vegetation. Colonel Waring states that he has used this for some years on his own place at Newport with eminent success. "These flush-tanks, made of iron, and with all their appliances complete, are now for sale by the agent of the patentee. They cost thirty-five dollars."

Basement floors should be so underdrained as to prevent the possibility of water entering the cellar; and where this is not practicable, the cementing of the floors and walls should be resorted to. It is always well, however, to give the floors sufficient slant, so that in case any dampness should enter, the water may flow to one point, from which there should be a drain; and the fact that there is not sufficient descent from the house to accomplish this, is an obvious reason why such a location should be avoided.

Areas also require draining; but when natural drainage is impracticable, by filling a few feet below their surface with broken stone or coarse gravel, the water collecting here will filter through.

Wash-trays or water-closets should never be placed in the basement, unless there be a decided slope from the house to the cesspool; for the fact that a sewer must start from a point below the basement floor, not only necessitates going to a great depth with the drains, but enters the cesspool at so low a level as to render the latter comparatively useless, for it is evident that the moment the fluids—which must enter near the bottom—rise above the mouth of the drain, they are liable to back up into the pipe.

Great caution should be used in the laying of soil-pipes; as, in the event of settlement, their joints are liable to open, causing the escape of gases. It is well, therefore, that those within the house should be entirely of iron, and their joints calked with lead. Outside soil-pipes should always be laid on solid bottom, as, when placed on made ground, they are liable to settle.

The matter of grading is of much importance, and great economy can be practised by placing the earth from the excavations exactly where we shall want to use it. A gentleman who had had but little experience in this matter, in superintending his own work went to much expense in having the earth removed; and when he came to grade, he discovered that he needed it all, and was put to the additional expense of bringing it back.

One thing should always be observed—that foundations should never rest upon made ground, as this takes years to settle, and, in fact, may never be considered as firm as the original strata. On side hills we are often obliged to excavate considerably into the bank, bringing the earth forward in order to make a level plateau on which to place the house, one half resting on the main bank and the other on the new

Design No. 3.

ground. Here the temptation is great to rest the walls on the new grade; and if builders are not closely watched, they are very apt to transgress in this particular. Another serious difficulty in grades of this description is, that the new earth, resting upon the bank, which is necessarily on an incline, is apt to shift, when, if our rule is not strictly observed, the shifting bank is liable to carry the foundation with it.

There is often serious trouble with our roads and the general lay-out of the grounds by terraces shifting in this manner, to avoid which, the original bank should be stepped, inclining somewhat inward, which will effectually prevent accidents of this kind.

Walls to protect terraces are often insufficient, unless they be built on the principle of "retaining walls," battering on each side; or if for good reasons it is thought necessary to build the outside vertical, the inside should have an additional batter, or incline. Indeed, this rule should apply to all bank walls, as the frost exerts sufficient pressure to throw them out of line, unless this method be adopted.

Area walls especially should be built as retaining walls, as, being exposed to the cold, the frost is liable to penetrate their entire depth; espe-cially as builders are in the habit of carrying these down but a few inches below the cellar bottom, regarding them in the same light as the foun-dations of the house. These, being protected on the inside, prevent the frost from striking down, which renders a few inches below the cellar bottom sufficient; but the condition of an area wall is different. The in-side not being protected, the frost may extend its usual depth below the area floor, which makes it important that these foundations should extend two or three feet lower; and the same rule holds good with area steps.

Side hills, in addition to the facilities already offered for draining, pos-sess other advantages for building; for when the slope is sufficient, one side of the cellar can be above ground, serving as an outlet in case of over-flow, and by this means cheerful kitchens, located above the surface, may be obtained. If these rooms, however, are to be occupied, it is always well to have a subcellar; not only on account of the dryness, but because this is the proper place for the heater, giving the benefit of registers in the basement, besides keeping the ashes and coal-dust out of the way.

In regard to water supplies, the best system is to bring the water in from some higher level, by which an impetus to carry it throughout the house may be obtained. Unless, however, there is a regularly constructed reservoir, it is difficult to find it in sufficient volume without collecting it in a tank in a situation above the living-rooms. The attic is generally the best place for this, as in a tank arranged outside the house the water is apt to freeze. A reservoir, however, might be constructed on higher ground, from which the water could be carried through pipes laid below the frost, and this, I think, would be a desirable method.

There are situations where even wells are not to be had without great expense, in which case the ordinary cistern will prove an excellent sub-stitute. In a house erected for my own use, where water was difficult to obtain, I built a cistern twelve feet square, in which I constructed a filter, which consisted of a simple four-inch brick wall built across one corner, through which the water percolated, and by a force-pump, was brought into the house as pure and clear as from a spring. In fact, it was difficult to discern any difference in the taste. The cistern, which was fed from the roof, never gave out. I even supplied my neighbors with water during a very severe drought; and in rainy seasons, had there not been an overflow from the top, I might have experienced serious inconvenience. These overflows are better discharged upon lower ground than into a sewer or cesspool, for in the latter case the gases are liable to enter the cistern; for, however well protected with traps, which are, at best, of but little use, they are much of the time dry. When the lower end of this drain is exposed, it is well to protect it from the entrance of reptiles and insects by a wire gauze. This also serves the purpose of admitting fresh air, while the foul exhalations find an escape through the leader-pipes from the roof.

When springs on a sufficient elevation are not at hand, the hydraulic ram placed in a running brook will answer the purpose. The ordinary method of raising water into a tank by means of a force-pump is perhaps the simplest; yet there are various mechanical contrivances for saving the manual labor involved by that system. A small Ericsson engine, placed in the cellar at a trifling cost, is an excellent arrangement; and its cheapness and economy in fuel especially recommend it. There is also a small steam-engine manufactured by Baker & Smith, which is put up in connection with their furnace, and, being supplied with steam from the same boiler, is worked without extra expense. The cost of each of these does not exceed two or three hundred dollars.

The favorite system of raising water by windmills, although very effective in its results, I think, in an æsthetic point of view, should be condemned, for they are sure to obtrude themselves most offensively upon the sight; and to see these awkward, spider-like structures dancing fandangoes before our eyes disturbs the repose, and mars the landscape of our otherwise beautiful homes. If these could be constructed in a picturesque manner, in imitation of some of the old Holland windmills, they might become a pleasing object in the landscape. I have seen an arrangement propelled by wind, and enclosed in an ornamental cupola, placed on top of a dwelling-house, or an out-building, which, while adding a pleasing feature to the architecture, kept up an adequate supply of water with scarcely an hour's work a day. These spiders, however, have an advantage mechanically, as, by presenting a greater surface to the wind, their capacity is increased, which, where great power is a consideration, as in the manufactory, is an argument in their favor.

DESIGN No. 3.

First-floor Plan.

1. Living hall, 18×18; 2. Parlor, 14½×21; 3. Dining-room, 14×18; 4. Kitchen, 14½×16; 5. Back hall; 6. Store-room.—*Estimated cost*, $6000.

This cottage has recently been erected at Montclair, New Jersey, for Mrs. A. C. Connelly, and, with some slight changes, at West Brighton,

Staten Island, for Mr. C. Dubois, Jun. Its principal feature is the square entrance-hall, with its irregular staircase, landing on a raised platform which constitutes a bay-window. This bay, which is conspicuous from the entrance, is nearly filled with stained glass, and is made large enough for the accommodation of plants (the lower part of the sash being clear glass, in order to admit the sun), and running up sufficiently high to light both stories. The vignette shows a similar hall recently constructed at Staten Island, the plan of which is reversed from the present design.

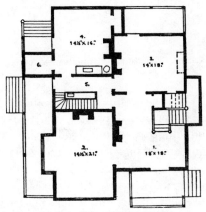

First-floor Plan of Design No. 3.

The dining-room and parlor communicate with the hall by double doors. The latter has the upper part of the bay-window, which is opposite the doors, filled with stained glass. The butler's sink, in this case, is placed in the back hall, which, as a matter of economy, has its advantages; though, as a general thing, we would advise having the butler's pantry separate. There are four large bedrooms and bath-room in the second story, also two bedrooms and billiard-room in the attic. The tank, which is large, is sunk below the attic floor, in order to admit the water directly from the roof, and, being floored over and well lighted, affords space for a trunk and store room.

CHAPTER IV.

PLANS.

Views.—Exposure.—Estimates.—Architect's Supervision.—Commercial Value attached
to a Well-arranged Plan.

THE next step, after the site is selected, is to provide proper plans or
working drawings. There is no doubt that every one who intends
building has some general idea of what he wants, and frequently sketches
out an arrangement of the various floors which he fancies is just the
thing. There can be no particular harm in his doing this; on the contrary, it frequently enables the architect to judge somewhat of the number and size of the rooms needed, and the general requirements of his

Hall and Staircase of Design No. 3.

client. Still, there is this danger; he is too apt to be wedded to his own ideas, thus tram-
melling the professional man in
producing the best arrangement
and effects. These amateur designs should be taken as suggestions simply, nothing more.

It is the duty of the architect, studying the desires and
needs of his client, carefully to
manage the design in all its
parts, so as to fit into, and harmonize with, the lives to be
spent under its roof. He will
first arrange the rooms in re-
gard to exposure. For example, the parlor or living-room — that most
occupied by the family — he would place toward the south, being the
most cheerful, which, while being sheltered from the bleak winds of winter, receives, also, the prevailing summer breezes.

Should the gentleman be a reading man, it would be well to place the library at the north, in order to acquire a steady light. The dining-room may properly be situated at the western side, giving a view of the sunset at the evening meal. North of this should be the kitchen, occupying the least-desirable exposure. If the verandas are limited, the most valuable position would be on the east side of the house, on account of the shade the greater portion of the day. For the contrary reason, the conservatory should have a southerly exposure. The plumbing should also be located at a warm side, to prevent its freezing. And this is not all that is to be taken into consideration in a well-studied plan. It is essential that the rooms most frequented should command fine views, and their arrangement should be such as to form a pleasing exterior as well, the important parts to present the most imposing appearance. Again, a constructional motive should be considered. The arrangement of supports, the disposition of doors and windows, the intersection of roofs, and the general outlines of the building—all have a bearing upon the arrangement of the rooms, which should suggest themselves to the architect in the first conception of his plan. After these preliminaries, he should submit the sketch to his client, which may not prove altogether satisfactory. It is either unsuited to some of his domestic requirements, or not in accordance with his original intentions. Should these prove solid objections, it would be the architect's duty to alter his sketch, and, while transgressing no general rules, conform more with his client's notions. This settled, he next proceeds with his working drawings, which consist of the floor plans for each story, and the four exterior sides or elevations. These, in connection with the specifications, are sufficient for obtaining estimates from the various contractors. It is often considered by the uninitiated that mere sketches or preliminary studies are sufficient to obtain correct estimates of the cost. But this is a most dangerous plan to work upon, as it is almost certain to mislead; for no builder can have a clear conception of what the building really is to be, until regular plans and specifications are matured. These estimates being received from reliable parties, the owner may then go on with a certainty of what the building will cost.

No work of any importance should be carried on without the general supervision of the architect, for rarely is there a plan so perfect that improvements cannot be made, and they are likely to suggest themselves as the building develops. But the most dangerous thing an owner can do is to allow alterations to be made without consulting the original designer, who has fully studied the plan in all its bearings, and one slight change may affect the composition in twenty different ways, both of a constructive and æsthetic nature. The architect is always willing to make changes when the owner desires them, and he alone is able to make them in conformity with the other parts of the plan.

I can cite, as an exemplification of this, an instance of an expensive dwelling, for which an architect had prepared the plans, on the line of one of our metropolitan railways. The design was prepared with especial reference to the rules to which we have alluded, and he had laid out the house on the ground accordingly, ready for the building to proceed. Upon visiting the place a few weeks after, he found, to his dismay, that, for some trivial reason, suggested by the mason, it had been turned and made to face in a different direction. Immediately all the advantages of exposure, view, and the general appearance of the building—so much studied, and from which he had expected such good results — were entirely lost. One point on which he had depended making a favorable impression was that from the railway, from which hundreds of passengers daily commanded a view of the building. Another was from the highway leading from the village. The side of the house least considered was the north, from whence it was little seen, and had no particular view, where he had located the kitchen. Imagine his chagrin, then, at finding the picturesque grouping turned entirely away from the points upon which he had calculated, and in their place those parts he had most endeavored to conceal. The kitchen seemed to have been the object of especial pride to the owner, as it was this he had placed fronting the railway, and it now occupies the agreeable exposure designed for the living-rooms. There shortly after offered just the opportunity for rectifying the blunder, as, wishing to enlarge this department, he could build a tasteful addition, relieving its gaunt and meagre appearance. But instead of consulting his architect, he was again guided by his builder, who assured him that the way to accomplish his design was to lengthen the kitchen portion some ten or twelve feet. Then the error assumed a magnitude truly sublime, for the blemish was intensified at least tenfold, as it overpowered and destroyed all the proportions of the house.

This is the solution of the question I have so often heard asked, as we ride by in the cars, why Mr. B——'s house so much resembles a prison or a lunatic asylum ; and, I might add, had not his obstinacy stood in the way of his interests, the building might, in case of trouble, have brought him a fair profit, instead of a loss of fifty per cent. on the original investment, and the architect's reputation might not have suffered, as it invariably does when these charlatans thus distort his plans, and the damage he sustains overbalances by far any pecuniary advantages he may derive.

There are times, however, when buildings are so remote that it is impossible for the architect to visit them, or, if at all, perhaps not more than once or twice during their construction. In such cases, by retaining copies of all the drawings and specifications, with a practical superintendent upon the grounds, the architect may be consulted almost as well as if he were making constant visits to the works. I have at this time buildings in Canada, Tennessee, and Texas, which I am superintending in this manner, the results of which are entirely satisfactory.

Design No. 4.

There is a commercial value to be attached to a well-arranged plan and carefully studied grouping of the exterior of a house; for it is evident that a dwelling built on these principles requires no more material or labor, but is simply a scientific rendering to produce harmonious and convenient results; and the difference between a house of this kind and one of ordinary construction, when placed in the market, is invariably apparent. I remember a neighborhood in New Jersey which had been built before the present decline in prices, but, owing to the results arising from the panic, many of the houses were offered for sale for which not more than half their cost was realized. Now, had they been constructed with a greater regard to these principles, it is certain that this sacrifice would not have occurred; for there was one instance of a gentleman who had built a house no more expensively than the others, but in which the arrangement and proportion had been better studied, and the price realized at its sale was sufficient to pay a fair profit.

Frequently persons bring their own plan of arrangement, which materially transgresses these principles; and when their attention is called to the fact that certain rooms have no closets, they state that they require none for this apartment, or that there is one in the adjoining hall. When it is remarked that certain rooms are inaccessible except by passing through others, they answer that, although it may be in violation of general principles, yet in their particular case it is especially suitable. It is then suggested that though this may be so, yet, should they desire to sell the house, such an arrangement might prove an insuperable objection to a purchaser. But the answer generally is that the house is not built for sale. It is intended for their own use; and as their children are small, there is not the occasion for much independent privacy. I then remind them that in case of their demise they little know what disposition may be made of the establishment, and it would be well, at any rate, to consider it as an investment for their families after they are gone; also, that their children will not always be young, and as they advance in years they will require different accommodations from those of the nursery. But suggestions and arguments are in vain. They will follow their own no-

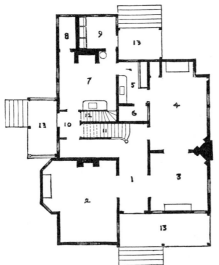

First-floor Plan of Design No. 4.

tions, and when, from some unexpected calamity, they are compelled to sell, they find, too late, the warnings verified.

DESIGN No. 4.

First-floor Plan.

1. Main hall; 2. Parlor, 14×20; 3. Library, 14×14; 4. Dining-room, 14×18; 5. Butler's pantry; 6. Store-room; 7. Kitchen, 14×15; 8. Pantry; 9. Laundry; 10. Vestibule; 11. Main stairs; 12. Back stairs; 13, 13, 13, Verandas. — *Estimated cost,* $6500.

This building has recently been erected at Montclair, New Jersey, for M. F. Redding, Esq., and is a specimen of how a simple square structure may be broken up into picturesque outlines. The hall is of the L shape, having double doors near the entrance, connecting the parlor and library. A broad pier is left in the parlor for a piano, and a similar one in the library for the bookcase, while the dining-room has a special niche for the sideboard. The butler's pantry contains sink and dresser, and communicates with an ample store-room. The kitchen, though small in itself, has a large pantry, and is connected with the laundry, where much of the rough work may be done.

There are four large bedrooms and one bath-room in the second story, together with finished rooms in the attic. The main staircase ascends to a landing, at the top of which there is a stained-glass window opening on to a second-story balcony. The house is of frame, sheathed on the outside and clapboarded. The panels between the windows are smooth-ceiled, upon which flower patterns are stencilled. The gables and attic walls are covered with ornamental cut shingles, the whole having a broken and varied effect.

CHAPTER V.

BUILDING MATERIALS.

Brick.—Stone.—Concrete.

THE site being determined and the drainage established, it becomes necessary to decide upon the material for building. In most of the Eastern and Middle States stone is very abundant; and unless it can be utilized in the building of walls, it is necessary to dispose of it in some other way, which is both expensive and troublesome.

The vast forests which formerly covered the land, from which timber could be procured, are rapidly becoming things of the past; and lumber is now brought from Maine or Michigan, at an expense for freightage of more than half its value. Why not, therefore, instead of going hundreds of miles for building material, utilize the stone which we dig out of our cellars? In many cases, it is true, it is of coarse quality, and shaped in ill accord with jointed ashler; but, however rough it may be, a clever mason can always make it appear well, even if its sides are not plumb or its bases true. Rubble or random courses often present a better appearance, especially if the material is of somewhat rough character, in which case it is well, instead of making the pointing flush, to sink it as deeply as possible within the recess. By thus emphasizing the irregularity, we show a more honest construction and secure a certain picturesqueness of effect; and here creepers and climbing vines have a better chance to cling than if the stone were dressed. The difficulty in working some of this unyielding material is in adapting it to the openings and corners; for these parts it may prove economy to import a better quality of stone. Bricks may sometimes be used effectively in the angles, and are cheap, for the reason that they require no cutting. One of the chief expenses in stone building is in elevating the material; for which reason, the custom of building the masonry simply to the second story, and finishing the remainder with wood, has become quite common in England, and seems to be appropriate for all attempts at such work. There are many cases, however, where stone is difficult to obtain, when we would suggest, in order to carry out this motive, brick or concrete should be used. It has been sometimes argued that houses of these materials were damp, but, if properly constructed, our experience has not proved them so; and when we consider that in England and on the Continent these are the only materials used, and that in the principal cities of our own country wood as a building material is prohibited, we do not see why the dampness should be peculiar to our suburban buildings, especially in so dry a climate. There are methods, however, by which capillary attraction may be prevented, and one is the laying of a course of slate in the wall above the ground, on a line with the water-table or first-story beams. This is, perhaps, more effective when laid in with hydraulic cement.

When the stone taken from the ground is more than is needed for building purposes, it can be disposed of in the beds of our roads and walks; for if excavated to a depth of from three to six feet, according to the amount of material at our disposal, and the larger stones placed at the bottom, graduating up with the smallest upon the top, the foundation being below the frost, the road will in all weathers be firm and dry, and the bottom, being open on the principle of a blind ditch, serves an admirable purpose for drainage. These road-beds often solve the embarrassing problem of what we shall do with our rubbish, for here seems a catch-all, not only for rocks and stones, but for stumps, shavings, and other débris. Indeed, if we place earth or gravel upon the surface, shavings or salt hay will prove a useful covering to prevent the earth

from washing down; otherwise, after every rain we are liable to find the road full of holes; and shavings, especially those of cedar, will remain for years without decaying.

Much has been said recently on the subject of concrete for building, and one of the English

Design No. 5.

journals went so far as to offer a premium for the best design for a cottage in this material, and has published a number of papers on the subject. They propose building, not only the exterior walls, but the partitions, floors, and even the staircases, of it. The smoke flues can be constructed by drawing up a cylinder as the work progresses: the staircase risers to be of illuminated tile; the tread, balusters, and hand-rail made of Roman cement; some of the floors and wainscots to be of tile, and the cornices and trimmings of cement.

The staircase, trimmings, and pavements of the Gilsey House, New York, are of this material. The balusters are ornamental, and the heavy newels and hand-rail—which latter is simply capped with mahogany— attest its adaptability for this purpose.

The chief difficulty in the use of concrete is, that, as it sets, it is liable to shrink; and, when the wall is of great length, it is very apt to crack. It is proposed to overcome this by using iron anchors through the walls, which may show with an ornamental head on the surface. The walls may further be sustained by a system of wooden battening, resembling some of the half-timber constructions of an Elizabethan cottage, these battens to be bolted on the inside. However well this may be adapted to England, where they enjoy an equable climate, we think it would scarcely be so here, where we are subject to such extreme changes. If the shrinkage is suggested as an objection with them, how much more of one would it be here! And the very system by which they propose to strengthen the walls—iron ties—would with us soon work ruin, where the climate, varying from twenty degrees below zero to a hundred and one in the shade, would cause contraction and expansion of these metal anchors; and if cracks should occur, the water entering them would cause disintegration, and, if then exposed to frost, would soon make such havoc as would be difficult to repair. Stucco, of course, would be some protection to the exterior, but even that has proved far from satisfactory in this country. It is true that in some parts of New England this has been applied with considerable success, but (whether owing to the climate, material, or mode of working, it is difficult to say) it has proved a failure in other sections.

Some fifteen years since, I planned a house which was built of concrete brick. This, in a measure, overcame the difficulty of shrinking, as what under the other system would have occurred the entire length of the wall was here distributed in each brick, which, being subjected to great pressure, became very hard and durable, so that the house still stands in good condition. But it is difficult to determine the quality of the concrete. One builder may produce an excellent and satisfactory article; while another, either from want of experience or proper material, will make it in such a manner that it will scarcely last a season; although its weakness may not become apparent until some time after the house is completed.

However good this method may be for contractors, it is certainly bad for owners; and unless a builder and locality have an established reputation for sound work of this character, it may be regarded as little better than an experiment. The material possesses this advantage, however—it seems to be thoroughly fire-proof. When floors and partitions are constructed of it, especially if the trimmings and mouldings are of the same, it gives a sense of almost absolute security in this respect.

DESIGN No. 5.

First-floor Plan.

1. Hall; 2. Parlor, 15×26; 3. Library, 14×15; 4. Dining-room, 15×16; 5. Butler's pantry; 6. Store-room; 7. Kitchen, 15×20; 8. Lavatory; 9. Coat-closet; 10, 10. Verandas.— *Estimated cost*, $8000.

This represents a house on the Erie Railroad, a few miles above Paterson, the residence of Wheeler W. Philips, Esq., in the thriving and picturesque town of Ridgewood. The first story is built of stone, above which the material is of wood, framed in the ordinary manner and clapboarded. The junction between the wood and the stone is covered with a bold dental cornice, running around the building; the gable separated from the second-story wall by a similar cornice of the battlemented type. The gables are covered with vertical boards and wide battens. A peculiar feature is the chimney showing on the outside, with panels relieved with bands of black brick.

The parlor bay-window, too, is somewhat peculiar, owing to its being octagon below, terminating with a square gable above.

The roof is of purple slate.

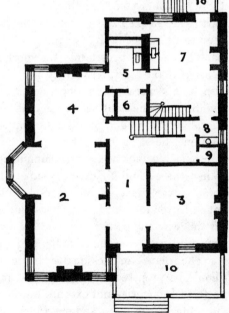

First-floor Plan of Design No. 5.

The wood-work is of a warm olive color, trimmed with chocolate, the finer lines being picked out with black and Indian red.

CHAPTER VI.

SPECIFICATIONS.

Estimates.—Contracts.—Mechanic's Lien.—Foundations.—Rubble-work.—Pointing.

THE tedious and somewhat thankless task of preparing the plans being completed, it becomes necessary to draw specifications of the workmanship and material pertaining to the different trades, after which the obtaining of estimates is in order. The usual system of submitting these to competition is, no doubt, the best, although it is frequently dangerous to award the contract to the lowest bidder, as it often proves the dearest in the end. It is always well, in obtaining estimates, to allow none but those in whom you have thorough confidence to compete, as irresponsible parties are in the habit of estimating low in order to obtain a contract, and then securing themselves against loss at the expense of the owner. Work done by the day is certainly the most satisfactory, and, although more expensive at the start, frequently proves an ultimate economy. We would also, as a general thing, deprecate the system of giving out the entire building to one contractor, for it is too much to attribute to one man a thorough knowledge of all the complicated branches of building. If, for example, he be a carpenter, he is liable to let out the other trades to irresponsible men whose recommendation is simply that they are cheap. When there is no architect to superintend, of course it is well to employ some clever " jack of all trades;" but if the architect is accessible, it is much better for him to supervise and let out each of the trades separately. In this way the owner may use his own discretion in the selection of his men, and still have the advantage of the work at first cost.

The plans and estimates being finally approved, careful contracts should be prepared stating terms of payment, and binding the contractor to furnish material and execute his work according to the true intent and meaning of the plans and specifications, and to the satisfaction of the architect, who should give a certificate that the work is complete before the various payments are made.

One of the greatest bugbears in the way of building is what is known as the mechanic's lien law, which, in most of the States, seems to be entirely one-sided, intended only to protect the mechanic; and owners, if they are not particular to guard against its penalties, are more than likely to become victims.

I once knew a couple who, after an industrious and frugal life, had, as they supposed, accumulated sufficient to keep them from want in their old age, and, retiring from business, determined to build for themselves a modest home, and thus realize their life-long dream. The building was completed and paid for; but imagine their dismay when they found that, in consequence of the irresponsibility of their contractor, they were called

Design No. 6.

upon to defend a series of lawsuits from parties who had furnished both work and material for which they had never been paid. The result was that the unfortunate couple completely lost their home, and what remained of their savings was consumed by their lawyers; so that their dream, instead of being realized, proved the agent of their destruction. It becomes as important, therefore, for those inexperienced in building to employ an architect, as it is to have a lawyer conduct a lawsuit.

The first thing an architect should attend to, in the execution of his work, is the laying-out of the building upon the grounds. This should be done under his own supervision, in order to secure the best grades, views, drainage, etc.

Foundations are of paramount importance; for if they are not substantial, the mistake is of the most radical nature. How many buildings have we seen, in other respects thoroughly good, where this fatal blunder, if it did not imperil their safety, at least became a grievance of most sore description! One church, we remember, had its tower taken down twice in consequence of insufficient foundations.

The walls on the underside of the frame or water-table, constituting the underpinning, should, if possible, be laid with dressed stone, cut in square blocks, not necessarily of a size. It is true that there is an expense attending this which may be overcome by introducing what is known as rubble-work. The peculiarity of this is, that, though inexpensive, it may be made to appear well by a judicious use of pointing, which should resemble as nearly as possible the natural color of the stone. But here, perhaps, arises an objection that the pointing becomes a sham, covering up the ragged edges of the stone and giving them the appearance of a closely dressed joint. We would therefore advise, if possible, that a better kind of work should be exposed to view. Still, as this seems a pardonable deception in inexpensive work, a slight description of its method might be advisable. The best way to imitate granite, or blue stone, is by a composition of cement and well-washed sand, colored with lamp-black, Spanish brown, and Venetian red. (Lamp-black being liable to fade, blacksmith's cinders or coal-dust might be substituted.) Regular joints may then be struck with white-lead, imitating those of nicely jointed masonry. These lines should be perfectly horizontal and plumb, and as nearly as possible in the centre of the pointing. Sometimes the cement is sprinkled with pulverized stone, which is pressed into the pointing while fresh. The color for the entire work should be mixed at one time, as there is always a difficulty in reproducing the exact shade.

In timber buildings the walls should be at least eighteen inches thick ; if of stone, the basement walls two feet, allowing a shelving of three inches within for the beams to rest upon, and projecting three inches on the outer side. This projection should be capped with a cut stone water-table, which may be bevelled to an angle of forty-five degrees.

In regard to foundations, much depends on the natural bed upon which we are to build. Rock, as may be supposed, is the most substantial, and next to this, gravel, or hard-pan. Large, flat stones should be placed at the bottom, and when these do not get a perfect bearing, they should be imbedded in a layer of cement or concrete, the thickness to depend upon the nature of the substratum.

When there is any part of the foundation resting on rock, it is necessary, if practicable, to run all the trenches down to this ; for in case the portion resting upon the ground should yield, that upon the rock remaining solid, the structure must settle unequally, thereby materially injuring the building, and throwing it out of level.

Chimneys, owing to their extreme height, but also to the fact that but little attention is usually paid to their foundations, are apt to settle, and where they join the walls of the apartments we almost invariably find cracks extending throughout their length.

DESIGN No. 6.

First-floor Plan.

1. Vestibule; 2. Main hall; 3. Library, 14×14; 4. Parlor, 14×20; 5. Dining-room, 14×18; 6. Butler's pantry; 7. Store-room; 8. Kitchen, 14×16; 9. Main stairs; 10. Back stairs; 11, 11. Verandas.—*Estimated cost,* $6500.

This is a frame cottage, with four rooms and a hall on the first story, four bedrooms and bath on the second floor, and good accommodations in the attic. The hall is well lighted by the staircase-window over the landing, which is sufficiently high to admit of a vestibule underneath. It is nine feet wide, and the rear is enclosed for the accommodation of the back stairs, which run from basement to attic. The butler's pantry, though small, has two dressers and a sink, and is connected with the store-room. There are two windows placed over the dressers for light.

The fireplace in the parlor is opposite that of the library, while in order to give the chimney the appearance of being in the centre of the room, there is a break in the ceiling, forming a transom, on a line with the library wall. This may be effectively treated with curtains, and, at the same time, improve the vista, by allowing the chandeliers to range on a line.

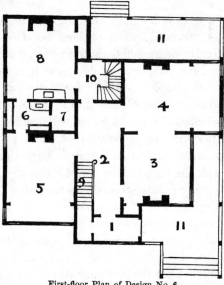

First-floor Plan of Design No. 6.

CHAPTER VII.

FRAMING.

Timber.—Furring.—Cellar Partitions.—Covering a Frame House.—Seasoned Lumber.

THE foundation being complete, let us now take up the subject of framing. The old method, where large timbers were not constructively put together, and no precaution taken against settling, seems mostly to have gone out of date, and to have been supplanted by a lighter and more simple method. It is evident that a stick of timber ten inches square can be divided into four sticks five inches square, and two of these, scientifically put together, will sustain a greater pressure than the original stick, put up regardless of these principles. One of the points to be guarded against in timber construction is that of shrinkage; for however well the foundations may be prepared, if the frame is liable to shrink, an equally disastrous settlement, causing the cracking of plaster and a general derangement of doors and windows, is sure to follow. The old system of placing the sill on edge, with the beams resting on independent girders, each liable to shrink from a quarter to half an inch, necessarily caused the house to settle. Being unequal in its bearings, the floors not only became unlevel, but the resulting strain had a serious effect upon all its parts, causing the external joints to open and the roof to leak.

There was a mode of framing invented by our pioneers with a view to obviating this difficulty, in which the green timber was so manipulated as to avoid shrinkage; and by a nice calculation of its bearings all the strength of the heavier method was attained with a small amount of timber. Advocates of the unscientific mode ironically styled it the balloon system. Yet, notwithstanding all the ridicule to which it was subjected, it has steadily grown in favor, and is now, in a modified form, accepted by our best builders. The system upon which it is based is simply to avoid, as far as is possible, resting the frame on girders or interties. The sill, instead of being set on edge, is laid flat, reducing its shrinking properties to three inches instead of ten. This method has also the effect of distributing the weight over a greater surface of the foundation, and supplying a sort of cap or binder to the wall. The studs and posts, instead of being cut at each story, and surmounted by a lateral timber or intertie, which is liable to shrink, are run continuously up to the roof, interties being omitted altogether. Thus, instead of thirty or forty inches of timber across the grain, we have but the sill and plate, in both of which, being placed flat, the shrinkage is reduced to eight inches only. It is a well-known fact that timber shrinks across the grain, and not lengthwise.

Design No. 7.

All timbers receiving lath should be about sixteen inches from centres, in order to give the lath, which is four feet long, four bearings for nails. Furring strips might be placed at the distance of twelve inches, giving five nailings to each lath.

It is generally a good principle not to lath immediately on the underside of the floor beams, as the shrinking of these timbers is likely to cause irregularities and cracks. To prevent this, the system of furring, in which there is a series of strips, say one by two inches, nailed across the joists, may be introduced.

In regard to roof timbers no particular suggestions need be offered. The plate may be of pine, laid flat as before described; the sloping rafters, 3×5; rafters on decks, 3×8, each 24 inches from centres; hip rafters, 2×8; valley rafters, 3×10; ridge pieces, 2×9.

We would here observe that the cellar partitions in all first-class buildings should be of stone or brick instead of wood, as the dampness of the cellar is apt to rot the wood, making the foundation, in time, insecure.   It is true that brick piers every six or eight feet form an excellent substitute, but in this case the intermediate weight necessarily comes upon the girders, which have to be heavy in order to prevent sagging, and the increased size offers a greater surface for shrinking.   Brick arches over piers are a good construction, as they not only give the entire superstructure an equal bearing, but do away with solid partitions, which obstruct both light and air.   I have sometimes seen iron rails, such as are used on railroads, placed on top of these piers.   These make a thoroughly solid and fire-proof bearing, not being liable either to shrink or decay.

The old plan of filling in the frame with brick has proved objectionable, inasmuch as it is found to collect moisture, making the house damp and thereby hastening decay.   Brick filling, therefore, has been abandoned and the process of sheathing substituted.   This is simply a covering of plank boards nailed diagonally over the outside, which adds so much to the strength that the frame may be made considerably lighter, and consequently less expensive.   This sheathing is covered with thick paper or felt, and is then ready to receive the outside clapboards.   In houses built after the old plan, the frame, in shrinking away from the bricks, was apt to leave numerous seams through which the wind and cold might penetrate, while the felt, a perfect non-conductor, being wrapped around the entire building, acts like a blanket, keeping all warm and dry within.

Great care should be taken, in covering a frame house, that there are no joints in the trimmings that will admit rain or snow.   The upper members should always overlap those underneath, on the same principle as a shingle or clapboard.   Thus the upper trimming of a door or window should have a lip, or, as it is known in carpentry, a rabbet, that may run up under the siding, as should every horizontal joint throughout the exterior of a building.   I have often heard carpenters say that their joints fit so tight that no water could be admitted; and when you speak of shrinkage, they say their lumber is so well seasoned that you need have no fears on that score; but no greater fallacy than this can exist.   In our days there is no seasoned timber, and even if there were, it would shrink. I have known of wood that has stood for half a century, which, when worked over and a new surface exposed, has both swelled and shrunk. Therefore it is useless to accept the theory of non-shrinking of wood, even after it is painted.

Of course, the better seasoned the lumber is, the better chance it has; and as the difficulties of procuring seasoned timber are so great, if time were not an object, it would be better for the owner to purchase his material a year or so before it is needed, and stack it up to dry. Usually, however, the great point is to have the building completed in as short a time as possible, as our minds are rarely made up till the last minute, when everything is wanted in a hurry. In fact, if a house could be simply enclosed so as to protect it from the weather, and the lath put on, and so remain for six months or a year before plastering, the whole would have an opportunity to settle and shrink—a process usually going on after the house is completed—and cracks in the plaster would, in a great measure, be prevented. In the same way the interior wood-work and trimmings might be prepared, and have the advantage of being seasoned before being applied.

DESIGN No. 7.

First-floor Plan.

1. Veranda; 2. Main hall; 3. Library, 15×15; 4. Office, 8×9; 5. Living-room, 15×28; 6. Dining-room, 15×20; 7. Butler's pantry; 8. Store-room; 9. Kitchen, 14×20; 10. Servants' hall; 11. Servants' porch; 12. Back stairs; 13. Principal stairs.—*Estimated cost*, $8000.

This is a simple frame cottage of small cost, such as many of our American people might build. The living-room is large, surrounded on three sides by a wide veranda. The dining-room connects with the kitchen through a butler's pantry, out of which opens a store-room. The kitchen has two closets, and there are back stairs. The library is of good size, communicating with the gentleman's "growlery:" both these rooms open on to the veranda. The second story has four bedrooms, bath, and two dressing-rooms; the servants' apartments are in the attic. From the staircase landing a very

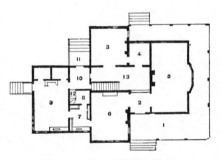

First-floor Plan of Design No. 7.

pretty effect is obtained by a triplet window of colored glass, lighting the first and second stories, and showing conspicuously from both. The left-hand window communicates with a large balcony, covered by the main roof. Another unusual feature is the bracketing-out of the main roof over the sitting-room veranda, in order to cover the second-story balcony.

In this climate, supplementary roofs, tacked on promiscuously, are objectionable.   Balconies, canopies, dormer-windows, and even veranda roofs, necessitate much work, and are a continual source of annoyance and expense, owing to leakage.   Roof decks are also productive of much trouble, especially in our climate, where we are subject to heavy falls of snow.   They should be abandoned, if possible, and the roofs carried up to the ridge, sufficiently steep for the snow to slide off without obstruction.   The nearer we get to the form of a tent, the nearer we arrive at perfection in this respect.   Here the Queen Anne system comes to our aid, and seems to offer the method that most fully meets our requirements.   Designs Nos. 10, 12, 14 are examples of this.   In these the main roof covers everything, even to the balconies, dormers, and verandas.

CHAPTER VIII.

ROOFING.

Metals.—Shingles.—Slate.—Testing Slate.—Sheathing.—French Method.—Oiling Slate.
—Painting Roofs.—Tiles for Roofing.—Crestings and Finials.

I ADVISE that the walls be covered before the roof is built, as I have
frequently known the latter to be carried off by the wind, when the
sides of the house were not protected. The further to exclude draughts,
it is well to enclose the door and window openings with rough boards or
temporary sashes, at least on the side toward the wind. The openings
on the leeward side act as an escape, or safety-valve, in case of danger
from this source.

In regard to the material for covering the roof, much depends upon
the angle of inclination. It is obvious that if flat, with sufficient pitch
only to shed the water, slate or shingle would be impracticable, as driving
storms would be apt to force the rain or snow under them. It is generally considered that these materials are not desirable if the angle be less
than thirty degrees. Metal forms the best covering for roofs that are
inclined to be flat. Copper is no doubt the best material, but it is little
used on account of its expense. Tin, in our climate, answers as an excellent substitute; composition—such as tar or other materials—we would
not advise on good work, as its only merit is its cheapness. It is generally advisable that roofs of dwelling-houses should be of sufficient pitch
to admit of the use of slate or shingles. Split shingles, although more
expensive, serve their purpose better than the kind known as sawn shingles, as in the former the fibre runs the entire length. The advantage
gained by their use is that the moisture, in following the line of the
wood, is less likely to penetrate. In sawn shingles, the surface is frequently across the grain, rendering them not only more liable to break,
but, the ends of the fibre being exposed, they more readily absorb moisture, which induces rapid decay. It is an erroneous idea that rafters must
be boarded before the shingles are applied; as much air as it is possible
to procure is necessary for a shingle roof, both above and below, in order
to keep it dry and free from rot. A shingle roof will last much long-

er if simply laid on slats placed at the proper distances to receive the nails.

The numerous quarries of slate which have recently been developed throughout the country offer, we think, the most desirable material for roofing. The best slates supplied at present are from Pennsylvania and Vermont, although there are other quarries furnishing excellent varieties. Perhaps those of Virginia may also rank among the best. Their grain is so close and even, that they may be made thinner, and consequently lighter. At the same time they present a smooth surface; and their color, which is excellent, is less liable to fade.

A good slate may be known by its ringing sound when struck. Hardness is thus indicated, which is a most desirable quality. Such slate possesses small power of absorbing water. The contrary property is generally found in those whose surface is smooth and greasy. "The quantity of water absorbed by slate in a given time is a sure test of its quality, the best being that which retains the smallest possible amount. In selecting a roofing slate, therefore, a safe plan would be to weigh each variety before placing it in a tub of water, when, after several hours' immersion, and being again weighed, that which has gained the least will prove the most durable." The great advantage possessed by slate roofs lies in the fact that they are not affected by damp. Another is, that slats need not be employed. Here sheathing is not only legitimate, but between this and the slate thick felt may be placed, which is a protection from heat and cold, and acts as a barrier against wind and snow; for, although the lap of the slate may be sufficient to exclude rain, snow will always be forced into every crevice in case of wind.

In roofs of this kind it is always desirable that the grain should run lengthwise, rather than across, for, as the slates are usually secured by two nails near the top, they are apt, in case of cross grain, to break at these points during violent storms.

The French method of laying slate, as given by Viollet le Duc, has a great advantage in this respect. It consists of a strip of metal which lines the slate and is turned up at the bottom, space being allowed at the top for the nails. Thus each slate is secured in its position without the necessity of punching holes, which invariably impairs its strength.

It is usually a custom, after the slating is completed, to cover it with a coating of oil. This seems to clean it off, and gives it a dark appearance, and the slater will assure you that it prevents its fading. This, however, is an expedient entirely unnecessary in good work, for poor slate alone will absorb the oil, and only this quality is liable to fade. Oil on sound slating, therefore, remains on the surface only until it is washed off by the rain, and is then conducted into our cisterns, and we wonder what is the matter with the water!

Another folly that we might as well condemn is that of painting roofs; we mean particularly shingles, for these, if left to themselves, will naturally assume a color which improves every year by exposure; while paint not only appears unnatural at the outset, but looks worse and more rusty as each season passes. Another objection to paint is, that although it is used to protect the shingles against the weather, it in reality promotes their destruction; for the shingles in their natural state allow the water to run free, whereas paint fills up the cracks or water-courses, and forms certain ridges, which prevent its escape; consequently it remains in the wood.

Design No. 8.

There is a certain sympathy between shingles and the changes of the weather which renders them especially suitable as a covering. Not only do they assume a harmonious color through exposure, but in dry weather they shrink and give ventilation to the roof; and in wet weather, when it is necessary to keep out the storm, they swell again and become tight.

Perhaps it is too much to say that shingles *never* appear well when painted. I have seen shingle roofs improved by being painted something the color of red tile. They have thus much the appearance of tiles, and, while less expensive, they require no additional construction to support their weight. I learned, however—and I have since tried the experiment—that the shingles were dipped in a tub of paint before being applied. This not only does away with the usual objection of filling up the cracks, but coats the shingle on the underside and edges, so that the tendency of the paint is rather to preserve than destroy.

Tiles, for the purpose of roofing, although much used in the Dutch colonies of this country a century or two ago, seemed to have fallen into disuse until within the last few years. That they possess much merit cannot be denied. The greatest difficulty hitherto appears to have been the expense, although we understand that those used on the building erected by the State of New Jersey on the Centennial Grounds were nearly as cheap as ordinary slate. Tiles certainly are very ornamental, and when of a color complementary to the exterior of the building, produce a decidedly picturesque effect. By this we would imply that when they are red they should not be used on a building the external walls of which are of the same color — as brick, for instance. Here green or purple would present the best contrast; but in case the walls were of darker material, say blue granite or limestone, the red is desirable, and seems to warm up the cheerless effect, as brick trimmings relieve the coldness of blue stone. In England some beautiful effects in crestings and finials have been developed in this material (kindred specimens may be seen on St. George's Hall at Philadelphia), and seem, in a great measure, to have superseded the cast-iron structures which have hitherto "out-Heroded Herod" in obtruding their fantastic proportions against the sky.

The dipped shingles, as before described, producing the effect of these tiles in color, may have a ridge of wood somewhat resembling the tile cresting in outline, and painted the same color. This cresting should cover the ridge on the principle of a saddle, and, when properly secured, it may do away with the necessity of metal flashings. The beauty of tile roofs seems, however, to consist in simplicity. When worked into fancy forms, tiles lose their dignity, and have a frivolous, tawdry effect. In fact, the less we emphasize the roof the better, as it should be the chimneys which give prominence to the building.

DESIGN No. 8.

First-floor Plan.

1. Hall, 15×18; 2. Parlor, 14×18; 3. Dining-room, 14×18; 4. Butler's pantry; 5. Store-room; 6. Kitchen, 15×16.—*Estimated cost*, $5000.

The peculiarity of this design is the absence of verandas, which are superseded by a large porch some fourteen feet square. This porch has all the advantages of a room, and may be made secluded by an arrangement of rolling shutters, to let up or down at pleasure. Here the family may sit in groups, instead of being stretched out in a line, as must generally be the case on a veranda. It is true, if the veranda be of sufficient width, social circles may be formed, but not without obstructing the space appropriated as a promenade, which is the chief reason why a veranda is preferable to a porch. Perhaps the best arrangement, therefore, in order to meet both these requirements, is to have a veranda constructed on the principle of bays, where groups may assemble without interfering with those who wish to enjoy a walk.　An arrangement of this kind is attempted in Design No. 9.

Passing the entrance porch, the large square hall with its low landing staircase, lighted by a triplet bay-window of stained glass, becomes the prominent object of interest.　This hall and porch, therefore, would naturally become the favorite gathering-place of the family, while the parlor would serve as the reception and music room.

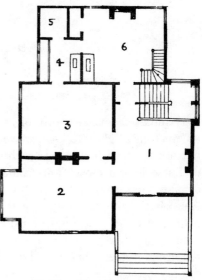

First-floor Plan of Design No. 8.

The butler's pantry, store-room, and kitchen are arranged in the usual manner.　The second story has four sleeping-rooms, bath-room, and the customary accompaniment of closets, one of which, connected with the chamber over the hall, is of somewhat unusual dimensions, being the space enclosed by the lean-to roof over the porch.　Owing to the peculiar slope upon which this house is built, the rear of the cellar coming above the ground, the kitchen might easily have been located in the basement, allowing the one indicated in the design to serve as a dining-room.　This was objected to on account of the too great exertion required in going up and down stairs, so the basement was converted into a laundry.

CHAPTER IX.

GLASS.

Plate-glass.—Stained Glass.—Prismatic Glass.—Blue Glass.

IN imitating ancient example, as was said before, it is not incumbent upon us to give up all that we have gained in the course of centuries, but to adopt and incorporate with the old everything that has been proved desirable in the new. For example, in Queen Anne's time, small panes of glass were invariably used, for the simple reason that they had no large ones; but for us to go back to the use of small panes, only because they belong to the style, would be ridiculous. We should not only injure our view by cutting it up with these little checkered squares, but would miss the brilliant effect that we might obtain from that most beautiful of modern inventions, plate-glass.

Plate-glass in a country-house will add a greater richness than anything else. Its reflection from the exterior is so clear and perfect, that it instantly attracts the attention of the passer-by; and as it is approached, its delineation of the lawn and distant scenery is a picture which none but the Great Architect could paint. From the interior, plate-glass is so absolutely translucent, that no obstruction seems offered to the view; so that, in case of a window glazed with a single light, it is often supposed that the sash must be open, which is the acme of the effect to be produced. I remember a circumstance of a gentleman entertaining some of his friends at a lawn party, where a very ludicrous scene occurred. One of the company, a clergyman, went into the house to procure a croquet set; and, seeing the window, which extended to the floor, open, as he supposed, he attempted to walk out that way, when, to his dismay, he crashed through an entire pane of glass. And here a scene followed which, but for the serious consequences that might have ensued, would have been laughable in the extreme. The sash, being suddenly relieved of its load of glass, flew up like a shot, and the poor gentleman came within an ace of being carried up with it. As it was, he was sent flying out on the lawn; and had it not been for the croquet-box, which intervened between himself and the glass, he might have been severely injured. In order to prevent the repetition of such an accident, the owner had illuminated on the centre of each pane the monogram of the different members of his family.

In windows only intended to give light, and not in a position to command a view, it would be proper to use small panes, or even stained glass with leaded sash. This would be allowable, for instance, in windows over a staircase landing, and indeed in all sashes above the height of the eye. Though this idea is borrowed from the Gothic, and seldom found in the examples of the Queen Anne, yet we do not hesitate to accept it as being extremely beautiful, and capable of the most artistic treatment. I have recently fitted up a dining-room, where the upper sashes are thus treated. Designs of fruit, game, convivial scenes, and texts of good cheer furnish appropriate decorations.

Staircase windows particularly offer an opportunity for stained glass. When they are placed above a landing, thereby coming into a central position between the two stories, they serve the double purpose of lighting both, as is shown in several of these designs. When introduced in a proper hall—I mean, one serving more as a room than a passage —stained glass is appropriate, even if not

Design No. 9.

admitted to any other part of the house. In the panels of the hall door, also, instead of having the unmeaning and at the same time expensive material, known as figured glass — in which the figures, by-the-way, are almost always execrable — stained glass would be appropriate, as its obscure effects would serve the purpose of preventing passers-by from seeing in, which is the only object of ground glass. Upon the fan-lights it could also be well applied, and the green curtain or the *chef d'œuvre* of ornamental paper might be dispensed with.

Many think that stained glass gives a house too much the appearance of a church. This was formerly, and with good reason, said of furniture and interiors treated in the Gothic style. This perhaps suggests one reason why the Queen Anne rendering is so popular; every detail seems so fitted for domestic use. Stained glass has also an adaptability to domestic purposes, which has been developed in this style. Instead of a dark and dim religious treatment, the colors are usually light and transparent, and the leading, instead of being diamond-shaped, is square. The material used is that known as "roll cathedral," which, from the unevenness of its surface, has a brilliant and sparkling effect. We would warn our readers against using plain or enamel glass for this purpose.

There are some windows in the Café Brunswick, New York, which are examples of this style, and seem appropriate to the decorations and furniture. They are good specimens of this work.

Sometimes, when the openings are small, the light may be increased by using prismatic glasses, similar to those in a dead-light over an area. A small aperture is frequently all that is necessary to give a large amount of light when treated in this manner; and could we realize how minute a glass, properly placed, will suffice to light a large space, as in the apex of a dome, we would more readily believe that we have not yet reached the perfection of lighting.

Stained glass in our houses seems such an innovation that the majority of people, taking custom only as their guide, are astonished at the mere suggestion; and, true to the religious instincts of their forefathers, who so long banished it from their temples of worship, it seems difficult for them to become reconciled to it in their dwellings. It sometimes becomes necessary for the architect, in order to accomplish such a reform, to resort to subterfuge; and the mania for blue glass, in the healing properties of which so many were gaining faith, afforded the desired opportunity. A true artist might at one time have felt especially favored if he were in possession of some fanciful or hypochondriacal client. Now, however, it is generally conceded that the fact of the glass being blue has very little to do with its healing properties, although it is, no doubt, efficacious to resort to such a device, in order to induce people to submit themselves to the rays of the sun. There is little doubt that a sun-bath of any color, or of no color at all, would produce the same effect. Physicians say that the sun is as necessary to the health of animals as to the life of plants; and if people would expose themselves more to its influence, there would be fewer aches and better health, both mental and physical. There is little doubt if our dwellings could be arranged more on the principle of conservatories, where we might sun ourselves, as well as our plants, we should find a corresponding improvement.

Blue glass, viewed æsthetically, may act as a foundation to artistic treatment in design—either leaves and flowers, with an occasional medallion, or a Japanese rendering of storks and rushes—while it gives a liquid or atmospheric effect to the background.

The chief objection urged against stained glass is its expense; and although but a portion of the sash need be thus treated, a dollar and upward per foot (according to the work) soon amounts to a sum which an economical estimate will not permit. Variations, however, may be given to an upper sash of clear glass, by making the sides of geometric patterns; and with a simple transparency suspended in its centre, a good effect is often produced. These transparencies may be made the entire size of the sash, so that they can be removed at pleasure, and are often convenient where plate-glass is already in, and where any permanent change would be undesirable, as in a hired house or flat.

DESIGN No. 9.

First-floor Plan.

1. Entrance-hall; 2. Living-hall, 18×20; 3. Parlor, 14×20; 4. Dining-room, 14×18; 5. Butler's pantry; 6. Kitchen, 14×16; 7. Back hall; 8, 8. Verandas.—*Estimated cost,* $6000.

This study, which was suggested by a house designed by Mr. Rutherford Meade, of this city, and built for Mr. Herrick at Peekskill, New York, though similar to that mansion in outline, differs in plan and detail. In the original, there are three living-rooms and a kitchen; in this, however, there are but two living-rooms proper, but a hall, lighted by a staircase window, is arranged in the rear of the house. Being closed from the vestibule by a screen, it is sufficiently retired to make a pleasant family-room, and is rendered the more effective by the staircase bays being in full view of the entrance. The window, being placed obliquely, has ample accommodation for plants in the triangular space at the corners, without interfering with the landing.

First-floor Plan of Design No. 9.

The parlor, entrance-hall, and dining-room are *en suite,* opening into one another by means of folding-doors. The butler's pantry is spacious, with a dresser for china running across the rear. It might be thought that the dresser would interfere with the windows, as this is the only direction from which light can be obtained. To obviate this difficulty the dresser is made low, which renders it not only easy of access, but leaves space for the windows, which are placed above. By this method both light and closet-room are secured without the one interfering with the other. As the difficulty of reaching the windows without a ladder still exists, they are arranged to open and shut on the principle of those of a greenhouse, which work by the turning of a crank.

A recessed balcony, with coved ceiling, opens from the billiard-room in the attic. The exterior of the house may be painted in neutral tints, with darker trimmings; the shingled gables of a middle tint, produced by an equal mixture of the two former; while the receding part of the balcony may be painted in stronger colors, the coved panels being of ultramarine blue, relieved by trimmings of Indian red.

CHAPTER X.

CHIMNEYS.

Painting Chimneys.—Chimneys on Exterior of Houses.—Draughts.—Security against
Fire.—French System of laying Floor Beams.—Smoke Flues.—Hot-air Registers.

HITHERTO chimneys have been treated too meagrely: they have invariably been low, and usually too narrow and thin; and when attempts were made at embellishment, they were placed upon a clumsy base, rendering their disproportion only the more apparent. We would advise, unless economy be an object, not building a chimney on the principle of a parallelogram, but, like the Gothic column, broken up into different members or shafts; in fact, each flue should be treated separately, if possible.

Painting chimneys, and brick-work generally, should be avoided. There is not the excuse for such treatment that exists in buildings of wood, where paint is necessary for their preservation. Brick is an honest material, and when of a good color appears well. Paint, when not used as a protection, has the appearance of covering up defects. Indeed, we think it as absurd to color brick-work, as to besmear cut stone with paint or whitewash. There are other legitimate modes of relieving brick, if it be thought necessary. The introduction of stone or tile makes a very pleasing contrast, as also bricks of different color, such as blue, black, or buff; and, if used sparingly, they do much to relieve the monotony. Black pointing has hitherto been considered *de rigueur*, as white, in the opinion of many architects, conveys a raw and disagreeable effect. This idea can, however, be carried to an extreme, as white pointing may often enliven a wall which might otherwise present a gloomy appearance.

Lateral bands are usually objectionable in the treatment of chimneys; their lines should, as far as possible, be vertical; and now that moulded bricks of any form may be obtained, different varieties may be grouped satisfactorily. Plain chimneys, however, may appear well by the simple introduction of buff or black bands. Black here seems to harmonize with any color, and a good effect may be obtained with but little cost. Sometimes buff bands, if edged with black, may be used to advantage.

Chimneys show their purpose, and serve as a relief to the monotony, by being carried up on the exterior of the walls. They not only form an ornament by having their projections on the outside, but save room within.

The two points most to be considered in the construction of chimneys are, first, a good draught; and, second, security against fire. The greatest difficulty with which we have to contend in obtaining a draught, is that of friction. The flue should be made as smooth as possible and of uniform size; and, as smoke ascends spirally, if it could be built round, like a stove-pipe, a considerable advantage would be gained. A bend or turn also serves to create friction, and thereby injures the draught.

In regard to danger from fire, it is essential that the wood-work should be kept at a safe distance from the flue. It is usually the custom to have but four inches of brick-work, and allow the timber to be placed directly against it. This, especially with flues that are overheated, as by a range or furnace, is a very unsafe method. On the front or ends of a fireplace, where it is free from the wood-work, this is not objectionable; but on the back, against which the studding is likely to be placed, not less than eight inches of brick should be considered safe. The great mistake with builders is making the chimney openings too small in framing, so that the wood-work comes directly against the masonry. When there are but four inches of brick, the beams should be placed at least three inches distant; and if but one inch has been left, it is well to fill the space with plaster of Paris, which serves as a non-conductor.

Notwithstanding our being in constant anxiety as to the danger of having our buildings destroyed by fire, this subject has, strange to say, heretofore received little or no attention in our country-houses, and we are continually erecting tinder-boxes, exposed to fire from stoves and chimney flues. We are generally satisfied with a policy of insurance; and although fires usually occur in cold weather, we do not appear to consider the loss of a home, or the misery of being turned out-of-doors during a wintry storm. The children and the infirm may be driven from their beds without clothing, or may be stifled, and perhaps lose their lives. Money, of course, is a great soother in case of loss; but how many things are there endeared to us by old associations which are impossible to replace!

In our cities we are compelled by law to build houses somewhat with reference to the prevention of the spread of fire. Not that the houses themselves cannot be destroyed, but we are obliged to build part of the walls heavy; so that in case our own dwelling is consumed, those of our neighbors may escape. Would it not be well, therefore, in this nineteenth century, to do something to prevent the constant recurrence of fire?

Professor Chandler, of Columbia College, at an Architectural Convention held at Delmonico's, related the following incident: Some years ago, while seated comfortably at dinner in Paris, the alarm of fire was raised in the building. With his American ideas that the entire structure must be in danger, he took his hat, and hurried with all speed into the *porte*, expecting every minute to see the steam fire-engines approach, and, as a consequence, a deluge of water, smashing of windows, and a grand rumpus generally. But, to his astonishment, very little excitement prevailed, and no engines made their appearance. The simple and primitive system of extinguishing fires—that of passing leather buckets of water—was resorted to, and was sufficient; and although the smoke issued in considerable volumes from one of the windows, he could not see that the fire was making any headway. It was actually confined to the apartment in which it originated, and died away almost of itself, after the combustible material in the room had been burned.

Design No. 10.

This was before the depredations by the Commune. But when those Vandals attempted to burn the city, and hundreds of barrels of petroleum were used, still it was almost impossible to induce the conflagration to extend beyond a single building. In fact, there seems to be little or no dread of fire in European countries, simply because, in putting up their buildings, special care is taken to render them fire-proof. Even their country buildings are not only composed of stone, but the cellars are vaulted, the interior partitions are of brick, and the roofs and floors are generally made of iron, cement, and tile. The exterior walls, instead of being furred to prevent the dampness striking through, are built hollow, with the plaster put directly on the brick-work.

A system laid down by Viollet le Duc demands that the floor beams be made square and placed in the walls diagonally. The upper sides, by this arrangement, are made to slope, and serve as a skew-back for brick arches between the beams. These are cemented over, forming a flat surface to receive the floor boards or tiling, while the underside is plastered directly upon the bricks, forming a corrugated ceiling, and presenting a constructive appearance. This is easily decorated, and is, at the same time, thoroughly fire-proof.

Our system of placing the floor joists edgewise, with plaster beneath and boards above, besides showing a false construction, allows each space not only to act as a paradise for rats, but also to prove most dangerous in case of fire, as a flue. If we *must* continue building these fire-traps, there is no doubt something should be done to make our houses somewhat more secure.

After the joists are laid, instead of stupidly filling them in with mortar an inch or two deep, which serves no other purpose than that of deafening sound, let us enclose these timbers, as well as the underside of the floor boards, with a coating of plaster of Paris, and then use wire-cloth on the underside of the floor beams, which answers as an excellent substitute for lath. To prevent the spaces acting as channels for fire, let both ends be enclosed with a slab of roofing slate, which can be easily imbedded in the plaster of Paris. This also prevents the entrance of rats.

Apropos to the subject of isolating smoke flues, we would also call attention to the necessity of protecting the wood-work from the hot-air flues of the furnace. These are frequently run through floors and stud partitions in the most reckless manner, without any arrangement being made to prevent their scorching and eventually setting fire to the wood-work. Where these flues come in contact with this material, it is always well to make them double, allowing a space between to be filled in with plaster of Paris or brick, by which means a greater degree of safety is secured. Another and perhaps more simple mode is to cover the exposed timber with tin, and, instead of wood, iron lath may here be used. By this means the flues may be made larger and also less expensive, on account of their not being double.

Register boxes, also, should be protected by a skirting of soapstone let into the floor, and beams should never be permitted to abut against a hot-air flue. As for the building of timbers into chimneys, it should be regarded as a crime ranking with that of incendiarism or arson.

DESIGN No. 10.

First-floor Plan.

1. Entrance porch; 2. Vestibule; 3. Lavatory; 4. Water-closet; 5. Main hall, 13½×26; 6. Dining-room, 16×21; 7. Butler's pantry; 8. Kitchen, 17×19; 9. Kitchen pantry; 10. Back hall; 11. Library, 15×17; 12. Sitting-room, 17×24; 13. Veranda.—*Estimated cost*, $8500.

This cottage, designed for some picturesque site where the scenery is of a varied character, is irregular in plan and somewhat broken in sky lines, in order to be in greater harmony with the natural objects amidst which it is placed.

However plain a structure may be, it is well to have some little extravagance in a prominent part, to which the rest of the work may appear subordinate.

In the present instance, I have selected the column at the entrance; and as there is but one, we can afford to have this of the best; therefore let the shaft be of polished

First-floor Plan of Design No. 10.

Scotch granite, and the capital and base of marble richly carved in foliage pertaining to the locality.

There are four rooms on the first story, five on the second, and four on the third. The sitting and dining rooms are placed opposite each other. The main hall is roomy, and may be also used as a sitting-room, being but slightly reduced in size by the stairs. These occupy an alcove of their own, and protrude into the hall only so far as to show agreeably, without taking up too much space. We should strongly object to having the staircase entirely shut off from the hall, as it seems to belong to it by old association, and to suggest invitingly that there are comfortable apartments above. So, too, the superseding of the spacious fireplace and hearth-stone in our family sitting-room by the modern hot-air furnace is an abomination grievous to be borne by those who remember fondly that

Vignette of Design No. 10.

ancient symbol of domestic union and genial hospitality. Indeed, if our means would allow, I should prefer to have a fireplace in the hall itself; and instead of the little, narrow, hard-coal grate, with the inevitable marble mantle surmounting it, a generous, old-fashioned open chimney, large enough to sit in if one so desired. But in a house of this size such a chimney would require too much space; and I have preferred to carry out the idea in larger dwellings, as represented in some of the designs that follow elsewhere in this volume.

A gentleman, by frequent communication with his architect, necessarily, to a great extent, imprints his own character upon his house. This is one of the most important æsthetic ends of the art, and proves how possible it is to express, in the construction of a dwelling, even the most delicate idiosyncrasies of human character. It is the duty of the architect to study the desires and needs of his client, and to manage the design in all its parts, so as to fit into, and harmonize with, the lives to be spent under its roof.

The house we are considering will, we think, at once impress the beholder with the conviction that it is the habitation of a gentleman of small family and means, yet possessing education and refinement, and an appreciation so delicate for the scenery amidst which he lives, that he would have his very dwelling-place in harmony with it.

The library, occupying the central portion of the house, would naturally be his favorite room. From it he can easily approach his drawing-room on the one side and his dining-room on the other. Evidently he is rather a man of nice literary taste than a close student, for this apartment is too liable to intrusion and household noise to serve the purpose of a study, strictly so considered. The size of his drawing-room indicates his fondness for society, and the arrangement of the folding-doors, by which the entire first story may be thrown into one apartment, gives evidence of generous hospitality and large social qualities.

The vignette shows the two-story bay-window on the parlor side of the house. This may appear somewhat peculiar, as the first story is octagonal and the second square. This digression is pleasing from its variety, and was very common in buildings of the Queen Anne period.

CHAPTER XI.

COST OF HOUSES.

Miscalculation of Expense.—Simple Rule for making Estimates.

"FOOLS build houses, and wise men live in them," is a trite and familiar saying, and certainly has not lost its appositeness in the present day. We are too much in the habit, in this country, of going beyond our means in building. This, in a great measure, arises from ignorance by no means confined to novices, for many shrewd business men are deceived in this respect. Why is it that a man having determined upon an expenditure of seven thousand dollars finds his completed residence to have cost him ten, or even more? When a man intends building, he begins to "count the cost," and decides how much he will expend. He then usually sketches his idea of the general arrangement and the amount of accommodation necessary for his family, and settles himself down to the belief that these ideas may be carried out within his original notions of limit.

I have frequent application from persons whose means are small, to build houses of such character and dimensions as none but the rich should think of attempting, and they consider it very hard when they ask for a design of a most extravagant character, and give an exceedingly low figure as the price they intend to pay, to find that the two are entirely incompatible. They frequently give no figure at all, and are much astonished, when the plans are completed, to find the estimates far exceed their limit. In this manner, persons not infrequently, in having their houses built by the day, never realize the cost of the work until it is done. When it is too late, they discover, to their amazement, that the expenditure has overrun their estimate fifty, and sometimes a hundred, per cent.; and the result is that but a portion is paid for, the remainder being left on mortgage, whereby their income, as well as their principal, is assailed. This sometimes works well enough. So long as business is brisk, the extra interest is not felt; but when troubles come, and business is depressed, the owner finds great difficulty in making both ends meet; and if it were not for the encumbrance already upon his place, he might not only save the interest, but find his dwelling a convenient medium for obtaining loans. Frequently it becomes necessary to dispose of it altogether; and at such times our proverb is verified, for the wise men are ready to pick up for a trifle what has cost the embarrassed owner, besides a large sum of money, an endless amount of trouble and vexation.

There is no greater misdemeanor on the part of an architect than to lead a client to believe that a building may be constructed at a certain cost, when, in reality, it must far exceed that amount. We cannot imagine any professional man of standing being guilty of such deception. It is frequently the case, however, that when a design is offered which the architect honestly believes can be executed for a given sum, the owner is continually making alterations or expensive additions—matters which, though perhaps small in themselves, amount to a formidable bill of extras in the end. Often, as mentioned above, nothing is said about the expense. In one instance where application was made to an architect by a wealthy client to design a residence of considerable pretension, in order that he might not be disappointed in the cost, the architect concluded to ask him frankly what amount he expected to spend, and was answered about $20,000. He assured the gentleman that the building could not be carried out in the spirit of the design for that sum, and advised him either to reduce his ideas or be prepared for a greater outlay.

Design No. 11.

The client sarcastically remarked that he was aware that it was to the architect's advantage to run up the cost, not only to make a reputation for himself, but to swell his commissions, and that he need go no further until the matter had been thought over.   The following day brought a letter announcing that he had consulted with another architect, who had confirmed his ideas regarding the cost, and he had placed the matter in his

Balcony from Within, in Design No. 11.

hands.   The one consulted in the first instance, though suffering the loss of his commission, had the satisfaction, after the building was completed, of receiving an apology from the gentleman, who stated that the house had, in reality, cost a sum far beyond the original estimate, adding the friendly assurance that the loss the architect had sustained on that occasion would be made up by the confidence he had inspired.   The result was that this gentleman remained thereafter one of his best friends and most valuable clients.

It is often imagined by those who desire to build economically that beauty is an extravagance in which they cannot indulge, and therefore that a cheap cottage can have no pretension to elegance, and must barely suffice for the comfort and shelter of its occupants; and no higher aim is attempted.   This error arises from the false but prevalent idea that beauty and grace are extraneous considerations, rather matters of ornament than of proportion and symmetry.   For this reason, many small houses, whose owners wish them objects of taste, are loaded down with unmeaning and expensive decorations, or so frittered away with cheap and ready expedients of boards sawed, cut, and otherwise tortured into utter uselessness and absurdity, that the entire building becomes subordinate to its appendages, and the arrangement of its important masses is lost sight of.

When the architect is called upon to design a very cheap building, he must be content to express his art in the fitness and proportion of all its parts; and he should combine beauty with the strictest utility.

There is a simple rule which enables any one to approximate the cost of a house he intends to build.   It is to find one of the general character and finish of that proposed, to calculate the number of cubic feet it contains from the basement floor to the top of the roof, and to divide the cost of the building by its number of feet, which gives the price per foot. This, for a simple rule, is perhaps more reliable than any other where a regular estimate is not made; but it should not be confided in too implicitly where the finish and little extras known as "modern improvements" are concerned. Another thing that should be taken into consideration is, that the house upon which the calculations are based was built at a time when the prices of labor and material were similar.

DESIGN No. 11.

First-floor Plan.

1. Vestibule; 2. Staircase hall; 3. Parlor, 15×25; 4. Library, 15×19; 5. Dining-room, 15×18; 6. Butler's pantry; 7. Store-room; 8. Kitchen, 15×16; 9. Back hall and stairway; 10. Veranda, 15×17; 11. Library balcony.—*Estimated cost,* $8000.

This design is of somewhat larger character than those previously described. The rooms are of good size, with a spacious vestibule, from which, if the main hall is used as a sitting-room, the library and parlor may be entered direct. The chimneys in hall, dining-room, and library are grouped together, so that they may be carried up in a single shaft—a matter not only of economy in construction, but in winter (when fires are required in the living-rooms) all the heat may be thereby retained. The kitchen chimney is so arranged as not to heat the house in the summer. The staircase landing is lighted by the triplet window of stained glass. Under the landing is a lavatory, which is approached by descending a few steps from the back hall. From this there is an exit,

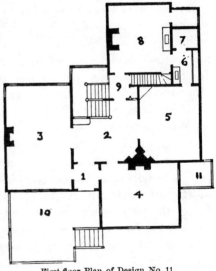

First-floor Plan of Design No. 11.

which is on a level with the main grade, and also serves as a rear entrance to the kitchen. Here, again, the veranda is arranged on the porch system, being about fifteen feet square; while the balcony from the second story is grouped in with the porch, and sheltered by the same roof. There is an opening to the front from the upper balcony; while the side, acting as a gallery, is in communication with the porch below, as seen in the vignette on the preceding page.

CHAPTER XII.

ARCHITECTS' DUTIES AND CHARGES.

American Institute of Architects.—Preliminary Sketches.—Plans.—Specifications.—Detail Drawing.—Supervision.—Speculative Building.

WHEN a person is sick, it is customary to seek the advice of a doctor; and having confidence in his ability, it would be the height of folly not to follow it.   Now, an architect should stand to his client in very much the same relation as the physician to his patient; but instead of the client going to the architect and asking what he *ought* to do, he generally tells him what he is *going* to do—writing, as it were, his own prescription for the doctor to fill, or laying down the law to his lawyer.   An architect who is accomplished in his profession has studied quite as hard, and learned as much by research and experience, as one of any other profession; but the fact that he is so trammelled by the obstinate whims of ignorant clients is the reason why he may fail in what might otherwise have been a successful effort.

With persons who attach so little value to professional skill, it might become a question as to the propriety of employing an architect at all—whether his scientific aid, artistic design, or administrative control of expenditure be worth his commission.   In such cases, perhaps, it may be as satisfactory for one to get up his own design, leaving the practical working of the plan to his builder.   Such was not unfrequently the case in times gone by; but now it seems to be generally conceded that the architect's skill is not only important, but necessary, as the combinations of builder and architect are becoming less and less common.   In fact, the typical builder is continually growing to be more of a mere contractor, ceasing even to supply the knowledge of his craft except through the medium of his foreman, and, as professional skill advances, he is left far behind.   Some years ago there was but little affiliation on the part of the architects, each seeming to be suspicious of the other, and each apparently willing to take advantage of his neighbor.   The builder architect, in the public estimation, ranked the same as the professional, and they were loud in boasting of the superiority of the practical man

over the one who simply knew how to make pictures. It was not surprising, under this condition of things, that the moral standard of the
profession was at a low ebb, and that there were many so-called architects
who made a practice of obtaining business through a system of under-
bidding, charging less than the services of a competent architect were
worth, and making up the deficiency by taking commissions from the
other side, who, in turn, expected to reap their reward by the architect's
accepting inferior work at an excessive charge. By this means the owners were doubly defrauded; and while they imagined they were saving
money by employing an architect at one-half the usual commission, they
were indirectly paying three or four times as much, and getting in return inferior service. In fact, so low had sunk the name of architect,
that the public had begun to look upon it with suspicion, until it became
necessary that the honorable members of the profession should band themselves together for mutual protection. Thus they determined to establish
an institute which should be responsible for the honor of its members,
and see that their employers were fairly dealt with. It was resolved
that no member should accept any commission outside that of his em-
ployer, and that he should charge a sum that would fairly pay him for
his work—that is, five per cent. on the entire cost of the building. This
on some things seemed high, and on others proportionately low; but as
the profession in all other civilized countries had for many years considered five per cent. a fair average, the American Institute of Architects
established this as their rate on all work exceeding five thousand dollars.
To this percentage when the building is remote from the city, travelling
and hotel expenses are to be added.

The reason that many think this a high charge arises from their ignorance of the work performed by the architect. Some even think that a
mere sketch, or preliminary drawing, is all that is necessary; and although
this embodies the entire expression or idea of the subject, the practical
work is not yet commenced. The plans have to be drawn with such ex-
actness that every stone and each timber are considered, and every detail studied out carefully; and these, when completed, in no way convey
to the uninitiated an idea of the amount of labor and calculation required. Then the specifications in the same way have to describe every
detail in the most minute manner; so that when the contract is taken
there may be no chance of extras. It is generally supposed that when
all this is accomplished the office labors are ended. Little is known of
the amount of work involved in what are called detail drawings, in which
every portion of the building has to be drawn out full size. In a struct-

ure of any magnitude, these drawings often cover from fifty to a hundred sheets, each containing from fifteen to twenty superficial feet. After these are completed and the work under way, the architect is obliged to superintend the building from beginning to end. Not only has he to see that each party performs his contract, and to give the certificate of payments, but there are continual emergencies arising wherein his adjustment is necessary, in making the different trades fit in and work harmoniously. It being advisable to have a separate contract for each specialty, the architect's duties involve the scope of artist, lawyer, engineer, etc.

In making the preliminary studies, too, much more labor is expended than would appear; for, in arranging the groupings and foreshortenings, it is necessary that each elevation should be studied in perspective, in order that the artist himself may feel satisfied that his work will appear in proper proportion from every point of view.

Design No. 12.

Some of our city buildings are specimens of what was formerly done by the tyros of whom we have spoken; and even at the present time they are, in their arrangement, far behind those of similar pretensions in the country. The back staircase, the lavatory, and cloak-room are seldom seen. The bedrooms are of the most hap-hazard kind, as regards their possibility of furnishing. Then, as for the domestic offices, they are frequently dark, ill ventilated, and musty. If a house happen to be on a corner, instead of the rooms taking advantage of this exposure and light, it is an even chance that the staircase and hall are located here. Even when such errors have become apparent, block after block is erected with little or no improvement.

No doubt the chief cause of these shortcomings is that city houses, instead of being built by their occupants, are put up almost entirely by speculators, frequently irresponsible, and often most ignorant, who have very little idea of the refinement of living, and consider that a person who can scarcely write his name is competent to draw a plan. The more ignorant these designers are, the more cheaply their services may be had, which is an obvious reason why draughtsmen of this class are so popular; and the consequence is, a competent architect is seldom employed in this sort of building. It has been discovered of late—the speculator's theory to the contrary notwithstanding—that where the best arrangements are executed with the highest skill and first-class material, they yield a profit to the owner far in advance of these flimsy and inartistic structures.

Messrs. Duggin & Crossman, of this city, have demonstrated this theory; and a large number of first-class dwellings, conveniently arranged with admirable appointments and superior workmanship, have given them such a reputation that the fact of a building constructed by them entitles it to command a much larger price than others of perhaps greater pretensions.

It may be thought difficult, where discrepancies already exist, to have them repaired. There is no question but that, in starting a new building, there is much greater chance in a good architect's securing a happy result. Yet many existing difficulties may be overcome by the master's hand. The accommodations spoken of in the country-house may be added; light may be admitted, ventilation improved; and the house, instead of being a dark, musty abode, may assume a freshness and cheerfulness which will add greatly to the comfort of the family.

Where bedrooms are concerned, it is seldom that a skilful architect need hesitate to promise, without anything like structural derangement or heavy expense, a transformation which will double the convenience of that portion of the house. Sometimes the addition of another story will literally double the capacity of a house; for it is evident that the same living-rooms and domestic offices will serve equally a large or small family, if the sleeping accommodations are sufficient.

DESIGN No. 12.

First-floor Plan.

1. Carriage porch; 2. Veranda; 3. Main hall; 4. Dining-room, 15×20; 5. Library, 15×15; 6. Parlor, 15×18; 7. Butler's pantry; 8. Store-room; 9. Kitchen, 14×15; 10. Back hall; 11. Kitchen pantry; 12. Servants' porch; 13. Conservatory.—*Estimated cost*, $8000.

In this design we have three rooms, besides a greenhouse and a kitchen on the first story. The rooms are placed opposite, allowing the breeze to circulate unobstructed through the living rooms of the house. The

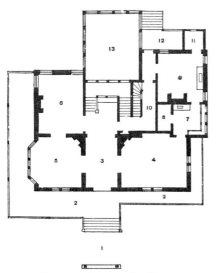

First-floor Plan of Design No. 12.

veranda, being exposed to the morning sun, is protected by an awning, which, while affording ample shade, is at such an elevation as not to cut off the view. This awning can, of course, be raised when the sun has retreated so as to leave the piazza in the shade.

It will be observed that the chimneys come in the corner of the rooms. There is often an advantage gained in such digressions from stereotyped customs, as they can be treated as agreeable and novel features, and, if thought advisable, the opposite corners may be made to correspond, as shown in our plan of the library. Yet we have no hesitation in accepting the situation, and coming out boldly with this corner treatment, and abandoning symmetry, especially when there is an evident motive. The object in this case is to bring the chimneys together in the attic, so as to unite on the roof in a single stack.

One of the most important features, and one peculiarly susceptible of bold and artistic treatment, is the main staircase. In the present instance, as shown in the vignette, it is at the end of the hall. The first landing being raised but six steps, gives the appearance of an elevated gallery or dais, beyond which, and agreeably terminating the vista, there is a spacious greenhouse. The principal newel is plain, and is surmounted by an appropriate gas standard. The niche between the flights, not serving as a passage, is occupied by a seat of simple construction, covered with an ornamental leather cushion. Through the door at the right we pass down six steps to a lavatory, beyond which, under the greenhouse, is a

billiard-room. This may be consid-
ered somewhat objectionable on ac-
count of the dampness from the watering of plants; and unless great
care be taken to keep the ceiling
thoroughly water-tight, it would be
better to have the billiard-room in
some other position, and use the
space as a potting-room or general
workroom connected with the greenhouse.

This is another example of how
a simple square cottage may be made
picturesque, without any straining
after effect. Each line seems to fall
naturally into its place, and the whole

Main Staircase, Design No. 12.

appears a legitimate outgrowth of the requirements suggested by the peculiarities of our climate.

It is often remarked that these broken and irregular roofs are pretty
enough to look at, but very uncomfortable to live under. This is because
the ceilings of the second story are frequently cut off and made to follow the sloping lines of the roof, so as to interfere with the head; and
being directly on the rafters, there is not sufficient space to protect the
room from the external changes of heat and cold. But these inconveniences are far from being unavoidable. They are simply builders' blunders, and can always be avoided in a well-studied plan. The roof in this
design not only permits the second-story rooms to be square, but serves as
a protection from heat and cold by covering the triangular space over the
veranda, which may be readily utilized as closets.

The attic has a similar protection in a loft, which is lighted and ventilated by louver boards in the peak. This may be roughly floored and
used as a storage or trunk room.

One of the most effective and convenient features of this design is the
recessed balcony coming under the main roof. This to the chamber is
like the veranda to our living-room, where in pleasant weather much of
our time may be spent.

CHAPTER XIII.

PLUMBERS' BLUNDERS.

The Overflow of Tanks.—Boiler Explosions.—Leaky Gas-pipes.—The Lightning-rod Man.

THE confessions which people are sometimes obliged to make of the errors committed in building are often more amusing to the auditors than to the victims. A gentleman was narrating to me some of the perils he had undergone from the results of bad planning and inferior workmanship. He said that the difficulties and annoyances he had sustained from the blunders of his mechanics were too much for Christian endurance.

The plumber seemed to be his especial *bête noir.* Among other instances, he cited that, in order to carry a two-inch waste-pipe from the laundry-tubs, the plumber had cut a hole large enough for a sally-port directly under one of his main piers. The consequence was, that the walls began to settle, and every lintel throughout the height of the building was cracked. He believed the entire structure would soon have fallen, had he not immediately summoned his mason to put in temporary supports and fill up the aperture. This plumber, he said, seemed to have excelled himself in the enormities he committed. He continued:

Recessed Balcony.

" We had been but a few weeks in the house, and were congratulating ourselves, during a heavy shower, that our tank was filling, thus obviating the necessity of using the force-pump, when, to our consternation, a flood of water came rushing down the attic stairs; and, had the storm not abated, we should have stood in imminent peril of being deluged. When I went up to ascertain the cause, I discovered that the overflow-pipe to the tank, instead of being sufficiently large to carry off the surplus, was of a much smaller size than the inlet. Of course, the water being admitted so much more rapidly than the waste-pipe could carry it off, an overflow was a natural consequence. This tank was to have been of a certain size, commensurate with the weight which the foundations were able to support; but, consistently with his foolhardy incompetency, he had made the tank three times the dimensions calculated. The excessive weight began to show its effects by the settling of floors and the cracking of ceilings. The pipes also were laid upon the cold side of the house; so that during the first severe snap they not only froze solid, but were of such light material that they burst in every direction.

"My wife, one day while superintending some operations in the kitchen, ordered the cook to have a quick fire, when she was called away. This proved to be providential; for while detained in the parlor by unexpected company, she heard a terrific explosion. Rushing to the kitchen, she found the room filled with steam, while fragments of windows and furniture were scattered in every direction. Upon further investigation, the poor cook was found lying upon the floor in a senseless condition. Of course the excitement was intense. Neighbors flocked in, and physicians were summoned. It was well for the plumber that he had shortly before left for Colorado. He would scarcely have escaped lynching by the indignant crowd, for the cause of the disaster was only too evident. The boiler, which had been specified of a certain weight, and had been relied upon as standing any amount of pressure, had, in consequence of the additional heat in the stove, exploded. On examination, we discovered that it was made of the lightest material, while, to carry out the deception, a sufficient amount of lead had been placed in its bottom to bring it up to the specified weight.

"Then, on the principle of 'give a dog a bad name,' every one had something to say against the unfortunate blunderer. One of the ladies, in virtuous indignation, proceeded to relate how this individual, manifesting a stupidity almost criminal, had spoiled her new parlor carpet. It seems that after laying the gas-pipes, he had neglected to prove them, and not until the plaster was on, and the inspector came with his air-pump to test them, was it known that they were imperfect and leaked badly. There was no alternative. The walls had to be ripped off and the floors opened, in order to find the leaky joints.

"The process of the investigation was in this wise: Soapsuds were liberally applied with a brush upon all suspected places, and then, by pumping air through the pipes, wherever there was a leak, a bubbling effect was perceived. For a month, at least, did that indefatigable gas-man go around with his pail of soapsuds and air-pump, before he could make those everlasting joints secure; and, after all, he was compelled to tie them up with rags and putty, till they presented very much the appearance of sore fingers.

"This—my friend was willing to believe—would meet the exigencies of the case for a time, at least. He was anxious to get rid of the nuisance, as the completion of the house had already been delayed for several weeks. The family were impatient to get settled; the carpets and furniture had been ordered some time before, and were all ready to be put in their places. The mechanics once fairly out of the house, there was all haste and excitement, laying down and arranging these in time for a house-warming, the date of which had been previously appointed. The hostess dreaded to see the fatal plumber again in the midst of all this; but there was no help for it, for it was necessary that the chandeliers should be hung. The first room he went into was the parlor, and—but we will use her own words: 'I was determined to go with him, to divert further mischief, if possible. The fixture having been raised to its place, nothing remained to be done but to unscrew the cap at the end of the pipe. But, horrors to behold! the cap was no sooner removed than a horrible black substance spouted out, deluging everything in the room, and utterly ruining my beautiful carpet, just fresh from Stewart's! Imagine my consternation if you can! I was speechless with indignation and despair, and looked vaguely from him to the carpet, and back again. The black and greasy pipes, oxidized by the application of water, had converted the soapsuds, so persistently applied, into a fluid the color of which was like ink, and equally indelible, while its stench was nauseous in the extreme.'"

After experiences like these, it is not surprising that one pauses before entering upon the sea of troubles involved in the complicated business of building, for the plumber is by no means alone in his liability to err. Indeed, this seems peculiar to the building trade.

There is one individual rather more remarkable than the rest, with whom one has to contend, whose ignorance and conceit are only equalled by his pertinacity, and who is a type so peculiar that he may be set down as a character, excelling even the sewing-machine agent or the Yankee clock-peddler. This is the lightning-rod man. He seems to penetrate the inmost depths of country retirement, and the mountain nook and sequestered valley are not proof against his invasions. Neither need you imagine that you can rid yourself of him by putting him off, or refusing *in toto* to have a lightning-conductor. If he asks you fifty cents per foot, "lay not the flattering unction to your soul" that you can shake him off by offering twenty-five, as he requires not a moment to consider before he takes you up. Finally, if all fair means by which to accomplish his ends fail, this irrepressible mortal will resort to strategy; and the ingenious devices of which he is capable show a fertility of resource and imagination worthy of a better calling.

Design No. 13.

One gentleman was telling me of his having erected some cottages for sale. He had somehow become the particular mark for the aim of these agents, but had bravely resisted, until at last he found himself caught by a most ingenious trap. One of the fraternity called upon him in the guise of a purchaser, and, having looked through the building and understood the terms, professed to be so pleased that he closed the negotiation, and instructed the owner to call at his office at a certain time to execute the papers. When the man was about to leave, taking a final look at the exterior, he observed, with some consternation, that there was no lightning rod upon the house; that he certainly could not consent to move his family into a building where there was not this safeguard. The owner promptly assured him that if that were the only objection, he would have them adjusted at once, which seemed to satisfy the apparent purchaser.

A confederate soon after drove to the grounds, with the usual rods and fixtures in his wagon, and a contract was made to furnish the house with rods. At the appointed time the owner went, papers in hand, to meet the proposed purchaser, when, to his dismay, no such office or man could be found.

These men, who pretend to follow a scientific vocation, are in reality the most ignorant of their kind. They put on the rod by the foot, simply with the idea of distributing as many feet as possible over the building, without the faintest notion of how it should be applied; and when you speak of insulation or non-insulation, or of the upward or downward current, they evince a most unpardonable degree of ignorance.

DESIGN No. 13.

First-floor Plan.

1. Entrance porch; 2. Main hall; 3. Library, 14×14; 4. Parlor, 14×18; 5. Dining-room, 14×20; 6. Study, 13×17; 7. Back hall; 8. Butler's pantry.—*Estimated cost*, $10,000.

This building was designed as a residence for the Hon. Lyman K. Bass, the well-known Member of Congress from Buffalo; but owing to

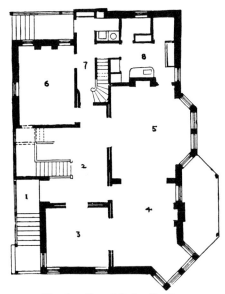

First-floor Plan of Design No. 13.

an attack of illness occurring shortly after the designs were prepared, it has not, as yet, been erected. Although of a somewhat rustic character, it was considered sufficiently town-like to be placed on one of the main avenues of Buffalo; for, from Elizabeth down to the Georges, this style has been adopted in the finest thoroughfares of several of the European cities, such as Chester, Rouen, and some of the old parts of London.

The first story is intended to be built of Baltimore pressed brick, which, with its dark, rich color and black pointing, presents a sober and substantial effect, appropriate for a foundation or basement. The walls above were to be covered with ornamental tile hanging, placed on brick-work of a rougher character; the roof to be of red slate from the Vermont quarries.

The first floor has four rooms, and are so thrown together by means of sliding-doors, that they form a continued suite in every direction. The staircase landing extends into an overhanging bay, sufficiently high not to obstruct the carriage-way beneath. There is a carriage porch at the rear entrance. Of course, in a city lot, where the space is limited, verandas or extended wings must necessarily be avoided. The house is therefore made narrow on the front, while the depth is increased; and as it is necessary to make up in height what we lose in breadth, the basement is finished, containing kitchen, laundry, and domestic offices, among which is a servants' hall. These halls I would especially recommend in every house where more than two servants are required, as giving them a place to sit and take their meals, without intruding upon the province of the cook. The kitchen may be made correspondingly smaller, while the hall adds to the independence and contentment of the servants generally.

CHAPTER XIV.

HEATING AND VENTILATION.

Large Furnaces.—Open Grates.—Ventilating Shaft.—Ventilators in Windows.—Ventilating Soil-pipes.—Tin Flues in Dark Rooms.

HEALTH is the most important object to be attained in the construction of our dwellings. Dr. Johnson says: "To preserve health is a moral and religious duty, for health is the basis of all social virtues. We can be useful no longer than we are well." Perhaps the most essential agents of health are proper heating and good ventilation.

Modern improvements are excellent things until used in excess, when they become more troublesome than useful. This is especially true of ventilation, for, however complicated an arrangement may be requisite in a public building, in a dwelling the more simple the method, the more effectual will it prove in operation.

It has hitherto been generally conceded that the ventilating flue should be situated at the base of the room. The theory was that the breath expelled from our lungs in the shape of carbonic acid gas, being heavier than the atmosphere, sank to the floor, and, in order to induce it to rise, a strong draught in the ventilating flue was required. Recent experiments, however, have shown that this theory, though plausible, is incorrect; for our breath is of about the same temperature as our bodies, or ninety-eight degrees, and, being so much warmer than the atmosphere of the room, naturally rises to the ceiling. Thus, if a flue be placed here, the foul air will be at once carried off. By being thus immediately expelled, we do not incur the danger of again breathing the same air in its vitiated condition; whereas the theory of floor ventilation is open to the objection that it remains in the apartment sufficiently long to cool and settle.*

Sometimes a small register, placed in the ceiling, giving somewhat the effect of a centre-piece, through which the air, heated by the gas, may also

---

* In this matter I have received some excellent suggestions from Mr. Carl Pfeiffer, the well-known architect, whose able articles on this subject must be familiar to many of our readers.

escape, will serve the purpose. This may be carried between the floor and ceiling by a simple tube, which may connect with the nearest chimney or ventilating flue.

I do not wish to be understood that floor ventilation should be abolished. Fires in open grates serve an excellent purpose, for, while securing a better draught, less heat from the furnace is required.

The old style of anthracite grates has almost fallen into disuse, soft coal being now preferred. This is not only more cheerful, reminding us of the good old days of wood fires, but its effect upon the air is not so drying. If wood or bituminous coal be used, however, the chimney flue should be built larger, as it is otherwise apt to become obstructed by soot.

Design No. 14.

In order that ventilating flues be made to work successfully, it is necessary that fresh air should be introduced. This is generally done by means of the registers, which supply heat from the furnace and fresh air at the same time. There is a great advantage in having the furnace large; for if too small, the radiating surface is apt to be overheated, thereby destroying the vital properties of the air before it is introduced into the rooms. With a larger furnace, a greater amount is admitted, which may be simply warmed, so that the fresh air flows throughout the building, in no way diminished in purity, but merely changed in temperature.

In the better class of houses, which are erected with such niceness of workmanship that not a seam or crevice is supposed to be open for the admission of air, a more elaborate system of ventilation is required, not for the rooms only, but also for the halls and staircases; otherwise the air from these must be drawn through the living-rooms. In Design 23, I have arranged a central shaft, in the centre of which I have placed an iron pipe, which may serve the purpose of a smoke flue from the furnace, radiating enough heat to cause a stronger draught. In this shaft, too, the plumbing pipes of the house may be placed. By this means any offensive odors are carried off, and in case of a leak no damage will ensue. They are also easily accessible for repair.

It is generally considered that direct radiation in a living-apartment is undesirable, as it simply warms the air, and, producing no circulation, the oxygen is consumed without the introduction of a fresh supply. Hence the drum, the gas-stove, and even steam heating-pipes are objectionable, unless some auxiliary system of ventilation be employed.

As flues are useless to carry off the foul air of the house, unless fresh air be introduced to take its place, so, too, it is obvious that a current of freezing air admitted directly upon our backs is in no way agreeable. It should, therefore, be warmed before entering the apartment.

We have frequently seen two pipes placed under the window-sash for the admission of air, furnished with dampers by which to regulate the supply. This is a clever means of introducing fresh air into the room, and, when accompanied by proper exhaust flues, performs its work effectually. Yet this does not overcome the unpleasantness, before mentioned, of cold air being introduced directly into the room; and although the inventor has ingeniously contrived a quarter-turn in the pipe to force it upward, and thus to prevent its blowing immediately upon the occupants, it does not fulfil its mission. The cold air, being heavier than the warm, naturally takes a downward course the moment they come in contact. I wrote to the patentee some time ago, bringing this fact to his notice, and suggested that if the air could be brought into the room slightly warmed, as from the register of a hot-water furnace, I believed his system would be perfect. He stated, in reply, that this would involve a complication beyond the scope of his invention, and gave the matter no further attention. The method of accomplishing this is, however, very simple. Let the steam radiator be placed directly under the window; then the fresh air introduced becomes warm in passing over it, and rises naturally of itself.

In regard to the ventilator which we have been describing, we would say that it is unnecessary to adopt these awkward-looking pipes, filling up, as they do, some eight or ten inches of the window, excluding the light, and obstructing the view. A simple quarter-turn moulding, about two inches high, placed at the bottom of the sash, to the top of which the window may be raised, secures equally good ventilation, with this objectionable feature avoided. Here the sash itself acts as a damper. Any carpenter can fit up this moulding, on which, owing to its simplicity, there is no patent-right.

An excellent method of ventilating rooms in which there is no fire-place is by means of a tin flue, open at the floor and ceiling, and terminating above the roof. If within the pipe a light be kept burning, it will so rarefy the air as to insure a constant draught. There may be arranged in front of this light a glass, so that the same flame may serve to illuminate the room. It often happens, especially in city houses, that the bath-room, water-closets, and butler's pantry must be in a part of the house where no daylight can be obtained; this is a ready means of supplying that deficiency. Frequently, too, particularly in houses built upon the flat system, where every inch of room must be economized, small bed-rooms are necessarily situated in the same position. Here this method of lighting could be adopted with especial advantage. A frame-work containing transparencies, hung before the light, would obviate the unsightly appearance ordinarily presented.

DESIGN No. 14.

First-floor Plan.

1, 1, 1. Verandas; 2. Hall, 8×32; 3. Parlor, 15×28; 4. Library, 15×17; 5. Dining-room, 15 × 25; 6. Kitchen, 17 × 17; 7. Butler's pantry; 8. Store-room; 9. Lavatory.—*Estimated cost,* $10,000.

The candor and simplicity of this design expressed in the picturesque breaking of its sky lines, with gables, hips, crests, and chimneys, and its fair acknowledgment of all constructive obligations, may serve as a good illustration of the progress which American rural architecture has made since the days of Puritan plainness. But few specimens are now left of the architecture of the "good old colony times." There is an old-world expression about these venerable buildings which recommends them to our interest as historical reminiscences; and it must be confessed that there is a truth and a solidity about their construction for which we look in vain, in the architecture of a later day. Undoubtedly they fairly ex-

press the solid energy, determination, and great-heartedness of the founders of a new empire in the wilderness. The straightforward respectability

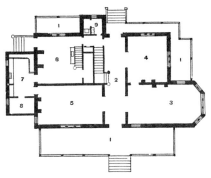

and honorable pride of the old governors are strongly imprinted upon
their mansions. Our prosperity, however, was too great and too rapid to
preserve inviolate this simplicity in
architecture, and soon pretentious display, without the refinement of education, became the aim, finally settling into the era, before mentioned, of
domesticated Greek temples and immense classic porticoes in wood. The
true refinement of the colonial aris-

First-floor Plan of Design No. 14.

tocracy, the hearty hospitality of the gentleman of the old school, seem to
have been overwhelmed by the conspicuous show and glitter of a society
whose "new-crowned stamp of honor was scarce current," and which naturally, in architecture, developed a
fever for base imitation.

The cottage under consideration
is one of the half-timber-and-tile designs of the Jacobite period. Like
its prototype, it is built of brick, at
least to the second story, where the
tile-hanging and half-timber work begins. As tiles, however, are difficult
to obtain in this country, shingles of
equal width and cut to a pattern may
be substituted. If these are of good
quality, neatly shaved and jointed,
they require no paint. Dipping them
in oil suffices to preserve and give
them a deep, warm color. These
might terminate on a moulded cornice, with dentals underneath, projecting about six inches from the
brick wall, the furring being arranged
so that the shingles may curve out-

Gable of Design No. 14.

ward. There might be a similar cornice and curve at the foot of the
main gable, and at the head of the gable-window. The roof, of course,

should be of slate; but it is better not to repeat this material on the walls; for even if a different color be used, a hard and rigid appearance is apt to be the result. The half - timbering of the library gable may be treated as follows: The principal uprights can be solid, the intervals filled in with brick, and then covered with a coating of cement. There is a difficulty here, however; for unless the timbers are thoroughly seasoned, they are liable to shrink away from the brick-work, leaving openings for the admission of cold air. Another method is to have the squares lathed in the ordinary manner, and then stuccoed. In this case there should be a channel cut in the side of the timbering, on the principle of a tongue and groove, which the cement will enter, so that in case of shrinkage the joint will not be exposed. In order to prevent dampness, it would be well to have the sill or bottom-rail rabbeted, as in the case of a groove here the water is apt to lodge, and thereby hasten decay.

As far as tightness is concerned, I think the better way is to carry the brick - work continuously to the roof. A series of planking, in lieu of half-timbering, may then be secured to the walls, and the bricks between covered with stucco. Still another way is to seal the walls with vertical boards, to which affix plank battens. The last two methods might be thought objectionable on the ground of imitating half - timbering, thus pretending to be what they are not, and so failing to preserve the truth, which, as we have before said, is one of the first principles of architecture. This appearance of sham, however, may be prevented by treating the planking on the principle of battens simply.

The ornaments represented in the panel should be stamped in the stucco while it is fresh, and then filled up with red or black mortar—a system known as *sgraffiti*. If wood be used as a backing, these figures might be produced by scroll-sawing, or even stencilled in red or black outline. If cement be used, the cove under the projection may be of the same material.

The vignette given on the preceding page illustrates the library gable, showing the half-timbering and ornamental panels on a larger scale.

CHAPTER XV.

STEAM HEATING.—ELECTRICITY.

Pure Air.—Automatic Contrivances.—Electric Signals.—Burglar Alarms.

THE steam apparatus has an unquestionable advantage over the hot-air furnace, as the former cannot be heated sufficiently to consume the oxygen. A greater amount of radiating surface, therefore, becomes necessary, and the atmosphere, consequently, is not liable to this contamination. It is impossible, as a general thing, to get a large amount of any commodity at a reduced price, without a corresponding reduction in quality; or, on general principles, if we have an abundance, and the quality of the best, we are compelled to pay for it accordingly : and it is so with the heat from our furnaces. We often hear of heaters, ranges, and stoves which give a maximum of heat with a minimum of coal, which, when the matter is sifted down, simply results in the fact that, when we find a heater which will produce this result with an economy of money, there is a corresponding extravagance in doctors' bills.

I was conversing with a friend only a short time ago who had been living in a luxuriously heated establishment in the city, and had been advised by his physician to remove into the country on account of his own illness, and general decline in the health of his family. He therefore purchased a small farm near the city, having on it a tumble-down rookery which he termed his cottage. Into this—so as to superintend the progress of his building—he determined to move with his family until his house should be completed. This picnic mode of living was all very well during the summer season ; but as his building did not progress as rapidly as he had anticipated, he was obliged to submit to the discomfort of remaining in the cottage during the greater part of the winter. He dreaded this chiefly on account of the delicacy of his children, particularly as no physician was near ; but what was his surprise to find that, notwithstanding the severe exposure, his family had never enjoyed such good health, and he stated that he actually had not had occasion to send for a doctor during the whole season ! It is a fact worth remembering that plenty of oxygen, which feeds combustion in our systems, is better for health and comfort than a large amount of caloric, minus this vital property.

Now let us consider how we shall obtain the largest amount of pure air which shall be warmed, without being allowed to pass over any surface whose temperature is sufficiently high to injure its life-giving properties. Steam or hot-water pipes are less liable to this objection than our ordinary hot-air furnaces. The former have also an advantage in the automatic method by which they are regulated. Nervous people might, with some degree of reason, protest against the presence of a steam-boiler in their cellars, if perfect safety were not insured by the adoption of these ingenious automatic contrivances. If, through the closing of several regis-

Design No. 15.

ters at once, the pressure upon the boiler becomes too great, the steam itself acts upon a regulator which reduces the draught of the furnace. There is also a safety-valve, through which the vapor forces an escape when the device just mentioned proves insufficient. This regulator is entitled to rank among the great triumphs of modern invention, for in case of a demand for extra heat its operation is reversed. Thus the business of attending to a steam furnace simply resolves itself into supplying the coal and removing the ashes, the amount of fuel consumed being governed entirely by the action of the regulator.

In these days, when the members of a household are compelled to suffer so much from the tyranny of servants, all automatic contrivances become a great source of comfort. Among the most valuable are those connected with electricity. The system of burglar alarms has become the terror of thieves, and adds largely to the security of buildings. The same battery which operates these wires may be made available for signals; for the system of telegraphy is rapidly superseding such primitive arrangements as bells and speaking-tubes. A gentleman may connect his wires with his stable, his gate entrance, and even extend them to the distant village or town; and the signal system, when properly arranged, may be made useful in various ways. I have seen it applied as a tell-tale to a tank, where, when the water had become low, it would set in motion a little bell, which would continue to tingle until the want was supplied; and when the furnace was in need of additional fuel, a similar announcement would be made. A guest arriving at the porter's lodge would be signalled in advance, and the gardener could not allow the greenhouse to cool, on a freezing night, without this little sentinel proclaiming the neglect. In fact, we may soon expect to see electricity so trained in our domestic service that it will announce when the baby wakes up, or the pudding is done.

A merchant can sit in his office and communicate with his different warehouses and factories. A wire can also be attached to his residence. Any one wishing a letter posted, or a message carried, can, by touching a wire, summon a messenger directly. Another signal at the same office brings a carriage or an expressman. This is, also, a means of protection in case of intrusion. A lady suffering annoyance from impertinent beggars or tramps can at any moment summon a policeman to her house. While the system is growing in favor in large cities, why should not this simple process be applied to our country homes, enabling us to communicate with shopkeepers and friends, or to summon a doctor at short notice, despite lame horses or bad roads? The fact seems patent that such an application of electricity to country houses would prove one of the most useful and economical of comforts.

Another great benefit to be derived is that, in a dwelling from which the family are absent for the season, the wires may be connected with the house of a friend; and, should a burglar enter, the alarm is sounded beyond his hearing. Our readers will probably remember the tragedy at Bay Ridge, where two burglars — who turned out to be the abductors of the child Charlie Ross—lost their lives in attempting to rob an unoccupied dwelling. The alarm having been arranged so as to sound in the residence of a neighbor, he, with his coachman and gardener, surrounded the house and awaited their exit, utterly unsuspected by them.

There has been the objection raised that these burglar alarms are frequently the cause of a panic, when there is no reason for uneasiness, nothing more dreadful having occurred than the mere opening of a window by some member of the household. Again it is said that burglars may effect an entrance through a pane of glass without raising the sash at all. Both of these objections, however, may be easily overcome by attaching the wire to the outside blinds. By this means the window may be raised at pleasure, and it would be impossible for any one to enter without opening the shutter.

DESIGN No. 15.

First-floor Plan.

1. Hall, 18×21; 2. Parlor, 15×21; 3. Back hall; 4. Kitchen, 15×16; 5. Kitchen pantry; 6. Butler's pantry; 7. Dining-room, 15×18; 8. Veranda; 9. Kitchen porch.—*Estimated cost*, $11,000.

This house, which has recently been erected for Mr. G. E. Hamlin, at Mountain Station, Orange, New Jersey, is a compact though liberally arranged dwelling, showing some of the advanced principles of building. The parlor is of good size, and is made the more spacious by its connection, through double doors, with a large, square hall, the fireplace of which stands opposite the parlor bay-window. This hall, containing the staircase, is somewhat similar to that in Design No. 3, though of a more elaborate character. Its fireplace and bookcase give evidence of its being one of the living-rooms.

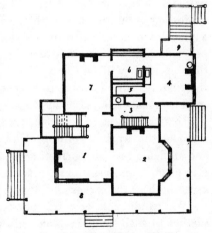

First-floor Plan of Design No. 15.

The window over the staircase, and the upper sash of the corner windows, are of stained glass. The latter has rolling blinds, which are coiled under the floor, and cover the plate-glass only. The parlor bay-window is supplied with similar blinds. There being no stained glass here, however, the coil is placed in the ceiling, by which means the entire window is protected.

CHAPTER XVI.

ALTERATIONS.

Remodelling Houses.—Self-styled Architects.—Saving Expense.

THE architect is often, in the discharge of his duties, called upon to perform many difficult tasks; but none more arduous than that of remodelling a country-house, where he is obliged to contend with the blunders and conventional distortions of carpenter's architecture, to develop harmony out of discord, beauty out of ugliness, and elegance out of the commonplace. Every day we see men of wealth, and sometimes of intelligence, employing ignorant builders—self-styled architects—to furnish designs for cottages, villas, and even mansions of great pretension. Among this class of mechanics some one may be found in every town whose ambition or conceit has led him to fancy that he may combine the profession of an architect with the trade of a builder. He may "draught a plan" which on paper may deceive the eye of his client, and actually persuade him into the delusion that, as it is the composition of the "practical man," it will appear well when erected. For many have thus, unfortunately, built in haste to repent at leisure.

The usual recourse in such cases, after the building is spoiled, is to apply to an architect of acknowledged ability, with the request that he shall remodel the work. With perplexed brain he sets about the expensive and difficult task of correcting a piece of work which, had it been properly done in the beginning, much trouble and vexation would have been saved both to the owner and himself.

We would not wish, of course, to dissuade those who have become victims to such blunders from calling upon a competent architect to remedy them. We would simply warn those who may contemplate building.

I often receive applications from persons occupying houses which have been "spoiled in the making," and it is then a problem as to how far it is judicious to alter them. Very often the owner imagines he will make a few changes, and begins with some of the simplest alterations. One thing leads to another, until finally, could he have realized to what excesses he should have been carried, he certainly would have decided to start anew.

One gentleman recently congratulated himself that he had purchased a fine dwelling at a very low cost, which only required a small amount expended upon it to make it exactly what he wanted. With the addition of a third story or a mansard, it would be sufficiently large, and then all it needed was simply the elevation of the first and second story ceilings. He was much surprised when I expressed the opinion that the house was not worth the alterations, though he admitted that an entirely new roof would be required, and the elevation of the ceilings would neces-

Design No. 16.

sitate the destruction of all the present plastering. The doors and windows, together with their trimmings, would have to be renewed, in order to suit the change, so that virtually it would be necessary to rebuild the entire house, and, in reality, all that would be saved was the cellar. Even then it would not be what he wanted, though costing as much as a new building, which might be arranged exactly to suit his wishes. Would it not be better, therefore, to let the old house to a farmer, and commence a new one on, perhaps, a better site? To this he replied that the present location was not only the most desirable, but the roads were already established, and the trees and shrubbery grown. Then I suggested that he might remove the old building, and put up a new one on the present site. My advice was accepted, and the result was that he had, at the cost of no greater sum than would have been necessary to alter the old building, a new one arranged entirely to his satisfaction. He, moreover, saved the expense of tearing down the original structure, and now had two houses, for the same price for which otherwise he would have had but one.

DESIGN No. 16.

First-floor Plan.

1. Hall; 2. Parlor, 15×22; 3. Library, 15×20; 4. Bedroom, 15×17; 5. Dressing-room; 6. Dining-room, 14×21; 7. Butler's pantry; 8. Kitchen; 9. Back entry; 10. Milk-room; 11. Back hall; 12. Staircase; 13. Veranda.—*Estimated cost*, $17,000.

This building has been recently erected at Pawling, Duchess County, New York, for the Hon. J. B. Dutcher, an old resident of that place. The parlor and library are approached from the main hall, and thrown together by double doors, making an entire range of fifty feet along the front of the house, which is skirted by a piazza some ten feet wide. On entering the house, the first thing that strikes a visitor is the large stained-glass window lighting the hall. The bedroom, though not large in itself, has a spacious dressing-room, with liberal closets attached. This may be also reached from the back hall, which has its entrance from the basement, as shown in the perspective elevation, which gives the rear view of the house. The entire first floor is fitted up with hard wood, the living-rooms containing some fine specimens of Jacobean workmanship, executed by Messrs. Pottier & Stymus of this city. The plumbing and ventilation are of the most approved character, and the heating apparatus highly satisfactory, having been put in by Messrs. Baker & Smith, while the gas is manufactured on the place by one of the Springfield Company's machines. The fixtures, which are good specimens of the reform school, are from the house of Archer & Pancoast, of New York.

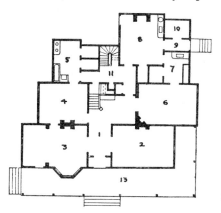

First-floor Plan of Design No. 16.

CHAPTER XVII.

LIBRARY.

Nooks and Cubby-holes.

PROBABLY the library, more than any other room in a house, reflects the master mind of the household. One person regards this apartment as simply a place in which to read newspapers, write letters, and

The Library, in Design No. 16.

keep slippers and dressing-gown. Another's idea is that it is like a museum for bric-à-brac, with showy bookcases and ample shelving for books, purchased by the yard, selected according to their backs. The real library is, of course, that in which the style and selection of reading matter convey some idea of certain specialties to which the *dilettante* or scientific possessor is prone. No doubt the most attractive collections are those in which are represented all classes of literature interesting to the general reader. In this case the alcove .arrangement, where volumes upon kindred subjects are kept by themselves, is undoubtedly the best.

This, however, is intended only for large collections, and these strictly the possessions of literary men. Home libraries, acting as a sort of rendezvous for social intercourse, may be far more cosy and inviting if arranged like a lady's boudoir. In some instances in England — as, for example, in the residence of Sir Walter Scott at Abbotsford — there are two rooms—one a large apartment simply for the deposit of books, the other a small study adjoining, arranged more in sympathy with the social disposition of the owner.

One of the first considerations in regard to the library is that of light. Light from the left is always regarded as more desirable for writing, and the advantage of having it fall upon the reader's book while he sits facing the fire has already been pointed out. Bay-windows in this, as well as in all other apartments, are desirable. These, like the fireplace, need not be placed directly in the centre of the room. Corner bay-windows, situated diagonally, are often effective in preventing stiff regularity, and giving grace to the room, while they form cosy retreats, and are "traps to catch a sunbeam."

Ventilation is also an essential consideration in a study or reading-room, these being the natural lounging-places for gentlemen who smoke, and because, in a close room, the gluing and pasting of the books are apt to become musty, unless proper precautions are taken to secure a good circulation of air.

In our observations on bookcases we shall describe somewhat at length the manner of their construction, size, etc. We would here say that, in order to prevent dampness, it is always well to have a bookcase raised a few inches above the floor, and made with solid backs, removed sufficiently from the wall to allow a free circulation of air.

As it is often the case that the library is appropriated by the master of the house, it is frequently brought into requisition as a business-room. It would, therefore, be well to have it connected with the dining-room, which could serve as a waiting-room for persons whose visits are of a business character.

When a house is sufficiently large, it is well to have a regular business-room, or office, where employees may be paid and accounts settled. Here, if the owner be of an agricultural turn of mind, might be placed a repository for pears and other fruits, which need to be carefully packed away in drawers, to ripen. This also seems the place for guns and fishing-tackle. Stuffed birds, shells, and curiosities may be added, as decorations to the apartment.

The reader might imagine, from the foregoing remarks, that a library is desirable only in rich and costly mansions; that such a luxury might be regarded as a superfluity in a cottage. It is not too much to say that every man owes it to himself, no less than to his family, to provide in his home a place where he may gather his dear ones for counsel and instruction. We would enlarge on this subject, which we deem so important, but prefer rather to quote the language of a distinguished writer of the day:

"We form judgments of men from little things about their house, of which the owner, perhaps, never thinks. In earlier years, when travelling in the West, where taverns are rather scarce and, in some places, unknown, and every settler's house was a house of 'entertainment,' it was a matter of some importance and some experience to select wisely where you would put up; and we always looked for flowers. If there were no trees for shade, no patch for flowers, we were suspicious of the place. But no matter how rude the cabin or rough the surroundings, if we saw that the window held a little trough of flowers, and that some vines twined about strings let down from the eaves, we were confident that there was some good taste and carefulness in the log-cabin. In a new country, where people have to tug for a living, no one will take the trouble to rear flowers unless the love for them is pretty strong; and that this taste blossoms out of plain and uncultivated people is itself like a clump of harebells growing out of the seams of a rock. We were seldom misled. A patch of flowers came to signify kind people, clean beds, and good bread.

"But other signs are more significant in other states of society. Flowers about a rich man's house may signify only that he has a good gardener, or that he has refined neighbors, and does what he sees them do.

"But men are not accustomed to buy books unless they want them. If, on visiting the dwelling of a man of slender means, I find the reason why he has cheap carpets and very plain furniture to be that he may purchase books, he rises at once in my esteem. Books are not made for furniture, but there is nothing else that so beautifully furnishes a house. The plainest row of books that cloth or paper ever covered is more significant of refinement than the most elaborately carved *étagère* or sideboard.

"Give me a house furnished with books rather than furniture; both, if you can: but books at any rate. To spend several days in a friend's house and hunger for something to read, while you are treading on costly carpets, and sitting upon luxurious chairs, and sleeping upon down, is as if one were bribing your body for the sake of cheating your mind.

"Is it not pitiable to see a man growing rich, and beginning to augment the comforts of home, and lavishing money on ostentatious upholstery, upon the table, upon everything but what the soul needs?

"We know of many and many a rich man's house where it would not be safe to ask for the commonest English classics. A few garish annuals on the table, a few pictorial monstrosities, together with the stock of re-

Design No. 17.

ligious books of 'his persuasion,' and that is all: no range of poets, no essays, no selections of historians, no travels or biographies, no select fictions, no curious legendary lore. But then, the walls have paper on that cost three dollars a roll, and the floors have carpets that cost four dollars a yard.

"Books are the windows through which the soul looks out. A house without books is like a room without windows. No man has a right to bring up his children without surrounding them with books, if he has the means to buy them. It is a wrong to his family; he cheats them. Children learn to read by being in the presence of books. The love of knowledge comes with reading, and grows upon it; and the love of knowledge in a young mind is also the warrant against the inferior excitement of passions and vices.

"Let us pity these poor rich men who live barrenly in great bookless houses. Let us congratulate the poor that in our day books are so cheap that a man may every year add a hundred volumes to his library for what his tobacco and beer may cost him. Among the earliest ambitions to be excited in clerks, workmen, journeymen, and, indeed, in all that are struggling up in life from nothing to something, is that of owning and constantly adding to a library of good books. A little library, growing larger every year, is an honorable part of a young man's history. It is a man's duty to have books. A library is not a luxury, but one of the necessaries of life."

Sometimes little nooks and niches may be converted into cupboards, or miniature closets, in a very artistic manner, often affording an agreeable surprise; and additional interest is frequently given by these cubby-holes, apparently panels, remaining for a long time unsuspected. There are spaces in the furring out of chimneys which may be thus utilized. There is one of this kind in the dining-room of Dr. Chadwick, of Boston. Over the middle panel of the fireplace hangs an old German picture (1525), whose frame is on hinges, rendering the service of a door to a small cupboard. Such cupboards prove convenient depositories for medicines, liquors, or valuables, and would, no doubt, be appreciated by our bachelor friends if devoted to the care of their pipes and tobacco.

Some of the old buildings erected prior to the Tudor period were rich in closets of this description. There were also sliding-doors, leading into secret chambers, passages, and stairways, some of which existed years before being discovered, and have many a romantic tale connected with them.

A lady mentioned to me, only a short time since, that the amount of anxiety she had experienced while living in the country, on account of having a quantity of family plate in her possession, kept her in a perpetual state of nightmare; and she and her daughter went tremblingly about searching the house, weapons in hand, at the slightest noise, construing the rustling of leaves and swinging of shutters into attempts at house-breaking. Finally she decided to utilize a waste space under the foot of the staircase, by converting it into a secret closet, the entrance to which should be a sliding panel in the wainscot. This hidden closet was in reality a greater protection against thieves than a burglar-proof safe with the manufacturer's guarantee. It is probable that in many cases the very fact of one of these safes being placed in a dwelling acts as an advertisement, making the house a mark for thieves.

DESIGN No. 17.

First-floor Plan.

1. Veranda; 2. Hall, 9×31; 3. Dining-room, 16×23; 4. Butler's pantry, 10×13; 5. Store-room; 6. Kitchen, 16×16; 7. Kitchen pantry; 8. Servant's porch; 9. Staircase hall; 10. Parlor, 15×22; 11. Library, 15×18.—*Estimated cost*, $14,000.

This design is somewhat irregular, having the entrance on the dining-room side, although the perspective is taken from the rear, or garden, view. The two front rooms—the parlor and dining-room—communicate by opposite folding-doors across the hall, forming a vista with the parlor windows at one end, and a niche containing the sideboard at the other. The library is a spacious room with a large bay-window. The hall, which passes through the house, is nine feet wide, and is unobstructed, the stairs being placed in an alcove at the left. Passing through this alcove, we come to the butler's pantry, containing two dressers and a sink. The pantry communicates with the store-room, kitchen, main hall, and dining-room. It is connected with the latter by a double door, swinging both ways, and closed by a spring, so as to shut off the view of the kitchen.

The second story contains five bedrooms and the family bath-room; there is also a dressing-room, with conveniences, connected with the front chamber. The hall in this story has a well-lighted alcove, intended for reading or sewing. The attic is quite roomy, having four good-sized bed-chambers. Two of these are in communication with a recessed balcony, which, owing to its elevation, may command an extensive view. These rooms are kept cool by a loft between the ceilings and the roof. Both attic and loft are thoroughly lighted and ventilated.

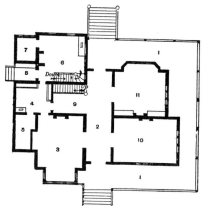

First-floor Plan of Design No. 17.

The building is frame, sheathed and clapboarded as described in Design No. 1. The vignette on the opposite page shows the rear porch or servant's entrance, with the kitchen pantry on the left. This porch is of good size, and provided with a settee.

The kitchen is accommodated with private stairs leading to the servants' room above. The advantage of this arrangement is that, when the family are absent, the domestics may be cut completely off from the main portion of the house, by simply locking the doors of the wing on each story, free access being still allowed them to their own apartments.

In small houses, where there is no private staircase, it is always well to have the main stairs out of sight from the living-rooms, so that the second story may be approached without observation. Except in houses of very small dimensions, we consider the back staircase indispensable. It not only saves wear upon the principal stairs, and keeps the servants retired, but it is very often a great relief to the lady herself to be able to reach her chamber before presenting herself to her guests, when suddenly summoned from household duties, to do the honors of the drawing-room. I have heard house-keepers frequently complain that the greatest inconvenience connected with a badly planned house—after the scarcity of closets—was the want of a private staircase. In fact, one lady went so far as to make the confession that she had not unfrequently been obliged to resort to the subterfuge of sending her servant up-stairs for a dress. First dropping it out of the window, the servant, in passing, would stop at the parlor door and state, with the usual ceremony, that "Missus" would be down in a minute. Then she would proceed to assist her mistress in her hasty toilet in the kitchen.

Servant's Porch, in Design No. 17.

CHAPTER XVIII.

KITCHEN.

The Comfort of Servants.

IT is a matter of dispute whether a kitchen is better above or below ground in a country-house. Many persons, especially if brought up in cities, claim that there is a greater degree of privacy when the kitchen and offices are below, and also that it is more convenient if they are on the same level with the vegetable, coal, and store cellars. In the vicinity of large cities, where land is too expensive to spread out much, of course this arrangement is best. It greatly reduces the cost of the building; for it is evident that the same foundation will support, and the same roof cover, a building, whether it have one or five stories. By this plan the entire roof and walls of a kitchen are saved, to say nothing of the cost of additional chimney shafts. There are others, again, who consider going up and down stairs the destruction of health and comfort, rendering the life of the house-keeper, who properly superintends her domicile, a burden. It is a recognized fact among house-agents, that houses with kitchens above ground will always rent or sell more readily than others.

The comforts and accommodations for servants in the country are matters which should receive more consideration than is usually accorded them. Nine times out of ten, unless basement kitchens have the advantage of a side-hill exposure, they are damp and gloomy; a fact liable not only to create dissatisfaction among domestics, but one by which their health is often seriously impaired. The old habit of putting them anywhere to work, and in some close or dismal garret to sleep, has justly excited rebellion among these necessary, and now independent, members of our households. This, no doubt, in a great measure accounts for the difficulties with servants of which we constantly hear house-keepers complain. Give them cheerful kitchens, exposed to light and air, and bedrooms comfortably warmed and furnished, with something to interest them during their hours of leisure, and the hue and cry against the tyranny of cooks and chamber-maids will become things of the past. It is generally thought that to warm their rooms is treating them with far too much consideration, and placing them beyond the sphere to which they belong; but the mistake house-keepers make in not providing for their servants' comfort is one by which they themselves are apt to suffer more than the servants.

The fact should be considered that people, even in the class of domestics, are human, and by no means without feeling and a need of sympathy. They are often taken to lonely parts of the country, and expected to be

Design No. 18.

contented to sit in a dreary apartment, without companionship or diversion, spending the long winter evenings like prisoners in the penitentiary. Many of them like to read, yet books and papers are strictly prohibited in the kitchen. Why should not music, games, pictorials, and other means of recreation be provided for our working men and women, to brighten their dull and monotonous lives, in which poor food and continuous labor, not only cause the intellect to deteriorate, but also impair the physical and moral health?

DESIGN No. 18.

First-floor Plan.

1. Main hall; 2. Parlor, 16×25; 3. Billiard-room, 15×21; 4. Library, 15×21; 5. Dining-room, 15×20; 6. Butler's pantry; 7. Store-room; 8. Kitchen, 15×18; 9. Back hall; 10, 10. Verandas.—*Estimated cost, $15,000.*

The illustrations which we give of this design show larger rooms and more liberal halls and stairways. The staircase, which is represented in the vignette on the opposite page, has a somewhat extensive conservatory on the landing, while in the hall itself the old wood fireplace reminds us of earlier days, when homes were as spacious as the hospitality they offered. From the first landing there is an alcove looking upon the billiard-room, from which visitors may witness the game, while the room itself is approached from the right of the stairs. Both room and alcove are protected and sounds deadened by the introduction of heavy hangings.

The antique wooden chest so common in old houses, which may be carved in imitation of old work, and bound together with ornamental straps and hinges, is introduced at the foot of the stairs. This would make a convenient receptacle for fuel, and its height may be sufficient to enable it to serve as a seat or hat-stand.

First-floor Plan of Design No. 18.

We would generally discourage the use of the modern appliance known as the hat-rack. It is an awkward thing at best, from whose pegs hats are continually falling. It seems much more convenient to place them upon a table, while the umbrellas may be deposited in a Japanese vase, such as that shown at the right of the staircase. Wraps and overcoats might with more propriety be placed in a closet, where they are secure, and out of the way.

The style of the hall has somewhat of a Japanese effect, though the fireplace is decidedly of the Queen Anne period; and it is remarkable how much similarity, or, rather, harmony of feeling, exists between the two. The Japanese joinery is of a thoroughly honest construction, a feature peculiar to the workmanship of that country. It is a notable fact that two schools of the same motive, though perhaps entirely different in

Staircase Hall, in Design No. 18.

treatment, always assimilate and appear well together; and, as honesty in building seems now the order of the day, any style which is based upon this principle should be fostered. This is manifested by the fact that some of our best cabinet-makers, who were first to introduce the Queen Anne motive in their manufacture, are now showing some delightful Japanese feeling in their productions.

CHAPTER XIX.

BILLIARD-ROOM.

Billiards as an Amusement.—Location of Room.—Tables.

IN a country mansion, especially if somewhat isolated, so that the occupants must, to a great extent, depend upon their own resources for amusement, a billiard-table is a great acquisition. The difficulty usually is, that it is in a room in some out-of-the-way part of the house, sometimes in the basement, but more frequently in the attic, approached by narrow stairs, and, at the best, having low ceilings directly under the roof. It is generally hot and uncomfortable. For this reason, after the novelty wears off, it ceases to be attractive, and is little used. The ladies of the family complain that the gentlemen exclude themselves, when indulging in this amusement, by ascending into doubtful regions, whither it would seem an intrusion to follow. To prevent this exclusiveness, why not accept the pastime as one of the social amusements, and give it the same prominence as music or cards, and let the billiard-room be situated on the parlor story, opening, if you please, directly into the sitting-room, where the ladies may feel free to enter, and join the game if so disposed? Any amusement that is relegated to gentlemen alone is apt to be considered—and perhaps not without cause—as dangerous and demoralizing; for the fact of young men assembling by themselves, without the restraint caused by the presence of ladies, no doubt often leads to dissipation, or, at least, coarseness. But there is no reason why billiards should not be enjoyed by both sexes; and probably the unpopularity of the game among ladies is often caused by the remoteness of the billiard-table, rather than any deep prejudice against it as an amusement. But if brought directly within our families, where the young and old may freely mingle, there is no reason why billiards should not be as innocent as any other game. It is certainly a healthful and agreeable exercise, and should be considered simply in the light of a harmless recreation. It is always a good practice, in order to prevent outside dissipation, to provide something more agreeable at home. But where children are strictly kept from games, for fear of giving them a taste for such pleasures, the very prohibition seems to add to the fascination exercised by amusements of this character, and, upon final emancipation from parental rule, they are indulged in to excess.

It was formerly supposed that a billiard-room must be built especially for the purpose, of such a size as to admit of a six-foot passage on each side of the table. Thus the fact of the old tables, being six feet

The Billiard-room.

wide, made it necessary to construct a room of formidable dimensions. Modern tables, however, are so much reduced that an ordinary room of fifteen by twenty feet will give sufficient space. In fact, want of room is no longer an impediment, as billiard-tables are now made to suit apartments of any size, and are so ornamental as often to be placed in one end of a parlor. Indeed, there is an arrangement by which a dining-table may, by a simple operation, be transformed into a billiard-table. The vignette given above shows the interior of a billiard-room, and a table, designed for Mr. H. W. Collender.

DESIGN No. 19.

First-floor Plan.

1. Porch; 2. Vestibule, 12×6; 3. Hall, 12×23; 4. Staircase; 5. Lavatory; 6. Library, 14×16; 7. Back hall; 8. Kitchen, 18×15; 9. Butler's pantry; 10. Store-room; 11. Dining-room, 18×22; 12. Billiard-room, 15×20; 13. Parlor, 18×20; 14. Veranda; 15. Side entrance.—*Estimated cost*, $16,000.

This is a design for a brick or stone dwelling, as indicated by the deep reveals to doors and windows, and the quoin construction on the external angles. The original idea was suggested by a villa designed by M. Aubertin, which appears in "Habitations Modernes," by Viollet le Duc. The present design, however, differs entirely in the internal arrangement, besides having, in addition, a tower and verandas. The entrance vestibule and hall are spacious, the two measuring some thirty feet. At the end of the hall is the dining-room, with a central door. Opposite this, and closing the vista, is a large bay-window, twelve feet wide and

Design No. 19.

four feet deep, with stained glass in the upper sash. The sideboard, in this case, is placed opposite the fireplace, a system objectionable in narrow rooms, but here admissible, as the dining-room is sufficiently wide to afford free passage between it and the table. The staircase is somewhat cut off from the main hall, being connected with it only by a wide arch opposite the parlor entrance. There is a stained-glass window over the landing, under which is situated the lavatory. This, while being out of sight, may be approached from the front vestibule, without passing through the main hall. It is also convenient to the library, which, acting the part of business-room or office for the proprietor, may be reached by a private entrance. In the absence of the gentleman of the house, the lady may find this a convenient boudoir, easily approached by the rear entrance, and near the kitchen portion of the house. The billiard-room is somewhat apart from the main

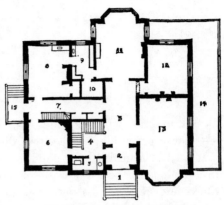

First-floor Plan of Design No. 19.

house, being connected with it by a private lobby; and its interior walls, if built of brick, will so deaden sounds that they will be scarcely audible in the adjoining apartment.

The second story has five bedrooms, and as many more may be built in the attic. The main stairs, which extend to the top of the tower, accommodate both attic and observatory.

CHAPTER XX.

BLINDS.

Inside and Outside Shutters.—Venetian Blinds.—Shades.—Wire Screens.

THE question whether blinds shall be placed on the outside of a frame house or within, has been in dispute since the time that wood was first used as a material for building. The great objection urged against inside blinds has been the waste of room occasioned by the furring out or thickening of the walls necessary to accommodate the boxes into which the blinds must fold. In stone or brick buildings this objection does not exist, as the necessary thickness of the walls affords sufficient room for

Interior of Bay-window.

shutter-boxes without furring. In single windows there can be but little objection to the blinds being arranged on either plan; but when windows are grouped with three or more openings, both are more or less objectionable. If outside blinds be adopted, the middle ones, when open, necessarily interfere with those on each side. It is also difficult to make the mullion wide enough to accommodate inside shutters without presenting a heavy and awkward appearance. In England, the difficulty is usually met by the adoption of blinds that are so arranged as to draw up; the Venetian, or rolling, blinds are also popular. The fault of these is, the first offer no protection from intrusion from without, and the latter are too expensive. There is an objection to each, however. When the upper sash is of stained glass, this, in itself, sufficiently excludes the sun. It would be superfluous to have, in addition, a shutter, thereby excluding from view the rich effects of the stained glass. In order to meet this difficulty, I have devised an arrangement by which the inside blinds may be made to slide downward in two sections, occupying the space between the sill and the floor, and, when raised, cover only the plate-glass portion. The centre openings in the vignette on the preceding page illustrate these blinds when down; those at the right when raised; the openings on the left show one section at the top and one at the bottom, none of which conflicts with the upper sash containing the stained glass. This vignette represents the interior view of the second-story bay-window of Design No. 7.

The objection to these blinds has been that the louvers, or slats, when open, are apt to bind against the pocket in which they are intended to slide, especially as the rod connecting them is some three-eighths of an inch in advance. A happy contrivance has, however, been devised by a firm in Hartford, in which the connecting-rod is dispensed with altogether, by the introduction of a ratchet running the length of the opening. This is imbedded in the stile, and is connected with the axle of each louver. The whole is worked by a simple button, which is sunk below the surface.

The same rule that applies to blinds when the upper sash is of stained glass holds good in regard to shades. They should be secured to the lower sash, and arranged to slide with rings on metal bars, above and below, as represented in the vignette. The material used should be some pliant fabric, such as silk or lace.

Sometimes, when there is an ornamental trimming about a window which involves the necessity of brackets extending over the blind, there is some difficulty in opening the shutters. There is a system, common in England, by which the upper portion of the blind is hinged at the top, so that, when raised, it has the effect of an awning, the lower part being arranged as usual.

There is a simple contrivance by which Venetian shades, made of black-walnut slats, turning like those of the ordinary blinds, are attached to the outside of the window with an ornamental cornice. They may be drawn up on the principle of the old Venetian shades, and can be extended out at any angle, and thus made to perform the duty of an awning. I have recently seen an admirable arrangement of rolling Venetian shutters, made by Messrs. Wilson & James, which seems an excellent substitute for blinds, applicable to the inside or the outside of a window. When attached to a veranda or porch, it has the effect of converting either into a room or open balcony at pleasure.

Blind doors, in addition to those of panel, are often of great benefit in warm seasons, as they are not only secure, but leave the air unobstructed.

Wire-gauze frames, arranged like doors, answer the same purpose, and possess the additional virtue of keeping out the flies. These are especially desirable for windows; but the manner in which they are usually arranged—which is, placed in the lower half of the sash—is thoroughly unscientific, as it is very desirable, in ventilation, to have an opening above as well as below. Therefore, by having a screen in both sections, the circulation of air will be more perfect.

Design No. 20.

A little knowledge regarding the principles of air currents may frequently do us good service. By merely setting a blind at the right angle, we may often capture a breeze that would otherwise pass by. For example, in a window facing south, if the easterly blind be open, say at an angle of seventy degrees, it will catch a westerly breeze and bring it into the room; *vice versa*, when the wind is in a contrary direction.

DESIGN No. 20.

First-floor Plan.

1. Main hall, 15 × 26; 2. Parlor, 15 × 22; 3. Billiard-room, 15 × 20; 4. Dining-room, 15 × 20; 5. Butler's pantry; 6. Store-room; 7. Kitchen, 15 × 18; 8. Back stairs; 9. Lavatory; 10. Library, 15 × 16; 11. Rear porch; 12. Veranda; 13. Carriage porch.—*Estimated cost,* $15,000.

Though somewhat unusual in character, we think this design embraces many points peculiarly adapted to meet our American requirements. The long, unbroken roof has the facility for shedding both rain and snow, and the broad verandas, projecting canopies, and recessed balcony afford ample shade at different points where fresh air and pleasant views may be enjoyed. The general irregularity of the design offers an opportunity for strong effects of light and shade, and may be made to harmonize with the varied and picturesque scenes of our country. The verandas are of unusual width, averaging from five to fifteen feet; thus giving ample space for groups to gather, without obstructing the promenade. The main entrance is

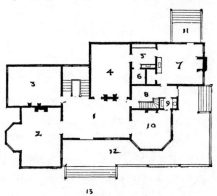

First-floor Plan of Design No. 20.

sheltered by a carriage porch sufficiently large to cover horses and vehicle. The hall is twenty-six feet long and fifteen wide, independent of the staircase, which occupies the L.

As in the former design, the library is convenient to the lavatory, rear entrance, and domestic offices, while the kitchen has a separate entrance, with a large porch in the rear for the benefit of the servants.

CHAPTER XXI.

CARE NECESSARY IN ADAPTING A ROOM TO FURNITURE.

Hot-air Registers.—Location of Doors and Windows.—Position for the Piano.—Gas-fixtures, etc.

SOME of the defects we notice in modern apartments arise from the fact that they have been built upon a half-digested plan, in which only a portion of the necessary requirements have been considered. An architect, in designing a room, should, as it were, live in it in imagination before pronouncing it complete. He should consider for what the room is intended, its proximity to other apartments and passages, the lights, the swing of doors; and, in fact, it might not be too much to re-

Design No. 21.

quire that every piece of furniture should be included within the plan. How often we see the hot-air registers come directly in the spaces provided for piano, bookcase, or bedstead. Often doors cannot be opened without interfering with passages, or encountering some obstruction. Then, again, there are some important pieces of furniture that are never calculated for at all; for instance, the leaves of an extension-table. These are never thought of, and are either set up on end in the dining-room corner, looking awkward and disconsolate, or else placed in the butler's pantry or china closet, where they are always in the way. The good old maxim, "A place for everything, and everything in its place," is one of the first principles of good house-keeping; and it is evident that a vast number of the many troubles to which we are exposed might be lessened by attention to these matters. It is not beneath the dignity of the man of science to study every domestic need, insignificant as it may appear.

A gentleman who had recently completed an expensive dwelling once complained to me that the neglect of such points as these had cost him endless annoyance and expense. He said that in his parlor there had been no adequate arrangement made for a piano or sofa; it was impossible to place either in the room without interfering with a door or window. The windows he did not so much regret, except that he was obliged to climb over the piano in order to raise or lower them; but his wife somewhat objected to having her seat obstructed, as she had anticipated a delightful view; while the draughts upon the instrument, before the season was over, had materially affected its tone; and when the tuner was called in, he discovered that the wires had become rusty, and that a new action would be required. He went on to relate, with some feeling, how a gas-bracket had been placed directly behind a door in the dining-room. The first time it was lighted was on the occasion of a dinner given to some of his friends, expressly that they might see the boasted perfections of his mansion. It afforded them much amusement, and himself unbounded chagrin, as the servant entered from the butler's pantry, to see the door strike against the gas-fixture, and a shower of glass ensue. Certainly the unfortunate host was excusable if he inwardly voted his gas-fitter a donkey and a villain.

DESIGN No. 21.

First-floor Plan.

1. Entrance porch; 2. Vestibule; 3. Main hall; 4. Reception-room, 15 × 15; 5. Library, 15 × 22; 6. Parlor, 15 × 24; 7. Dining-room, 15 × 20; 8. Butler's pantry; 9. Storeroom; 10. Kitchen, 15 × 18; 11, 11. Verandas.—*Estimated cost*, $15,000.

This is a building on a somewhat liberal scale, having large rooms and spacious halls. The main porch is broad, and fitted up with permanent

seats. There is an alcove at the entrance, which could serve as a vestibule in winter. This has hat and
coat closets on each side, while the
lavatory is down a few steps, occupying the space under the stair-land-
ing. The reception-room is on the
left of the entrance, which might be
arranged as a library in case it should
be thought desirable to convert the
present one into a billiard-room. The
parlor is of good size, being fifteen
by twenty-four feet, independent of
the bay-window, which projects five
feet, and is eleven feet wide. I will here say that the bay-windows are
not included in the dimensions of the rooms heretofore given.

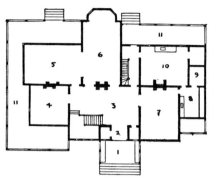

First-floor Plan of Design No. 21.

CHAPTER XXII.

THE MANSION.

Arrangement of Roads.—Natural Effect.—Planting of Trees.—View from Railway.

THE subject of roads is one that has seldom received sufficient attention. It is essential that our roads and walks should be as systemat-
ically arranged as the halls and apartments of our dwellings. The
great beauty of a domain depends upon the grace of its lines; for, like
the planting of trees, the laying-out of roads is sure to be formal and
stilted, unless great care be taken to produce a natural effect. It is,
of course, unnecessary, at this late day, to dilate upon the absurdity of
geometrical arrangement in this department. That curves are a necessity, both for amplifying and beautifying our grounds, has long since been
admitted; but to produce a curve which the wheels of a carriage would
naturally trace is something which but one person in a hundred is capable of achieving. Downing, in speaking of planting trees in a natural
manner, says that once, on account of a pressing engagement, he had not
the time to stake out the location of every tree; so he threw, at random, a peck of potatoes, one by one, and directed the gardener to plant
a tree where each potato fell. If this had not the effect of grouping
them scientifically, it certainly gave the appearance of natural arrangement. A rule similar to this, though rude of its kind, may be given to
produce a natural curve to the road. Drive your carriage, or even an
ox-cart, over the ground in the direction by which you wish to reach
the house, and the tracks which the wheels make will almost invariably
have an easy and natural. appearance, although, as in the former case,
perhaps the effect will not be as graceful as if the matter had been arranged by a landscape gardener.

As a general rule, the fewer roads we have on a small estate the better. The expense of making and keeping them in order is not only diminished, but the effect of an unbroken lawn is secured, and the grounds
naturally appear larger. For example, a winding road with the trees so

disposed as to lose certain views, and catch them again from another direction, presents the idea of different scenes. So, too, certain perspective effects may be produced by planting smaller trees, which have the effect

Design No. 22.

of being diminished by distance. Mr. Lowden, in writing on this subject, has gone so far as to suggest that a small breed of cattle should browse in an adjoining field; and he states that the Kerry cow is so small that it will nearly double the apparent distance.

A road which shall run around the house is to be preferred to the usual device of a circle in front. This not only forms an approach to the different entrances, but obviates the necessity of backing carts upon the grass—a difficulty which so frequently occurs, though easily avoided in a well-studied plan. It does not, however, necessitate the passage of business vehicles before the front door, as a private entrance to the stable is continually required, which may also serve as a passage for trades-people.

There is one point of view from which a country place is seen by passers-by more frequently than from any other; and, strange to say, this is most generally lost sight of in arranging our buildings and laying-out our grounds. The point in question is the railway; toward which — the main artery of travel — are usually turned our back yards and cattle-sheds. It is often remarked that we see but the poorest part of a town when passing through it upon the railroad, and the railway-station generally presents the least inviting aspect of any building in the town. This seems an extraordinary oversight, for the reason that we wish to give the public a favorable impression, in order to attract new-comers.

While on this subject, it may not, perhaps, be inappropriate to offer a few remarks on railroad improvements generally. It is now received as an axiom in political economy that the construction of railways from large cities through the rural districts, not only increases the population and industry of such districts, but must act as most effective agents of social reform. The natural overflow from the city into the country nec-essarily carries with it an element of refinement and culture, so that we find society, in every village which is touched by a railroad, slowly and surely improving, as is plainly shown in the vanishing of old prejudices

Grand Staircase, in Design No. 22.

in the matter of architecture, before the healthy example of the rustica-ting citizen who builds his elegant villa or picturesque cottage in the neighborhood. It is certainly reasonable to suppose that railway compa-

nies themselves, being thus the great civilizing agencies, would be foremost in setting examples of improved taste and culture before the people, by building stations along their lines, which
should be agreeable objects to look upon, and
stand as models of design. Such seed, though
thrown by the way-side, would not be lost, but
would surely bear its fruits in the increased refinement of rural sentiment, and the greater demand for country places. Usually, however,
these stations, even on
our most prominent
roads, are of the most
uninviting and even
ridiculous appearance.
When they are not beg-
garly, they are often ab-
surdly pretentious. We
are glad to note, how-
ever, that in some in-
dividual instances, evi-
dences of an improved
taste and a refined feel-
ing for elegance and
propriety is shown. We
wish that the stranger

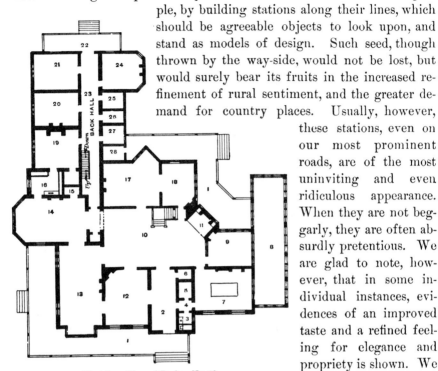

First-floor Plan of Design No. 22.

entering an American town or village were welcomed by something more
inviting than those rude sheds under which he usually shakes off the dust
of travel.

Perhaps nothing more readily attracts the attention of the American
traveller abroad than the beautiful little stations which, with endless variety, are dotted along the railway webs of Great Britain and the Continent. There travelling is a luxury, not only on account of the assurance
of safety and the splendid fitting of the carriages, but also by reason of
the tasteful little stations which, while they charm the eye by their agreeable exteriors, do not fail to comfort the weary traveller by means of the
perfection of their interior arrangements.

DESIGN No. 22.

First-floor Plan.

1. Veranda; 2. Entrance lobby; 3. Lavatory; 4. Passage; 5. Hat closet; 6. Elevator; 7. Billiard-room, 16×22; 8. Conservatory, 12×48; 9. Tea-room, 13×16; 10. Hall, 22×40; 11. Hall fireplace, 7×9; 12. Reception-room, 17×21; 13. Parlor, 17×34; 14. Dining-room, 17×28; 15. China closet; 16. Butler's pantry; 17. Library, 16×22; 18. Office, 13 × 16; 19. Kitchen, 15 × 17; 20. Laundry, 13 × 17; 21. Servants' hall, 14 × 17; 22. Servants' porch; 23. Back hall; 24. House-keeper's room, 14 × 16; 25. Store-room; 26. Boots; 27. Scullery; 28. Gun-room.

The mansion, as compared with the cottage, is like a full-grown man compared with a child. It not only surpasses the cottage in size, but also in general comprehensiveness and refinement. In the former, we expect to find all that can minister to convenience and comfort, as well as express the artistic and hospitable tastes of a cultivated family.

In this design the spacious porch seems to give an assurance of welcome as we enter. From the broad veranda, with its hundred feet of walk, admission may be had to the various rooms along its path by means of windows reaching to the floor. At the right of the entrance-lobby is a commodious dressing-room, with hat closet. Farther on is a lift, or hand-elevator, running from basement to attic, used for domestic purposes. Being near the front entrance, it can be utilized for transporting trunks and other luggage. It might be well if it were divided into two stories, the upper for the accommodation of old people and invalids. This is one of the modern improvements which has become regarded as almost indispensable in first-class houses. On the left is a reception-room, and beyond this the parlor, which, including the bay-window, is thirty-five feet long.

In the rear of the parlor is the dining-room. This contains a china closet and butler's pantry, the latter communicating with the kitchen. Beyond, and opening into the back hall (which is entirely cut off from the main house), are the laundry, servants' hall, house-keeper's room, store-room, scullery, boot and gun room. The library and office are separated either by curtains or folding-doors.

The principal feature of this house is the grand (or staircase) hall, from which all the living-rooms are accessible. The entrance vestibule communicates directly with the reception-room. The main hall is so retired that it may be used for family gatherings. Its great attraction is the generous old fireplace, ten feet wide and seven deep, forming a spacious alcove, in which settles may be placed, accommodating a party of six or eight persons. Here we realize the poetical idea of the chimney-corner, around which so many tender memories of early days are centred. There, in our childhood, our first Bible lessons were vividly impressed upon our minds from the texts and more remarkable events illustrated upon the old Dutch tiles around its margin. There we listened to endless ghost-stories, which made "each particular hair to stand on end," while we drew imagi-

Bedroom, in Design No. 22.

nary portraits of the goblins in the burning embers, and the legend of Santa Claus seemed not improbable while we peered up into that great chimney. It is pleasant, too, to recall the holiday games played without check in the old hall, while the yule-log burned merrily upon the fire-dogs.

It has often been argued that open fireplaces may be very picturesque and poetical, but that, in cold weather, they certainly do not warm our rooms; and we have often heard our grandmothers, who were brought up in the time of open fireplaces, and proportionately open crevices, state that while their faces were being scorched, their backs were freezing. Franklin, in endeavoring to estimate what proportion of heat from the ordinary fireplace of the period came into the room, and what escaped up the chimney, came to the conclusion that ninety-five per cent. was wasted. Out of this discovery came his great invention, the Franklin stove, which has gradually degenerated into the thousand-and-one so-called improvements of stoves now in common use, most of them serving only to consume the vital properties of the atmosphere, no arrangements being made for proper ventilation in the apartments where they are located.

I can remember in my childhood an invention of my grandfather's, which he termed the "iron back-log." It consisted of a cast-iron box, to take the place of the ordinary back-log. The air from without, being admitted into the cavity, became heated, and was introduced into the room through a pipe similar to that of the modern register. This, while detracting nothing from the radiation of the fire, secured a large amount of additional heat; and it may not be conceited for me to state that I believe this was the germ from which hot-air furnaces have been developed. Precisely the same idea is now carried out in connection with grates. In place of the usual back lining of soapstone, there is a small iron chamber introduced, from which the hot air is allowed to escape into the apartment through a perforation under the mantel-shelf. This is almost as economical as the stove, and it possesses the additional advantage of introducing fresh air into the room, at the same time affording means of escape for foul.

Worcester says, in defining the word "hall," that, as applied nowadays, it is perhaps improperly used. A simple passage-way from an entrance is not, correctly speaking, a hall. A few of his definitions read as follows: *Porch*, a covered station; *Portico*, a covered walk outside the building. A *vestibule* is a "fore-room," and a *hall* is the "first large room within a building, both serving as an entrance." During the Middle Ages, and down to the Georgian period, this apartment, with its spacious and curiously constructed fireplace, was always one of the largest in the mansion, and usually the most cheerful. It was the general assembly or living room of the family, from which the other apartments were entered. The stairs were elaborately carved, leading, with broad landings and unexpected turns, into chambers and corridors; and the irregularity of the stories were frequently overcome by an ingenious adjustment of these landings. The windows were never made to appear symmetrical on the outside, but were placed here and there, as the vagaries of the stairs required. Paint and plaster were but little known in the simplicity of construction common among our forefathers; and the rafters themselves, being forced to appear, were carved and moulded in various ways, thus becoming an ornament to the apartment. If the walls of masonry appeared cold, they were sometimes decorated with tapestry hangings, the bases being wainscoted with bold and honest panelling.

In attempting, therefore, to revive the ancient styles, it would be well to study the interior as well as the exterior of some of the dwellings of the period, and, when consistent with modern uses, adapt their distinctive features to the requirements of the present day. We have attempted such a revival in the grand hall. The tea-room, conservatory, and billiard-room complete the arrangement of this floor. The second story contains a hall similar to the lower one, which might serve as the children's playroom. This and the third story together contain twenty bedrooms, liberally supplied with

Corner Mullion, in Design No. 22.

closets, bath and dressing rooms. The attic is a full story, and has a loft over the entire ceiling.

The external walls of the building are of hard-burnt brick; the angles and openings of pressed, and the string-courses of moulded, brick. Black or colored brick, and even illuminated tiles, may be worked in with pleasing results. If thought desirable, tile-hanging might be introduced on the third or attic story, which would serve in a measure to relieve the height of the wall. As a good contrast, the main and veranda roofs might be of green slate, without pattern; and if the wood-work could be of pitch-pine, oiled, it would also harmonize. The ceilings of the veranda, porch, and balcony might be of ultramarine blue, picked out either with buff or red. On the kitchen-chimney panel I have designed a sundial. This was quite common on old buildings, and is both useful and ornamental.

A favorite custom in Gothic architecture is that of placing a series of windows near together, divided simply by lines or mullions. This is objectionable, inasmuch as they cut up the wall surface, leaving no place for furniture. In bedrooms, especially, we require broad piers, with windows on each side for the accommodation of dressing-tables; and unless we resort to the system, shown in the illustration, of placing the windows above the furniture, considerable difficulty is experienced. There is a similar objection on the outside; as here, by cutting up the broad surface, on which we rely for dignity and repose, the design seems to be attenuated and frittered away. The difficulty, however, may be happily overcome by the introduction of a very picturesque feature peculiar to this style, known as the corner mullion. It consists in placing the division immediately in the angle, and arranging the windows each side, instead of grouping them along the walls. The vignette showing the gable over the billiard-room illustrates the method by which this is accomplished.

Frequently in living-rooms, where two sides of the apartment are taken up with fireplace and sliding-doors, and the other two have windows, from the fact of these being in the centre there is absolutely no place for piano, bookcase, sideboard, or, indeed, any large piece of furniture. If, however, the windows are placed in the angle, the entire wall becomes available.

The vignette shows an interior in which ample space for a dressing-table between the windows is allowed, in consequence of the corner-mullion system having been adopted. Room for two bureaus, with a large mirror between, is also obtained. The glass could readily be made to swing, and sufficient space allowed for a hanging closet behind.

CHAPTER XXIII.

CITY ARCHITECTURE.

The Law of Alignment.—Amusing Story by the Rev. Walter Mitchell.

THERE is one point, connected with city architecture, which has been uppermost in my mind for some years past; that is, the incongruity of the buildings along our streets. We find every twenty-five feet a specimen of some artistic style of building which, if it pervaded the whole block, might give a breadth and grandeur to the entire façade. As it is, each man builds solely on his own account, without regard to the height and style of his neighbor. One, we will say, has put up a Néogrec building on lot 216, and his neighbor goes and builds along-side of him an iron structure of the Renaissance order. Now, if both were either Néogrec or Renaissance, although sufficiently different in design to mark the property of each, a good effect would be produced. Then, again, in order to give prominence, one makes his cornice tower above that of the other. Possibly a great deal more fault might justly be found with the architect than with the owner; for if the former had the strength of mind to come out boldly and oppose these heresies, a great amount of good might be accomplished. It is evidently the architect's duty, in designing a city house, to consider his surroundings, and, by a judicious adaptation of his design, to "sandwich" his building in such a manner as to harmonize with the neighboring masses. Clients are generally willing to be influenced by their architect; and if good reasons are advanced for opposing their pet notions, they are usually found to have their weight.

It may be thought that in our republican country—where it is the especial privilege of every citizen to commit whatever enormity he pleases —it would be considered egregious tyranny to have any legislation on the subject; but in France some of the finest architectural effects are the result of what is known as the law of *alignement*. We, in reality, have such a law, namely, that buildings shall not go beyond a certain line on the street. The French simply carry this a little farther by regulating the lines of stories, so that no cornice shall be built above a certain height. Thus, in order to attain greater accommodation, builders found themselves compelled to extend the roofs, which were frequently run up to the height of two or three stories. This was the origin of the Mansard roof. If our legislators would really take the matter in hand, and look to the ultimate advantage of beautifying our cities, they might, without tyranny, pass some law whose effect would be to encourage this reform. By granting an abatement of taxes, or some other privilege, many persons might be induced to submit their designs to the censorship of a commission, whose duty it should be to secure harmony as far as possible.

Design No. 23.

In a book of mine published some years ago—at the time when the New York Post-office was just commenced, and Barnum's Museum was still fresh in the memory of children and our country cousins—I expressed some of these sentiments on the laws of alignment. My remarks suggested to the Rev. Walter Mitchell the following humorous effusion:

"For the last six weeks we have been entertaining that intelligent Zulu whom Bishop Colenso 'took for his pal.' We have shown him our city by daylight and by gaslight. We have striven to impress upon him its wonderful superiority to the principal village of Pennsylvania and to the chief hamlet of Massachusetts. We have convinced him, aided by those statistical arguments so potent with his right reverend father, by the grace of mathematics, that all the world (west of the Atlantic) comes hither to buy goods, and that the remaining part (east of the same) is fast coming hither to obtain through emigration-tickets to Pike's Peak and Denver City. We have pointed out to him a drummer ensnaring a fly—we mean a spider entrapping a Western merchant; we have taken him to the American Museum (late Scudder's, now Barnum's), to the Central Park, and to the Washington Market. We have initiated him into our social life, shown him how our houses are built, lived in, and disposed of at enormous rents. At the close of our exhausting labors, we (this is not the *pluralis majestatis* of the editor's chair, but signifies self and chum) asked our friend what had most struck his fancy in the Empire City.

"Without hesitation he said, 'Your architects.' 'Our architecture, you mean,' said we, thinking it was a foreigner's natural blunder in our difficult language.

"'No, no,' replied he, 'your architects.' (We do not mind saying that this is our profession ; *vide* our design for new dressing-rooms at the Fifth Avenue Skating-pond.) We blushed crimson in our four cheeks, and were on the point of inquiring as to the opening in Natal for two young men of unquestioned genius and unanswered proposals, when our friend continued, 'Your architects have seized the dominant ideas of New York. Every stranger who comes to New York comes to buy or to sell something. The men from the West come to buy, the men from the East come to sell—their raw material, I think you call it—in the shape of muscle. Every Western man I have been introduced to appears to be inspired with two ideas; the first is to take a drink; the second is to build a city. The one he does on the spot; for the other, like Herbert in the story-book, "he looks about him." Your common shopkeepers put their goods in their windows, their advertisements in the newspapers, and send their drummers to board at the Cortlandt Street hotels. But your architects advertise themselves all over the streets. If a man wants to build a marble city, he can see a dozen patterns in one block. If he would rather build a brown-stone city, there are five styles between. If he likes a red-brick metropolis, next door there is a fine sketch in outline. If he prefers yellow brick, he has only to walk round the corner. I see in my walks that you do not build the whole house of your materials—only the parts, so that you can take down the old pattern, when it is dirty or cracked, and put up a new one. Your Broadway is the most superb pattern-card of new cities which I have ever seen. I walk down it till I get to the Park, and then I stop and rest my eyes at the fence which is built up around your new Court-house. I rest my eyes in beholding that splendid triumph of the printer—another great New York artist—which you told me the corporation have put up to teach the little street children their alphabets. I read that "Mr. and Mrs. Barney Will.—FAUST, New Op.—ET OF LEA THERMO S: T: X PLE AT A HORSTEREOPTICON" until my head goes round, and my eyes are very much rested indeed, and I think how exactly it represents in little what I have been looking at for three miles back, and which I ride on top of the omnibuses to enjoy. When I make my fortune in Wall Street, I will build a city. I will take my architect, and a large number of just-landed men of muscle, and we will walk up Broadway. He will point out to me the different patterns. When I decide, I shall only have to say to the intelligent gentlemen from Galway, "Build me a metropolis like 49 or 56," and they will answer, "Yis, yr' honor." "And go and build it—" Then we will all go and live there as soon as possible, and never come to New York again till we wear it out, or burn down our city, and want to see the latest spring styles or fall patterns once more.'

"I confess we were a little shocked at these heresies of the intelligent Zulu; and, to relieve our minds, arranged for a visit to the Central Park the next day. We went thither by that admirable institution, the Third Avenue car, holding on to small leathern straps, and contemplating high art in the pictorial embellishments of what my chum architecturally calls the frieze of those spacious and luxurious vehicles.

"We own to a thrill of pride as we looked down from the observatory upon that triumph of the topiary art. 'You have seen,' we cried, 'the Bois de Boulogne, Hy' Park, the Prater, the Thier-Garten of Berlin, and the Englische Garten of Munich, the lovely Cascine of Florence, and Boston Common; own, my friend, on the faith of a Kaffir, that they cannot hold a candle to this.'

"'My New York innocents,' replied he, 'I do not wish them to hold a candle or a calcium light, or even to offer a match to your Central Park; for surely it would then disclose that your diamond—and it is of the first (and Croton) water—lacks a setting. In my favored land, when a young beauty discovers that she is lovely, she suffers not her nose to lack a ring. When one of your beauties has a large jewel, she does not have it set in copper or in tin. Still less does she dress in a robe made of patchwork— a bit of *moire antique*, and a shred of lace, and scarf of *barège*, and a tatter of calico sewed into the same breadth. Paris has taught American ladies to dress; can it not teach their papas to build? Your Central Park is at present surrounded by a fine assortment of cellars and Irish shanties. It looks unfinished, but not deformed. Everybody accepts the long legs and rough coat of the colt as matters of course, and can see the future beauty of the winner of the Derby in its promise. But a thing once deliberately spoiled, especially a thing of beauty, is a nightmare forever. Don't set your diamond in tin. Don't dress your belle after the pattern of an Ojibbeway squaw. I'll tell you what I think of your Broadway. It reminds me of that torch-light procession you showed me, where there were a dozen military bands playing different tunes. There was a great noise, and it only wanted that each performer should play on his own account, without needing the key of his neighbor, to make the resemblance perfect. You surely are not blind to this. When your friend, the great dry-goods seller, whose villa you hope to build next summer (and I hope you may), gets through his work, he does not pile all his fabrics on the counter and stand looking at them for pleasure; he goes home to a dwelling where his curtains, and his carpets, and his bookbindings, and wall-paper, and pictures all harmonize. When your young friend Kit-cat wishes to draw a funny picture, I observe he generally puts a little fat man beside a tall, lean one. In his Academy picture last summer of the Seventh Regiment marching down Broadway, I noticed that the tops of their caps were tangential to a line as straight as his rule could make it, but the houses in his background were like the awkward squad of a country militia training.'

" ' But,' we broke in, ' you can't drill houses as you can the Seventh. Every man is his own master, and builds his house to suit himself. And after the houses or shops are built, you cannot shift them about till you get the right effect.'

" ' That is all as true as need be, my young Ruskin; but what is the need of being unaccommodating? Your people are naturally polite. I notice that in your omnibuses they keep their elbows to themselves and their feet tucked in. Why should Jones, who is to build upon that vacant cellar, insist upon having his rooms two inches higher than Smith, who will build next him? He may think brick, with brown-stone dressings and a French roof, prettier than white marble and a balustrade cornice; but, side by side, neither is pretty. In a country town, where each house stands in its own grounds, variety (within limits) is charming. So, in a concert, it is pleasant to have a ballad and then an instrumental solo; but think of an opera without a theme and without a plot—an opera pot-pourri of Mendelssohn, and Mozart, and Verdi, and Balfe, and Beethoven, and Meyerbeer, and Donizetti, and Adam, and Rossini, all served up in five-minute slices, just the same length to each composer, and the one strain cut short off for the next! That is what your city is. Jones has no right, I say, to spoil Smith's front by his own; and Smith has no right to spoil his; and you and I, who want to enjoy our Central Park, have a right to say that the two blockheads shall not spoil it for us. A park is the very noblest chance for display of architecture that can be had. Your narrow streets—and they *are* narrow—are ill-adapted for the best work, because it is never seen by anybody except the woman who washes the opposite windows. But a square—a park or place—is the architect's opportunity. Mind, I have no objection to a palace anywhere, if it *is* a palace. When Stewart wants one to put his silks and cottons in, I should like him to have one, taking ground enough to build it. When I first landed, I thought it was your famous White House we hear so much about in Natal; and I looked for the sentry-boxes at the entrance, and wondered where the big Swiss, with his cocked hat and mace, had gone to. But I do not admire palaces, *à la* sandwich, in slices.'

" ' All very well,' we replied; ' but what are you, or we, to do about it? Do you know the price of land per inch where those two little boys with a skate apiece are trying to rival the performers of the Park lake? Land in Natal is to be had for the asking; here you must carpet it with green-backs before you can lay a brick. Men build houses to live in, not to look at, especially as they go from them in a hurry in the morning and return after dark.'

" ' That will do for our down-town streets,' replied he, ' but not for our Park. The people who come here want something fit to look at. Your commissioners understand their business. They have done the best piece of work ever done in America. They have discharged a gigantic trust without a shadow of jobbing, with admirable good taste, with a large and liberal judgment. It is due them that their work be not deformed. I will tell you what you can do. There is a little book I took up the other day in your office—Hathorn's—no, Holly's "Architecture"—and I commend Plate 30 and what follows to your study. He talks of a public censor, and gives, I can't help thinking—though in Natal we fight shy of such officers—very sensible limits to the power and province of such a functionary. Now, give that office to your Central Park commissioners, and, for powder to your shot, enact that there shall be a certain reduction of taxes on all property erected according to their directions. That is it. One-half per cent. off if Smith and Brown will employ the same architect (and the committee choose him), and will let him design the exterior of the house. It will cost them no more—rather be a saving. You say they want their houses to live in, not to look at. Pray what difference.

then, does it make whether the fronts are brown stone or white marble? whether the sham cornice on top is two inches higher or lower? It is only to have his own way and say that the unlucky owner cares about. You architects dare not tell the truth, and say, "My dear sir, don't put a Louis Quatorze front beside your neighbor's Venetian one; you will make a fool of yourself if you do." No, you simper and approve, and go and do the work in bitterness of soul, and take your change out of him by accepting bonuses from all the mechanics whom you employ. You hate the business, but you dare not lose the patron. Why, the very tailor your customer employs has more self-respect, and will not let him put on ill-assorted colors. Since it is all a matter of pocket, let us go to the pocket. It is worth the city's while to take care of its splendid playground. It can appropriate liberally to build a public edifice, and nobody grumbles. Why not push the principle into a reduction of taxes to the same object? It is only shifting the thing end for end. You doubt if they have the power? Of course they have. It is only applying the right of eminent domain in a novel form. That right includes everything which the public needs. When a street is imperatively needed, it walks through a man's front entry. Why may it not pay him for good behavior when it is important that he should behave well, and he won't without being paid? Nonsense about power! Before your war, such talk would do for demagogue pettifoggers; but now you have learned what government means— that it means governing. Your Central Park means that you have decided to live in New York, not merely to sell goods there. It is a turning-point. Your city has had a narrow, a very narrow, escape from being a mere commercial railway terminus—a sort of Aspinwall on an isthmus between two vast seas of traffic. This Park means that you can, and will, live in New York, and love it as your city, take a pride in it, and make a home of it. Don't let it be spoiled. And—I sail for the Cape next week—drop me a line by-and-by to tell me how you succeed.' "

DESIGN No. 23.

First-floor Plan.

1. Main entrance; 2. Vestibule; 3. Main hall; 4. Staircase; 5. Parlor; 6. Reception-room; 7. Dining-room; 8. Butler's pantry, with store-room above; 9. Dumb-waiter; 10. Broom-closet; 11. Elevator; 12. Private staircase; 13. Skylight and ventilating shaft; 14. Lavatory.

Second-floor Plan.

15. Boudoir; 16. Bedroom; 17. Passage; 18. Dressing-room; 19. Dressing-room; 20. Library; 21. Billiard-room; 22. Lavatory; 23. Linen-closet; 24. Back stairs; 25. Elevator; 26. Broom-closet.

In city houses, where we are confined within lots averaging 25×100, and have to make the best of it, the requirements are necessarily very different from those of a cottage or country mansion, where the broad acres comprising the estate admit of a structure having the dimensions of a

Parlor, in Design No. 23.

five-story house, built all on one floor. We have previously attempted to illustrate the Queen Anne style as applied to country work, and now offer a design showing its adaptability to city architecture. In this instance,

Philadelphia brick and Ohio stone trimmings form the constructive color of the walls. This building is five stories above the basement, and might be allowed still another story without marring its proportions, which shows how admirably adapted this treatment is to buildings requiring great height—a virtue that the Gothic style does not possess. As a twenty-five-foot lot is insufficient for a building of this class, it is proposed that the owner should, if possible, purchase five feet of the adjoining lot, making his thirty feet in width, by this means rendering the avenue or bay-window front the more imposing.

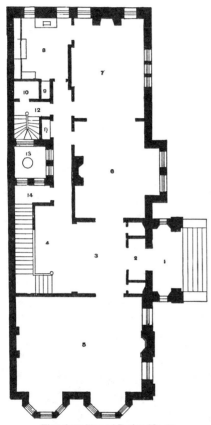

First-floor Plan of Design No. 23.

Ascending the entrance porch, which is some sixteen feet wide, we enter a hall-way of the same width, terminating with the grand staircase. On the left of this hall is the drawing-room, running the entire width of the house. This apartment, the interior of which we have illustrated, is twenty feet wide, independently of the two bay-windows, and has its wood-work of ebonized maple, with its lines picked out in a color resembling ivory. The chimney-piece is panelled the height of the frieze, and embellished with a bracket canopy, above which is a shelf for old china. The cove underneath is covered with stamped leather, while a low, bevelled mirror occupies the space between it and the mantel. Between the bay-windows is shown a cabinet for bric-à-brac, of the same style as the mantel.

In these interior views I have left out most of the furniture, in order that the architectural proportions shall be more clearly displayed.

Opposite the parlor is the reception-room, 18 × 20, including the bay-window. This connects with the dining-room, 16 × 20, including the niche for the sideboard. It is proposed not to separate these rooms by sliding-doors. In their place, there is a narrow screen standing out from the walls, which may serve as a frame for curtains. These screens always seem to add an air of cosiness to an apartment. Sliding-doors, on the contrary, look stiff; they give the room a barren appearance, and, like an awkward person's hand, are always in the way. I should prefer abolishing all doors where security does not demand them, and substituting curtains. In like manner, rooms divided by screens about two-thirds the height of the ceiling have a great advantage over those separated by partitions, inasmuch as each room seems larger, and has a freer circulation of air. The screens may be made to appear like pieces of furniture, and, if desirable, they may be portable, so that on occasion they can be removed altogether. Then if, as in the present instance, the dining-room be small, it can readily be thrown into connection with the reception-room, and the table extended so as to occupy both apartments.

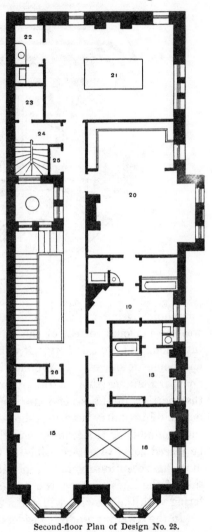

Second-floor Plan of Design No. 23.

Stained glass forms a prominent part in the decoration of this room; for as there is no particular view from the dining-room windows, the middle section alone is left clear. By also introducing stained glass into the panels of the screen, a light and brilliant effect is obtained.

As we ascend the grand staircase, we find that the second story is devoted exclusively to the lady and gentleman of the house. The boudoir is situated on the avenue front. This, being a lady's apartment, is fitted up in light woods, and the colors selected for the decorations are cheerful and transparent. One of the peculiarities of the room is the cove extending on each side of the ceiling, but not across the ends. This has something the effect of a canopy over the walls, apparently lowering their height, and giving an air of snugness to the apartment.

In a house of this character, a private parlor for the mistress is essential. Here she may receive her more intimate friends and transact all

Boudoir, in Design No. 23.

household business. The boudoir, or "lady's bower," of the olden time was the personal retreat of the mistress, where she escaped all noise and intrusion. At the same time, it was easily accessible from the living-rooms and domestic offices. In the city it is, of course, difficult to arrange such an apartment as this on the parlor floor; we have therefore placed it in that portion of the second story specially devoted to the mistress of the house. In country mansions, however, where there is sufficient room on the ground-floor to accommodate the domestic offices, the boudoir should be placed so as to be accessible to these, and also in a position to act as a morning reception-room. If possible, it should be on the south or east side of the house, where, if a conservatory can be arranged without interfering with the view, it will add a great attraction to the apartment.

In the dwelling under consideration there is a private passage connecting the boudoir with the bedrooms and dressing rooms arranged for the gentleman and lady respectively. Both are well lighted, and are accommodated with closets, bath, and toilet rooms. In order to carry out the healthy, and certainly comfortable, idea of sleeping in a cool room and dressing in a warm one, I have shown a small fireplace in each.

Beyond, and connecting with the gentleman's dressing-room, is the library. This is a cosy little apartment, containing a bay-window. An alcove for books is separated from the main room by a transom, beneath which curtains may be hung, shutting off the alcove entirely whenever complete seclusion is required. This room has an open timber ceiling, and parquetry floor covered here and there with rugs. The wall is panelled to the height of the door with old English wainscoting, and the mantel and fireplace are of Sienna marble, with opening and hearth of illuminated tile. The library is connected both with the toilet—adjacent to the dressing-room—and the billiard-room in the rear. On the floor above there are two bedrooms, each containing a bay-window. They have large closets, and are convenient to the bath-room. The remainder of this

Library, in Design No. 23.

story is devoted to the children. The nurseries for day and night are separated by dressing-rooms, and the nurse's room communicates with the children's sleeping-apartment.

The story above has a bath-room and seven chambers, all well lighted.

The servants' apartments are in the attic, which is accessible by a private staircase, the main stairs not extending to this floor. Here, again, we have the advantage of utterly excluding the servants from the main portion of the house by simply locking one door on each floor. Owing to the extreme height of the ceiling of the first story, it may not be necessary to carry the butler's pantry all the way up. Over it an *entresol* may be constructed, serving the purpose of a general store-room, which may be approached by a landing from the private staircase. The house-keeper, whose duties are chiefly confined to the lower part of the establishment, has her apartments on the basement floor. Her accommodations are suitable to a person who must be possessed of refinement and intelligence, in order properly to fill her position of responsibility and trust. Her little parlor, which is on the avenue front, has both fireplace and bay-window, and communicates directly with a small bedroom, closed off during the day with folding-doors. This opens into a spacious pantry, which is supplied with closets for hanging on one side, and a dresser, with drawers, on the other. Beyond this is a bath-room.

At the right of the house-keeper's apartments is the laundry, with stationary tubs and steam drying-room. The servants' hall is roomy; the kitchen contains a large pantry and well-lighted scullery. In this design, also, there is a lift which runs from cellar to attic.

INTERIOR OF DINING-ROOM.

PART II.
FURNITURE AND DECORATION.

CHAPTER I.

INDUSTRIAL ART EDUCATION.

The Necessity of it in the United States.—Impulse given to it by the Centennial.

PERHAPS no industry has suffered more from the want of technical education in our country than the building arts; and although architecture has made great progress in the last ten years, the artist has been

Fig. 1.—Frieze: The Lady of Shalott.

so lamely seconded by the workman as to sadly mar the effect of his designs. Until recently, it has been almost impossible to find skilled artisans; but the necessity has become so great, that we have finally been compelled to import them from abroad. The influence of their introduction has already been greatly felt, and some excellent work is now beginning to appear. It is natural to suppose, however, that but few of the best workmen would come to a new country when their talents are so much better appreciated at home. As a general thing, only the inferior mechanics are willing to emigrate; nor do these meet with much encouragement, as our people have been so educated in an atmosphere of bad art that they esteem good work but lightly. Unhappily, this state of things is likely to continue until some means is devised for improving public taste.

I remember going to a paper-hanging establishment, a short time since, the proprietor of which, while showing me designs from the famous Morris Company of London, mentioned that the taste of the public was at so low an ebb that it offered but little inducement for their importation. He remarked that the Americans were improving in this direction, however; for only a few years ago the worst designs of the European market passed current. As an example of this, he stated that at one time the figures generally selected were so large that it was not an unusual thing to do away with an important door, in order to avoid interfering with the pattern. It has become proverbial among European manufacturers that whatever is so wanting in good taste as to ruin it for the home market will do for the United States. In fact, Europeans have found to their sorrow the folly of sending their choice productions to what they, perhaps with some justice, consider a land of barbaric tastes.

Fig. 2.—Wall-paper.

Although it may seem heresy, in one born and bred in New York, to draw comparisons disparaging to his native city, I must say that in New England, and especially in Boston, art education has made much greater progress than with us. One indication of its advance is the erection, by a number of public-spirited citizens, of a spacious Museum of Architecture, not far from its kindred academy, the Institute of Technology. To this institution the public may have free access, and receive instruction in every branch of illustrative and practical art. It not only contains valuable collections of antique works, but the well-lighted galleries are hung with many elegant paintings, and the library is supplied with choice art publications. There are also apartments for drawing and modelling, and a large lecture-room. It is intended to make this institution serve in Boston the purpose fulfilled by the South Kensington Museum in England; and it is a crying shame that, with all this going on so near us, our own State should be so backward in recognizing the necessity of art education.

The effect produced by an institution of this kind is not merely of an æsthetic character. Its influence has actually a commercial value, as the experience of France will show. There the science of art has been introduced into all manufactures, and the consequence is that, notwithstanding the recent ravages she has sustained, France is to-day in a better commercial position than any other nation. There is an artistic beauty about the articles manufactured upon her soil that draws thither purchasers from all parts of the world.

England, prior to the International Exhibition of 1851, was almost in a state of barbarism as to the industrial arts. Seeing then and there how inferior her works appeared in comparison with those of other nations, she began seriously to reflect upon the cause, and concluded that it must be the fault of the English system of education. From this conviction resulted the determination to afford all classes an opportunity for improvement in the arts of design, by the establishment of technical schools. The consequences are that England at the present time possesses a class of artisans as ably qualified as those of any nation of Europe. Now, unpopular as the reflection may be, can we be considered in any way in advance of what England was in 1851? If not, it is certainly time that we, recognizing our deficiencies, should awake from our lethargy, and take up this subject in a serious manner. Such a school as the South Kensington Museum is sorely needed in this country.

The benefits accruing from such an institution are incalculable. They would extend to every class—from the wealthy, who might visit there for pleasure, to the adult mechanic, who would have the advantage of evening-school, with the best of instruction. Here the painter would be instructed in the harmonious blending of colors and the principles of design, practised in various countries in all ages —a form of education equally useful to the designer of carpets, draperies, and furniture stuffs. Here the carver, who might, perhaps, be able to

Fig. 3.—Wall-paper.

chisel out an ordinary Corinthian capital, with its eternal acanthus, but who would utterly fail to conceive or execute the spirited and ever-varying forms of Gothic scroll or leaf-work, would have eye and hand taught to appreciate and work out these graceful lines with feeling and power. The plasterer might here acquire the subtle touch of the artistic moulder; the fresco-painter would here get the "grammar of ornament" at his fingers' ends. The very stone-cutters might possibly be developed into young Ruskins, and the millennium of art might be speedily expected. The cabinet-maker, the glass-stainer, the potter, all would be nurtured in the love for the beautiful by our lyceum. Simply to enumerate the various trades that would reap its benefits would occupy more space than we can spare. It should also be remembered that the advantages of such schools are, in the end, returned to the patrons themselves, by the impetus given to the arts of every kind.

The Centennial Exhibition did more to stimulate art industry in this country than anything else has ever done. The specimens from abroad of furniture, carpets, hangings, and embroideries formed an opportunity for the art student such as may not occur again in many years. Most of our cities (except New York, which, in its greed for wealth, appears to have no time to give to the development of art) took advantage of the chance offered, and stocked their museums with works of this kind. Philadelphia especially seemed to appreciate her great opportunity, and the Pennsylvania Museum has collected within its art department some of the choicest articles brought from China, Japan, Turkey, Egypt, France, England, and Italy, among which are included bronzes, furniture, pottery, glass, and metal-work. The effect of this collection upon the future manufactures of this State will, no doubt, be most salutary; and we cannot but regret that, while other States are attempting to instruct their workers in design, that New York, with its characteristic apathy—as shown, for instance, in the matter of rapid transit—has been totally unappreciative of this golden opportunity.

The Gothic revival was the initial movement toward reform in domestic furniture. This style, although crude at first, has developed at the present day into one excelling all others for grace and beauty. I think some of the earliest efforts in this line were by Welby Pugin. One characteristic, however, of the furniture designed by him for Windsor Castle was that the finials, buttresses, and crockets were conspicuous in their detail. In these, Pugin himself afterward admitted he had violated nearly all the principles of Gothic construction. In his later efforts he produced some very legitimate work, which gave, perhaps, the first impetus to the reform which was taken up and improved upon by such men as Dr. Dresser, Eastlake, and J. W. Talbert.

Men of such genius could not, however, stand still nor remain in a groove. Mr. Talbert was one of the first to accept the lighter and more graceful treatment of the Queen Anne period. Of this his second book on domestic work affords some choice illustrations.

Any one who visited the Centennial Exhibition with the view of inspecting the various specimens of industrial art, must have been struck with the uniform excellence of the English furniture displayed. There were some half a dozen exhibits of British manufacture showing woodwork of exceedingly novel design, yet rendered in such a manner as to show great adaptability to various uses. Although setting at defiance many points claimed as essential by Mr. Eastlake, all the constructive principles were retained, while in many cases Jacobean details added a vast improvement to his method.

These specimens vied with each other both in design and workmanship; and all, with scarcely an exception, were good. In fact, England and America were the only countries which seemed to make much display in the line of this particular industry. But although the American exhibits were many, yet most of them—and not all our best houses were represented—compared favorably with the British. Those from Boston, Chicago, New York, and Philadelphia showed great progress in art manufacture.

Among the foremost houses in New York is that of Marcotte & Herter Brothers, whose designs are of the most chaste and elegant character. Messrs. Pottier & Stymus are also doing some beautiful work. Several English houses have recently established branches in our city, among which may be mentioned Cottier & Co., and Cox & Sons. These houses also furnish stained glass and pottery; and the former has done some of the finest Queen Anne decoration in this country, as evinced by numerous private residences, which have been entirely fitted up by this firm.

At the Centennial the exhibit of Robert Ellen & Co. showed some exquisite work; and, although the specialty of this house is carving—the excellence of which is attested by the new reredos and chancel wood-work of Trinity Church, New York—still their furniture is of the most honest and artistic character.

A set of furniture by C. R. Yandell, exhibited at the Centennial, was conspicuous for its coverings of stamped leather. This gentleman is now manufacturing some of the most beautiful specimens of this material in various colors. The stamping of plush also, for the same purpose, is extensively carried on by this house.

The author is indebted to the *American Architect and Building News* for some of the Centennial descriptions. The following extract from one of its articles on the furniture exhibits may prove interesting:

"The wonderful strides recently made in the revival of the earlier eighteenth-century work are seen everywhere. Under the names of Queen Anne and Free Jacobean, this seems too likely to become only a fashion, from which any change may lead to an abandonment of the really valuable constructive principles which underlie the style, and bring it into close alliance with the Gothic, or thirteenth-century, revival. Whatever may be said against the adoption of Elizabethan or Jacobean forms in external architecture, the objection will not hold with regard to the treatment of interior woodwork, and the construction of the furniture of those periods. Herein the two styles stand on common ground, the later style having the advantage of lightness of construction, while the other is pre-eminently great in the treatment of details — carving and decoration. The English furniture partakes largely of both elements. The works of Schoolbred & Co., Collinson & Lock, Cooper & Holt, William Scott Morton & Co., and Howard & Sons, may be classed together in this style, which is practised by all alike with remarkable harmony. Straight wood predominates in

Fig. 4.—Wall-paper.

all. Mouldings are worked on the solid. Mitred mouldings are used sparingly, and might better have been dispensed with altogether. They are generally around the tops of the larger pieces, and are not the huge cornices to be seen on so many American pieces, but fine mouldings of many members, having but slight projection, and therefore offering but little opportunity for opening at the mitres by shrinkage or swelling. Panel-decoration is sometimes carved, either in imitation of old work, or with original designs, and always in relief; sometimes treated with cast-bronze or *repoussé* work; sometimes with majolica, both in relief and painted; sometimes with paintings on vellum or wood; and sometimes on porcelain. Some of the most elegant panel-work is in inlaid woods."

Messrs. Pottier & Stymus have recently executed some very beautiful ebonized furniture for the residence of Judge Hilton, of New York. In it there is a striking contrast of white lines and decoration, which has much the effect of ivory inlay. Some of their ormolu furniture also is much admired.

CHAPTER II.

COLOR.

Interior Decorations directed by Architect.—Theory, Effects, and Gradations of Color.—
Symmetry.

IT has been said that he who designs the outside of a house should also
design the interior. I would go a step farther, and claim that, in order
to secure harmony, the same mind that conceives the original structure
should guide the arrangement of all its details, including color, decoration,
furniture, and carpets. This, however, seldom occurs. It is true that, in
building our dwellings, the assistance of an architect is called in; but
when the work of the carpenter and plasterer is finished, his services are
generally no longer required. An artist in the shape of an upholsterer of
totally different feeling is usually employed to complete the work, which
he may do in utter contrast with the original spirit of the design. Certain details, intended, perhaps, to be emphasized by distinction of color,
become subdued by being treated in a subordinate manner; and if one
style of architecture is employed in the construction, an entirely different
idea may be carried out in the decoration.

Color decoration, in particular, offers a broad field for the crude attempts of the modern tyro; and the unmeaning forms and less harmonious tints he employs, instead of gratifying, are likely to become an outrage
to good taste. Now, in order to overcome this difficulty, it would be well
to establish among first principles the theory of complementary colors;
and although we do not propose to make this volume in the least technical, perhaps a few remarks in regard to their harmony will not come
amiss.

We know almost instinctively that blue will not harmonize with green,
and that red will; but the theory upon which this contrast is based is but
vaguely understood. We remember studying in our "Natural Philoso-
phy" that white is the reflection of all colors; that is, that all the primary colors combined produce it. It is the general impression that there
are seven primary colors, viz., those seen in the rainbow; whereas, in reality, there are but three—blue, red, and yellow.

Green, orange, and purple are secondary colors, produced by mixing the primaries. Thus, blue and yellow make green; red and yellow produce orange; and blue and red, purple.

The mixture of these, again, creates what are called tertiary colors, such as citrine, olive, and russet. Orange and green form citrine; purple and orange, russet; and green and purple, olive.

A knowledge also of the quantities in which these colors may be made to harmonize is requisite. The whole art lies in combining them in the proportions which produce white. These, in the primaries, are five of red, three of yellow, and eight of blue; in the secondaries, thirteen of purple, eleven of green, and eight of orange; and in the tertiaries, twenty-four of olive, twenty-one of russet, and nineteen of citrine.

A primary color—say red—placed contiguous to the secondary green, which is its complementary (being composed of the two remaining pri-

Fig. 5.—Hunting Scene.

mary colors, blue and yellow), and arranged in the above proportion, produces the harmony required. It is also a fact that, in looking at any color, its complementary is reflected. Thus, green reflects red; and, when the two colors are placed in juxtaposition, both become more intense, whereby richness of effect is produced. To complete the formula, blue and orange, also yellow and purple, are harmonious; for in each case, when mixed in the right proportions, all the colors producing white are present.

By certain combinations, color may have an enlivening or depressing effect. For example, blue is a cold, quieting color; while red is warm and exciting. Each affects the mind in a different manner. Again, prominence or subordination may be given by their employment. For instance, blue produces the effect of distance, and, if placed upon the ceiling, causes it to appear higher, or, if in a recess, will deepen it. Yellow, on the contrary, appears to advance toward the eye; and, if used upon the ceiling, will seem to lower it, or, if upon a projecting moulding, will exaggerate its prominence. Red is the only color that remains stationary. Colors inharmoniously disposed are as painful to the practised eye as are discordant sounds to the musical ear.

It is generally admitted that furniture and costume show to a better advantage when the walls of an apartment are dark, while pictures look well upon a light background. In order to accommodate these requirements, the dado, or lower three feet of the walls, may be dark in color; the surface, where the pictures are to be hung, of a neutral tint; while in the cornice and ceiling any number of brilliant hues may appear. By this means a harmonious gradation of colors is achieved. Indeed, it would be well if this arrangement of colors were to be made the rule in decorating apartments. The heaviest and richest colors should be upon the floor or near it, and the lightest and most brilliant either upon or in the neighborhood of the ceiling.

A dark color, also, when applied to a skirting, or dado, gives the effect of strength, which is always desirable to suggest in parts bearing a superincumbent weight. Brown, rich maroon, dull bronze-green, or even black, may be used here to advantage.

Now, I think I hear some ladies object to this system, not only on the ground that, if the clear surface of the wall is too much broken up, the ceilings appear low, but that so many varieties of color destroy the dignity and injure the repose of an apartment. In answer to this, let me ask if the ladies, while exercising their usual good taste, do not exemplify precisely this same rule in their dress? Their shoes are dark, and their dresses neutral, while the gay and brilliant colors are reserved for their heads and shoulders.

This gradation of color from deep to gay is borrowed from the Great Architect; for, in nature, how often do we see the same system carried out; as, for instance, in a mountain capped by brilliant clouds at sunset! Or, take the tree, for example: the roots and trunk are dark and substantial, giving evidence of strength and durability; the branches are covered with leafy verdure, not pronounced in color; the blossoms, with their ever-varying and brilliant hues, are confined to the summit; while the sky (corresponding to the ceiling of a room) is blue—the color of all others which gives an appearance of distance. When applied to our rooms, blue has always the effect of enlarging them, and—to go on still farther in imitation of nature—if the ceiling be powdered with stars, or decorated with the figures of birds in the act of flying, we have a legitimate relief, and one that is, perhaps, among the most effective of all treatments. This system of wall decoration is nothing new; for, not only do we find instances of it in some of the rooms discovered in the recent excavations of Pompeii, but we know that it was practised by the ancient Greeks.

The association of color with strength claims a larger part in decoration than is generally supposed. Thus, the trimmings of the exterior of a dwelling, if painted a color darker than the body, seem to produce a constructive effect, and convey the idea of ribs and stanchions supporting the house. So, too, the frame of a panel, if painted darker, gives the idea of strength, while the panel itself, being light, appears to be supported.

A skirting or margin also, having in any way the effect of a frame, should be emphasized by a stronger color. This includes cornices and trimmings of doors and windows. These trimmings, or architraves, as they are called, should be of a color more pronounced than the wall, but not so dark as the surbase, unless black be introduced, in which case one or two narrow lines of bright color or gold may be added. When black is used, it would be well to have a portion of it polished, thus producing a contrast between a bright and dead surface.

Fig. 6.—Garden Scene.

The doors of an apartment should be darker than the walls — something in tone between them and the trimmings. Thus, if a wall be citrine, the door may be low-toned Antwerp blue or dark bronze-green; but in either case a line of red, being complementary to both, should be run around the trimmings.

The usual mode of treating sashes is in white, or, at least, some light color; but they may obtrude themselves less against a fine landscape if painted black. Then, by having the architraves the same color, and the jambs bronze, green, or olive, a very cosy effect will be produced. In this case we should advise that the stop-beads be of Indian red—a very beautiful color, formed by the mixture of vermilion and ultramarine-blue. Then, if amber-colored shades be used instead of white, no curtains will appear necessary. If the walls be of cream-color, with maroon and black surbase, the effect will have a completeness eminently satisfactory.

As regards symmetry in construction, Nature was always the model selected by the Greeks. According to Vetruvius, the Greek column was modelled after the figure of a woman, its diameter being one-eighth of its altitude—the same proportion which the female foot bears to the height of the body. The flutes of the column are supposed to represent her dress, devoid, of course, of the modern innovation known as crinoline, but hanging in graceful folds, as in the time of the ancients. The flowing outline of its capital may be readily imagined to represent the female head-dress.

It has been proven by actual experiment that there are certain forms which appear more lofty than others of an equal height, when treated irrespective of these laws of proportion. How many of us have tried to guess the height of a gentleman's hat! You are fully under the impression that this cylindrical piece of felt will measure nine or ten inches, which distance being marked upon the wall, and the hat itself adjusted to it, to your infinite amazement, you discover that it measures no more than six inches from rim to crown.

The perfectly formed human figure has pre-eminently this advantage. If the statue of Apollo and a plain cylinder were to be seen remote from each other, there would be found a marked difference in their apparent altitude, so that one would scarcely imagine they were the same height until convinced by seeing them placed side by side.

As I have said before, the principle of proportion, shown in the classic column, is that adopted by the ancient nations in their wall decoration— the frieze bearing to the wall the proportion of the capital to the column, the dado that of the pedestal. I contend, therefore, that the system of breaking up our wall surfaces, if carried out under these laws, adds to, rather than diminishes, the apparent height. This is no doubt the reason why, in England, the height of the ceilings is being materially lessened, the architect trusting to this method of embellishment to counteract the effect produced. Of course, in every case it is necessary to observe the correct proportions, otherwise the appearance of the room will be destroyed. Thus, in a high ceiling the width of dado and frieze should be increased. In great halls or public buildings, where the ceilings are unusually high, the frieze may sometimes be deepened to an equal width with the wall space, the advantage of this being that a greater amount of elaborate decoration may be displayed, and the figures drawn upon a larger scale. Men and horses may sometimes appear to a better advantage when drawn the size of life.

CHAPTER III.

PAPER-HANGING.

Selection of Patterns.—Adaptation of Colors.

A FREQUENT method of decorating our rooms is by the employment of wall-papers. These possess the advantage of being cheap, easily hung, and highly finishing in their effect—certainly great recommendations, if only taste be exercised in their selection. As I have said before, the architect is seldom consulted in these matters, and people generally use their own judgment, or that of their upholsterer, whose main object is to hit upon something "pretty and stylish."

One may choose a light-tinted paper for a dark room, or a small pattern for a small one; but, further than this, no rules are likely to be observed in the selection. The height, size, lighting, furniture, and purposes of the apartment are usually left unconsidered.

There is not now the excuse which heretofore existed for not employing wall-paper of a becoming pattern. Formerly that offered for sale was of so crude a character, that a simple whitewashed wall was far more agreeable. But, like most other industries that have come under the influence of the general advance in decorative art, the manufacture of wall-paper has greatly improved. The English, particularly, have paid special attention to the production of attractive wall-papers. The ablest artists are exercising their most brilliant efforts in developing this branch of industry. We were formerly almost entirely dependent upon the French for designs, many of which were considered very beautiful; but compared with those now produced by the English, they are as the American architecture of the early settlers to that of the present day. The breaking up of wall surface with frieze and dado is one of the peculiar characteristics of the English designs, and in this way some of the best combinations of color and pattern are produced. The dados are sometimes of a checkered chocolate pattern, relieved with gold and black; while the intermediate space above contains a neutral design, as introducing moss or delicate ivy. The frieze is of an utterly different treatment, sometimes Japanese in character, positive in color, and either conventional or natural in design. In some, storks, or other fowl, in various attitudes, seem gliding through the air. In others, vines and trellis-work, laden with vivid green and golden fruit, relieve the frieze, as if the intermediate space represented a wall or screen, over which various scenes of the vegetable and animal kingdom are made to show in bold outline.

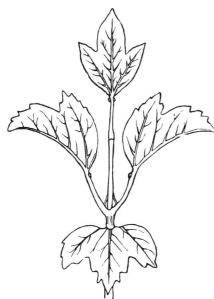

Fig. 7.—Guelder-rose for Wall-diaper.

For a room in which convivial conversation, wines, and viands are to be enjoyed, the color should never be light, but of neutral or complementary tint. In reception-rooms or parlors, the eye should be gratified, the senses of the palate not being brought into competition; and hence floral designs and gay colors —something of an enlivening nature—would be appropriate.

The late Owen Jones remarked that the flatness of a wall should be left undisturbed, and the decoration as little obtrusive as possible. But in how few instances is this rule observed! Instead of the flat diaper in imitation of stencil design, an attempt is made to show figures in relief with shades and shadows. This is in bad taste, and produces a disagreeable effect. Such vulgarisms are, however, happily passing away; yet the public taste is far from being cultivated in these matters; and paper, instead of forming a background to sculpture, pictures, and articles of *virtu*, is apt to assert itself far beyond its due importance.

A wall surface cannot be beautiful unless the forms upon it be of

Fig. 8.—Guelder-rose for Floor Pattern.

good design, and the colors harmoniously applied; yet even in good houses, we find walls which would often be effective if treated in plain tints, rendered offensive, rather than pleasing, by the decorations they bear.

It is not our province here to give special rules for the designing of wall-paper, yet one or two suggestions on this subject may not be inappropriate. A favorite treatment of wall-surface, either in paper or painting, is that of natural foliage, and here it becomes important to study the principles upon which Nature works. Mr. Dresser suggests that the walls being perpendicular, it is necessary that the plant should be viewed from the side, and have an upward direction, as in Fig. 7. This, however, would not apply to a carpet or ceiling, as it would not be in character to represent the flowers vertically. Fig. 7 is one of Mr. Dresser's designs, representing the guelder-rose, as seen from the side, and would be appropriate as a wall-diaper. Fig. 8 is the same spray as seen from above, or, to use the same form of expression, as would be appropriate if used as a floor pattern. Dr. Dresser is one of the leading wall-paper designers in England. One of his designs is represented in Fig. 2. Fig. 4 was designed by Walter Crane especially for the Centennial Exhibition, and, like the two former, was taken from the *Building News.*

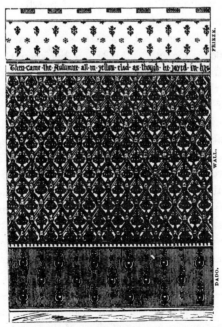

WALL DECORATION.

CHAPTER IV.

CEILINGS.

Cornices.—Mouldings.—Location of Chandelier.—Country Decorators.

THE plaster cornices, at one time so popular, are happily going out of fashion. They are frequently replaced by a simple gilt moulding only. From it pictures are sometimes suspended; but when there is no other decoration, the moulding appears too frail to support so much weight. It is better to employ a different means of attaching paintings to the wall, unless there is a frieze of some description. When this is present, however, it may be terminated with a moulding, from which pictures can be suspended with perfect propriety.

In decorating ceilings, paper may be used, provided tasteful patterns be selected. They should never consist of tawdry imitations of fresco, with cunning corners and marvellous centres.

The position of the principal gas-fixture is somewhat important. Frequently it is placed in a central position between the fireplace and the wall, without regard to the whereabouts of the windows and doors. Thus it interferes with the laying out of the ceiling. The proper position is at the intersection of lines drawn from diagonally opposite corners.

It may not be inappropriate to introduce around the ceiling a margin of some tasteful design in wall-paper—one, for instance, in which brilliant colors appear on a gold ground. In a large room, the effect would be good if this margin were the entire width of the roll. It might also be appropriately edged with a wooden moulding. These mouldings should be small and unobtrusive; and if an inlay of one or two inches wide be made to skirt the border, a moulding on both sides, covering the joinings, would appear to advantage. As a general rule, if light, transparent tints are used, the mouldings should be black. If a dark or maroon inlay is employed, gilt mouldings would make a pleasing contrast.* The remainder

---

* A large moulding on top of the dado may frequently be employed with advantage. It not only improves the appearance, but, if placed at the proper height above the floor,

of the ceiling, if low, should be of some tint calculated to give an appearance of elevation, such as, for instance, one of the many delicate shades of blue or violet. If, however, there be sufficient height to warrant it, a rose tint, or a buff, appears well, provided the general tone of the room will permit. Violet has the advantage not only of increasing the height, but it will also harmonize with paper of a green or olive tint, these being among the best colors for a wall.

In regard to tinting walls and ceilings, it is the custom to delay these finishing touches for a year or two, in order to allow the walls to season, as during this process there is always more or less danger of their cracking. For this reason, the final application of color and decoration is usually postponed until the house is thoroughly settled. We are, therefore, often compelled to endure the monotony of white walls for some time. The advantage of wall-paper is, that we can always order one or two extra rolls, so that, in case of any cracking, the blemishes may be easily repaired. The fresh paper can be so nicely adjusted as to prevent a possibility of detection; whereas, in painting, it is usually necessary to go over the whole room, it being nearly impossible to match the color exactly.

The necessity of waiting, if paint is to be used, is, in one respect, unfortunate; for in the interval one is apt to get out of the spirit of the design, and when the time arrives at which the walls are to be decorated, instead of applying to the architect to superintend this, the crowning part of his work, ninety-nine times in a hundred, as before stated, the owner calls upon the nearest fresco-painter, and verifies our previous remarks. Therefore, I suggest the use of wall-paper, in order that the finishing touches may be applied at once.

Painters, too, especially in the country, have so little idea of their art that it is almost impossible to get a satisfactory piece of work done. In this, as in other matters, it is frequently supposed that it is only necessary for the architect to give his ideas, and that an ignorant mechanic may be trusted to carry them out. The fact is, that unless he stands over the work, and virtually does it himself, he will hardly be able to recognize his own design. This business of gratuitously teaching the quasi-decorator the mysteries of his art is too often inflicted upon the professional man, whose only reward is the odium provoked by badly executed work. If

---

it will also serve to protect the wall from the chafing of chairs and other furniture. For the reason that we have before expressed—that the lower members ought never to be light—gilt mouldings should not be placed below the level of the eye. Therefore, black walnut or ebony are more appropriate here.

the same person would continue with the master, the latter would be able to reap some benefit from the instruction he gives, by getting subsequent work properly performed. In this case the teaching might be a pleasant task; but, in his next undertaking, another painter is usually employed, who exceeds the last in ignorance and stupidity. Thus the same ordeal must be gone through again.

The problem is yet to be solved how good work can really be done remote from cities, unless the architect assumes the position of "boss painter," and brings his own workmen. Usually, when he suggests that mechanics from some other locality understand the work better, he is met with the reply that there are excellent painters in the town, and he would be liable to give offense should he undertake to employ others. The country produces painters capable, perhaps, of doing external work; for here the colors, which are generally few, and neutral in their character, can easily be given by sample; but in the case of interior decoration, where a higher degree of skill is required, the ability of our country, and, perhaps, of most of our city "artists," may well be questioned. Indeed, it is scarcely too much to say that those possessing positive skill can almost be counted on one's fingers.

Wall-papers are a simple remedy for this difficulty, as, when the selections have once been made, all that is then necessary is to find a man who can properly apply them. But even here, when the architect selects the paper, it is well for him to make a drawing, showing where each particular pattern should hang, and also to give the matter sufficient attention during the work to see that, after all, the design is carried out.

A wall may be tinted with a distemper color or oil "flatted." The flattening, which is simply removing the gloss by means of stippling, is a great improvement; for shiny walls, like varnished furniture, are objectionable. Oil-color, on account of its durability, seems preferable. Another advantage is, that it can be cleaned without suffering damage. But, so far as delicacy of tint is concerned, water-colors are more beautiful.

A good effect may be obtained by the introduction of a gold background, upon which a small black figure or running pattern is placed. In such cases more gold than black should be visible. On a background of this kind, pictures in ebony and gilt frames appear to great advantage.

CHAPTER V.

BORDERS.

Ceilings.—Friezes.—Stamped Leather.—Legendary Decoration.—Wood-panelling.

CEILINGS are especially susceptible to ornamentation, for the reason that their entire surface may be seen at once. If we wish to limit the decoration of our rooms, let us expend our efforts here, as the walls and floors can be relieved by pictures and furniture. I would recommend the avoidance of structural members, and especially of that *chef d'œuvre* of plaster art, the centre-piece, with its impossible flowers and feeble ornaments. It would be better to use some flat design in color, making it the principal feature of the ceiling, reaching, if you choose, to within a few inches of the border: I say border, as the cornice, unless broad, is much improved by being extended with a margin of color. Now, these borders on the ceiling are like the dado on the wall, and have the effect of breaking up its broad surface. The same

Fig. 9.—Harbor Scene.

rule applies to floors. By surrounding them with a margin of darker color, a similar advantage is attained.

Friezes may be treated as elaborately as desired. They may be powdered, or, if divided into panels, richly colored, either in flat or in relief. If this system be adopted, subjects appropriate to the apartment should be chosen. If, for instance, the frieze of a dining-room be panelled, fruits and game would be in keeping; if continuously treated, some convivial assemblage, or perhaps a hunting scene, would be proper. In a parlor, flowers would appear well; or, if there are no panels, a mythological scene, introducing, for instance, the Muses, or other appropriate figures. In a library, portraits of authors would do, or, if continuous, scenes from historical or poetical works. A library by Messrs. Cox & Sons has the following lines from Tennyson's "Lady of Shalott," carried, as seen in Fig. 1, along the under side of the frieze:

"And there the surly village churls,
And the red cloaks of market girls,
Pass onward from Shalott.

"Sometimes a troop of damsels glad,
An abbot on an ambling pad,
Sometimes a curly shepherd-lad,
Or long-hair'd page in crimson clad,
Goes by to tower'd Camelot;
And sometimes thro' the mirror blue
The knights come riding two and two."

Each line which is illustrated fills a section, and the whole forms a pictorial text, reaching entirely around the room.

Fig. 5 represents a hunting scene taken from the catalogue of the same firm, and intended for a dining-room frieze. It is the work of Mr. Rossiter, and is a good example of his many happy efforts in wall decoration.

Some beautiful effects are obtained by the introduction of stamped leather. In some cases the ancient leather is used, which material, although much sought after by collectors, can still be obtained from some of our dealers in bric-à-brac at quite reasonable prices. In one house I have in mind, where the frieze was of this material, the wall space was covered with mediæval tapestry.

There is a quaint style of decoration, of which we give two illustrations. Being something of the Albert Dürer school, it is suitable for panels and stained glass. The garden scene (Fig. 6), from Cox & Sons, is by the celebrated J. Moyr Smith, the well-known illustrator of some of Marcus Ward's publications; and the harbor scene (Fig. 9), showing ships and fortress, is by Mr. B. J. Talbert. Both are striking illustrations of this style.

A great deal of feeling as well as effect may be shown by what is known as legendary decoration; that is, the working up texts and proverbs along our walls. Friezes offer especial opportunity for this. Sentences may also be placed over door-ways in such a manner as not only to express a sentiment, but denote the purpose of the apartment; as, for ex-

ample, "Welcome" over a reception-room; or "Hospitality" over a dining-room. Some very appropriate devices for fireplaces have been employed with significance and effect, such as, "Well befall hearth and hall!"

I have recently fitted up two dining-rooms, in which this style of decoration is worked into the stained glass. Among others, I selected the
following mottoes: "Hunger is the best sauce;" "Welcome is the best
cheer;" "Eat at pleasure; drink by measure."

Upon the walls of dwelling-houses of the sixteenth and seventeenth
centuries, a system of wood-panelling was employed with very satisfactory
results. The mouldings seldom projected beyond the surface, but were
cut in solid wood. The panel itself projected slightly, as illustrated in
the diagram (Fig. 10), which repre-
sents that over a fireplace. The
centre ornament may be carved in
wood, modelled in plaster, or stencilled on its surface. Should a low
mirror be placed beneath, it would
be in keeping to have the glass bevelled like the panels. The stiles
were frequently moulded with sunk-
en grooves upon their surfaces, resembling the ridges on old-fashioned gingerbread, a term first applied
to this kind of ornamentation, and
afterward to tawdry decoration of
wood-work in general. These, however, seldom returned, but ran continuously to the end of the member.
The ceilings were occasionally treat-

Fig. 10.—Wood Panel.

ed in a similar manner, but more frequently the rafters were left exposed, the edges being moulded and embellished with color.

After the introduction of plastered walls, this panelling was simply
applied as a wainscot, the usual height being from one-third to one-half
of the wall. Another system, also much in vogue, was that of hanging
the walls with tapestry. Haddon Hall, one of the finest baronial mansions of that period, was treated in this manner. One peculiarity of this
structure was the absence of wood-work around the door-ways, so that
when the doors were closed, being covered with the same material, they
did not produce a break in the pattern.

Another favorite custom of the Queen Anne period, before paper-hanging was invented, was to cover the walls, above the wainscot, with stamped leather. This system of decoration, as before mentioned, was productive of some of the best results. The ground-work was usually of silver or gold, upon the surface óf which scroll-work of the period was introduced in relief. This was frequently treated with some of the richest effects of color, the whole producing an exquisite result, and one which our modern paper-stainers have failed to achieve.

CHAPTER VI.

BACKGROUNDS.

Harmony of Colors.—Majolica Ware.—Bric-à-brac.

THE following remarks are taken from some of the leading English authorities: "Wherever pictures are hung, the hangings should be of one or two tones of the same color. Another important rule is: if one large picture forms the decoration, the dominant color of the paper should be complementary to that of the painting. For gilt frames, olive-gray and deep green are appropriate. It has been laid down by Chevreul that engravings or lithographs should never be placed beside colored pictures. The same rule holds good with regard to all monochromes, such as photographs, though we may often see the mixture in drawing-rooms, whose occupants would scorn to be told of their want of taste. A light gray, or neutral tint, or dark maroon is, perhaps, best adapted for engravings. The predominant color of the furniture should be studied after that of the pictures and other works of art. A 'harmony of analogy,' in which the colors of both walls and furniture enter, may be adopted, or, at least, a contrast between them. If mahogany is the prevailing material, the wall, as well as the carpet, should be devoid of reddish or orange tints. The walls and floors should agree by approximation of color, though of different tones, with that of the furniture; or, if a contrast be desired, the walls and floor may be of some color complementary to the furniture.

"For old china, if the prevailing color is blue, the wall-tints should be complementary—composed of red and yellow. Citrine and orange grays are best adapted. Greens partake too much of the color to afford a due contrast. Where objects of high art do not intrude, our walls and rooms should be studied solely with regard to architectural propriety, lighting, etc. For example, a suite of rooms, communicating by folding-doors or openings, should harmonize as much as possible. Thus, the dining and billiard rooms may, in many houses, if *en suite*, be treated in the same manner. They may have the walls painted or stuccoed of a gray-drab or chocolate hue, or they may be panelled throughout. For wood-panelled walls, parquetry or wooden floors are more agreeable than tiles.

"Woven wall-hangings, and stuffs for seats and curtains, need equal care in the assortment of the colors. The wood-work of the room, or the furniture, should afford a pleasing contrast with the stuffs, so that each may be enhanced. Thus, violet or blue stuffs contrast best with yellow or orange-colored woods, and green stuffs with red-colored woods, such as rosewood and mahogany. The same applies to grays in which either of these hues predominates. But depth of tone is another consideration. A deep-colored stuff is contrasted best with a wood-color of the same depth. If the tones are very different, the same color for both stuff and wood is desirable, or a harmony of analogy becomes best. The same with wood-panelling."

A friend of mine once remarked that he had never particularly admired faience or majolica ware until he visited the British Commissioners' Buildings at the Centennial Exhibition. There he was particularly impressed by the beauty of these manufactures, as the peculiar and somewhat subordinate treatment of the rooms, furniture, and decorations set them off to the best advantage. In every case the wall-paper harmonized so perfectly as to make them appear like jewels against its surface.

There are many families, having fine collections of china and porcelain, who lock them up carefully in a dark closet, or, at best, set them in a glass cupboard in the butler's pantry, where they are of no use and seldom seen. Now, did the possessors of these gems only know what exquisite effects might be produced by displaying them upon the walls of their parlors and living-rooms, they would not suffer them to remain long in obscurity. A rare piece of china upon the wall is often more effective than many ornaments or pictures. The dining-room of Mr. George W. Wales, of Boston, is an example of this treatment. The crimson walls, harmonizing with the green effects of the ceiling, make a good background for the many pieces of porcelain which hang there.

Mr. Charles W. Elliot, in his new book on "American Interiors," speaks of this room as follows: "With the exception of a few pictures lost among them, the walls are occupied with fine examples of Chinese and Japanese porcelain, a few pieces of European work, and some delft plates. Mr. Wales's collection of china is known as the largest and best in Boston, and the method he has adopted of hanging some small part of it is brilliant and effective."

CHAPTER VII.

ADVANCED ARTS ABROAD.

Some Descriptions of late English Work.

A SLIGHT description of some of the late English work that has grown out of the present revival may serve to illustrate a few of the more important principles of decoration. In the Royal Academy Exhibition of 1876, there was a view of the dining-room belonging to the residence of Mr. Henry Taylor, Avenue Road, Regent's Park, London, which has been recently remodelled from the designs of Mr. J. W. Brydon. The whole of the panelling around the room, including bay-window, the front of the sunken fireplace, etc., is of oak, stained dark and wax-polished, while the walls above the panelling are covered with stamped leather. The bay-window opens in the centre into a large conservatory, while from a window in the side opposite the fireplace most charming views of the grounds are obtained. The furniture, which is also of oak, a quaint bookcase in one corner, and a table at the bay-window, are especially worthy of notice. The style throughout is an adaptation of old English work, which seems to lend itself very easily to modern requirements. At the entrance to the grounds there is a picturesque lodge, also in the same style, built of red brick and half-timbered work, presenting a carefully designed gable-window toward Avenue Road.

Another of Mr. Brydon's designs at the Academy is the hall and staircase of a house at Salna, the residence of Thorsten Nordenfelt, Esq., one of the commissioners for Sweden. This is also a good study of seventeenth-century work, adapted to the requirements of a modern country residence. The staircase and the panelling of the hall are executed in pine, stained dark, and waxed. The chimney-piece is of American walnut; the coping around the hearth (which takes the place of the fender) and the jambs are of fossil marble; the sides of the fireplace and hearth are of tile. The floor of the hall is of oak, stained dark, with parquetry border. All the interior fittings, including furniture and decoration, have been most carefully worked out from drawings by the architect.

Another Academy drawing illustrates a dining-room designed by Mr. B. J. Talbert. A screen is shown in which stained-glass panels are introduced, the principal framing being oak with ebony mouldings. The oak, instead of being stained in the usual way, is, however, treated by fumigation, so as to get a dark-brown color from the wood itself. This is not merely on the surface, but penetrates for a considerable distance. The dado is of waxed pine; the walls are of a neutral-green color, with a small stencilled diaper of red and yellow, separated by gold lines. Above this, the frieze has panels with alternate black and gold ground, ornamented with fish, fowl, fruit, etc.

The green parlor at Doune Lodge, by Mr. J. Moyr Smith, is well worth noticing. The chimney-piece is of unpolished oak, with illustrated tiles of buff and brown. The subjects are selected from the industrial and historical designs executed by this celebrated artist. The tiles nearest the grate are of Dutch manufacture, and are ornamented with floral decorations upon a dark-blue ground. The subjects of the stained glass in this room are connected with Egyptian, Greek, and Gothic art, the actual painting being done by Mr. Smith himself. The wood-work of the windows, doors, etc., is painted a bluish green. The dado is of a rich color, chiefly composed of carmine and brown pink. The upper part of the wall is of a tint between a citrine-green and drab, the pattern being of a lighter shade of the same.

The following extract from the *Building News* is a description of Mr. Norman Shaw's dwelling at Hampstead:

"On a charming slope commanding an extensive dell of the landscape, Mr. Norman Shaw, A.R.A., has built himself a house of the thorough Queen Anne style. No one can mistake the authorship: the tall chimney shafts, with vertical strips of cut brick-work, terminating in a moulded cornice of brick, with their end faces relieved by pedimental compositions, rise from a tiled roof, and put us in mind of a dozen other works by the same architect. In plan the house is rectangular; the front is straight-faced, broken by two bays of singular difference in treatment, and for anything the casual observer may divine, the small, flat-faced, circular-cornered oriel of rough plaster and wood, breaking out from one side, may be an insertion of later date. On the other side, the bay springs from the ground, and is a bold semi-octagon in plan, the upper two stories being corbelled out from the lower portion by a very characteristic corbel of red cut brick-work, in which a deep cyma-reversa moulding is conspicuous. Over both bays are deeply moulded, painted, wooden barge-boards, with ornamental tile filling-in to gables, and between the larger bay and the angle of roof

there is a quaint cutting-back of the roof, with a weather-boarded front
and door—a sort of cosy belvedere or gallery, from which the landscape
may be surveyed over the parapet. The windows are irregular in height
and position, betraying a want of uniformity in the interior levels, and

Fig. 11.—Hall and Staircase.

are arched segmentally; the arches have the moulded label and keystone,
and the sills cut-brick fringings. Though entirely of red brick, there is
a pleasing contrast in the painted white wooden window-frames and sash-
bars and the circular-shaped heads and transoms in the oriel, while the
rough and weather-stained plastering between the windows of the latter

increases the piquancy. The dining-room has a novel and unique interior. It is, we understand, very lofty—fifteen or sixteen feet high; the fireplace is large and deep, forming a recess for 'side settles,' while above it an

Fig. 12.—"Anglo-Japanese" Parlor.

octagon-shaped bay-like projection, with a casement, protrudes, and forms a small retreat overlooking the room: access to this 'little sanctum' is obtained from a small door at the side of the fireplace. In another room of about eight feet pitch, projecting screens of wood-work slightly on the splay form a deep recess for the fireplace, on one side of which is an outlook with a settle, reached by a few steps from the floor level. To all intents, we have here an artist's house, in which conventional arrangements are superseded both internally and externally. Whatever the opinion of the ordinary passer-by may be, Mr. Shaw, in this instance, has allowed his artistic predilections full scope, and has shown, at least, how red brick-work and wide-barred sash-frames may be made picturesque by boldly rejecting all modern notions of house-building."

Perhaps one of the most remarkable specimens of decoration is a room which is now being executed in London by the celebrated artist, Mr. Whistler. The following extract from one of Mr. G. W. Smalley's letters to the *New York Tribune* gives an interesting description:

"London, Febuary 17th.

"One of the things in London most talked about for a week or two past has been Mr. Leyland's dining-room, to the decoration of which Mr.

Whistler has devoted himself. Friends of the artist have been permitted from time to time to have glimpses of it, but it is only quite lately that the work has come near enough completion for the layman to judge of the general effect. I have seen it twice, but I quite despair of giving anything like an adequate description of it. Mr. Whistler names it the Peacock Room, and calls his decorative work a harmony in blue and gold. These two colors, and these only, are to be seen on walls, and ceiling, and floor. The only design employed is from the peacock—either the bird himself, or his plumage, or his eye. With this severely simple *motif*, the variety obtained is very great. The room is, I should guess, thirty feet by twenty, and fifteen feet high. The ceiling is divided into sections, and upholds eight pendent lamps, which reach downward not more than three feet into the room. The lamps are each treated as centres, and from each is seen spreading a pattern invented from the eye of the peacock. The groundwork of the whole ceiling is gold, and on this the eye is repeated in different arrangements, alternating with a pattern from the breast feathers. Wherever on the walls there is a gold groundwork, the treatment is the same or similar—there are but the two patterns; yet so ingeniously are they varied, that at first sight you would say the patterns were a dozen or more. They are diversified in size, and the actual touch of the brush is never in two places quite the same; but from his fidelity to his pattern the painter never departs. I need not point out how much higher is the ingenuity requisite to attain a successful result with means so

Fig. 13.—Library Table.

simple than if the artist had permitted himself to introduce other forms. The eye reappears all along the lower edge of the cove beneath the throat feathers, with which the cove itself is overlaid. On the dado, or that part of the wall which rises for some three feet immediately above the skirting-board, blue on gold appears, as on the ceiling, the pattern sometimes larger and sometimes smaller, and the eye, the breast feathers, and the throat feathers being combined dissimilarly, with effects changing wherever you look, but always on examination disclosing the same secret.   On

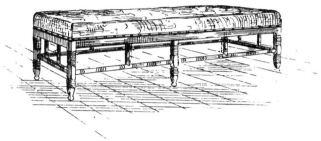

Fig. 14.—Hall Settle.

the walls, from floor to ceiling, light square shafts, divided by shelves and supported by corner brackets of quaint device, break the wall surface here and there on all sides into niches, which are to hold old Nankin blue-and-white china.   The unbroken wall surface is lined with leather, and colored deep blue; on this blue the eye and the feathers are revealed once more in gold.   The splendor would be quite intolerable if the blue and gold had everywhere met in small patterns or in any pattern; but the eye—I mean the human eye of the spectator—gets the repose it needs on broad spaces of pure blue at the sides, the floor again being covered with a carpet of blue, free from any figure or color whatever.   The shutters to the three windows on one of the long sides are closed, and down a gold ground the sweeping tails of three royal birds descend in blue waves to the floor.   At the farther end the entire wall above the dado is blue, but here the apotheosis of the peacock is reached, and the poem rises to its highest strain.   It is a peacock Valhalla, where two of them are fighting over again the battles of the earth—two gorgeous creatures, all gold, with ruffled plumage and eyes of flame, filled with such spirit and pride as no merely mortal birds ever showed to mortal man.   The eye of flame in one is an emerald, in the other a diamond.   At the opposite extremity of the room, over the fireplace, where a mirror is commonly found, hangs a peaceful portrait in oil of a famous Greek beauty, which left Mr. Whistler's easel many years ago.   The furniture is to be gold; the chairs gold, lined with blue leather; the dining-table to be laid with a blue cloth underneath, and the linen itself to be fringed with azure.   Whether the service will be all gold, or partly blue-and-white china, is an open question.   The only decorations over which Mr. Whistler's will cannot exercise its despotic sway will be the costumes of the men and women who are to dine in this room. I do not see how the men, at least, can be worthy of the occasion, nor even how the ladies, though each may be perfectly dressed as an individual at home, are to agree to harmonize their costumes with the room and with each other. It is possible enough that the discordant hues sure to come together will introduce just the element needed to set off to its height the splendor of the decoration.

"Of Mr. Whistler's success in his daring experiment there cannot be a question. Its least merit, I might almost say, is its absolute originality. Anybody can be original, after a fashion, but to be original, and violate no law of beauty and no canon of art, is a triumph of no common order. Every stroke of the brush is done by Mr. Whistler's own hand. He has not been content to design and leave others to execute; it is safe to say that, if he had, the room would have been something very unlike what it is. Here is to be seen the difference between upholsterers' tricks and the sincerity of an artist of genius. Nobody, not the most untrained eye, could mistake the touch here for that of a mere craftsman. Mr. Whistler has wrought with freedom, and the impression of individual power is as strong as the sense of fresh inspiration and unconventional courage. There may be, as has been said, something of Oriental feeling in his work, partly because he has left out the human element, partly because he has not shrunk from the magnificence nor feared to bring the fierce light

Fig. 15.—Parlor Sofa.

of the East into contrast with London gloom. But, East or West, there is no room like it, and it may be long before an artist of Mr. Whistler's force can again be found to give up half a year of his life to reproducing a scene out of Fairy land."

There are two architects in London whose works have done so much toward the advancement of this reform that it would not seem unfitting to mention them here. The first is Mr. J. W. Brydon, whose design for Mr. Henry Taylor's dining-room we have before described. Mr. Brydon, perhaps more than any other—with the exception of Norman Shaw—has done much to advance the Queen Anne revival. His hall and staircase of Salna House, Rochampton, Surrey, previously illustrated (Fig. 11, taken from the London *Building News*), is one of his many happy efforts at interior wood-work. The staircase and panelling are of pine, stained a rich brown color, and varnished. The chimney-piece is of American walnut, with fossil marble jambs, and fender. The hall floor is of oak, stained dark, with parquetry border. The works of Mr. E. W. Godwin, F.S.A., though not in this school, show some of the most successful attempts at adapting foreign designs to English usage, as Fig. 3, which illustrates the application of Japanese decoration to domestic wall-paper, will testify. Mr. Godwin has also made some remarkable adaptations of Japanese forms to English furniture, of which Fig. 12, also from the London *Building News*, is an example.

CHAPTER VIII.

FURNITURE.

Durability and Honesty in Furniture.—Treatment of Wood.—Graining.—Painting.— Staining.—Oiling and Varnishing.—The Arch.—Cross Grain.—Bent Wood.

HERETOFORE the exterior seems to have exhausted the efforts of the architect; but, with the advance of culture and taste, his province is extending itself over all important details. In order that harmony may be secured, the decorations, and even the furniture, are being designed by the same mind as the building.

We have already alluded, in a former chapter, to the bad taste frequently manifested in color decoration, and we now wish to call attention

Fig. 16.—High-backed Chair.   Fig. 17.—Substitute for a Curved Back.

to some of the prevailing errors in furnishing. Dickens, in his description of the Veneering family, stated that their character assimilated with their furniture: "They smelt too much of the workshop, and their surface was a trifle sticky." This might apply to much of the modern furniture. It appears thin, "shammy," and new, and, like the Veneerings themselves, is adapted to society of the mushroom order.

In furniture, the quality of usefulness stands first, and intimately connected with it is that of durability. The carpenter is compelled to do honest work, to select the best and strongest materials; but with the cabinetmaker deception is easy, and has become habitual. It is really as important that our chairs should hold together as that our walls should stand firm. A cabinet or a sideboard should be of as durable materials and as honestly constructed as a piano, the only difference being that frailty in the one case is ridiculously absurd, while in the other the cheat is not only practicable, but less readily detected. There is no economy in purchasing flimsy furniture. An article that will last a lifetime costs but little more than one which soon falls to pieces.

One branch on which art knowledge has a special bearing is the treatment of wood. A great evil is a want of honesty in its rendering. Veneering, graining, and marbleizing are shams which ought never to be tolerated. There is really no great advantage in veneered furniture, as ordinarily it may be procured of solid material at a little extra cost. The idea of covering an inferior wood with one of more expensive character is like Æsop's fable of the jackass flaunting a lion's skin.

There can be no objection to furniture simply painted. Flat colors, if treated harmoniously, may be made to produce effects which cannot be obtained in the plain wood. Staining, also, is an admirable treatment, as it brings out the grain, and, when relieved by certain lines of color, appears well. The present method of oiling and varnishing pine wood produces an excellent effect. Of course, in this treatment the wood must not only be of the best quality, clear and free from imperfections, but the workmanship must also be of a superior character; and, in order to avoid shrinkage, the greatest care should be taken to have it well seasoned. The method of kiln-drying—that is, subjecting the wood to a high degree of temperature for several days, in order to exhaust its moisture—is the only reliable means of accomplishing this end.

Paint and putty, applied to carpenter's work, have, like veneer, fostered bad workmanship, as imperfect material may be covered up with paint, and bad joints and knotty wood may be disguised with putty, so that, after the work is finished, it is difficult to detect its imperfections; but, like other shams, these devices are sure to reveal themselves in time.

Again, nothing can be more absurd than the practice of imitating in one material a mode of construction which is only legitimate in another, and of neglecting to avail ourselves of the particular method by which the best results can be obtained. The arch—a most ingenious invention —which affords the means of spanning a large space with small pieces, at the same time having great strength, is of the utmost utility in building; but in articles of furniture, where we have no wide space to span, and where wood possesses all the strength required, its use is evidently misplaced. The folly of this becomes the more apparent, when we reflect that the wooden arch is generally composed of a single piece, instead of a number of small ones; and that in order to form it, the wood must be cut across the grain throughout the greater portion of its length, whereby its strength is materially diminished. This we deem one of the chief objections to the Gothic treatment of woodwork. The arch and trefoil are continually rendered in this material, with the same confidence as though it were of the same nature as stone. We frequently see sweeping wooden arches span a Gothic building, giving the idea of support; while, in reality, being across the grain, they can do no more than act as a tracery to relieve an angle or decorate a truss.

Fig. 18.—Curved-back Chair.

This mania for cross grain is equally reprehensible in furniture. It is evident that a chair-leg formed on such a principle must be weak. Yet exceptions may be made to the rule, as in Fig. 16, where a slight curving of the wood is introduced in order to insure greater ease. Still, there are means of accomplishing this end legitimately, as in Fig. 17. Here the back is given an agreeable inclination without any sacrifice of strength being entailed.

Objections are sometimes made to straight work on account of its apparent stiffness. If curves are thought necessary, however, they may be effected in some cases by bending the grain, as in Fig. 18. This is accomplished by steaming the wood, which, after hardening, retains its new shape. Some very beautiful curved effects have been produced in this manner without violating the nature of the fibre.

CHAPTER IX.

LEGITIMATE WOOD-WORK.

Gluing.—Carving in Solid Wood.—Sideboard.—Marble Top.—Fine China.—Painting on
Pottery.

GLUE is responsible for many offenses against good taste. Without it, veneering would never have been invented. With it, the cabinet-maker is enabled to stick on mouldings, carvings, and raised panels after a

fashion that could never be accomplished by legitimate means. By this expression, the writer would be understood to mean that wood, to be manipulated legitimately, must be treated as it grows; that is, cut in the solid, and its nature in all cases displayed. As an example, I have shown a stair newel (Fig. 19), in which the panels and ornaments are worked out of the solid wood. But, it may be argued, by this method the work has all to be done by hand, and that, instead of advancing with the progress of the age, and taking advantage of machinery, we are retrograding, and returning to the primitive system of handwork. To this I reply, the moment art degenerates into mere mechanism, it is lowered in our estimation, as a chromo is but slightly valued in comparison with the original painting. Again, under the machine system, the ornamentation is apt to be excessive; while work done by hand, at the same price, is usually distinguished by its simple and graceful effect.

Another article of furniture, in which nearly every principle of good taste is violated, is the modern sideboard. In Fig. 20, I offer a design,*

Fig. 19.—Stair Newel.

---

* This sideboard was constructed for Mr. Lawrence Waterbury. Under the cove, which is covered with stamped

showing how this useful piece of furniture may be constructed on legitimate principles. Usually, scroll-shaping, machine-carving, and glued panels run riot, the cracks, fissures, screw-heads, and all other imperfections being filled up with putty, and the whole smeared over with shellac or polish, ostensibly to give it brightness, but in reality to conceal its flaws. A system by which defective wood and worse workmanship may be hidden with a coat of varnish certainly has the advantage of cheapness; but, like the man whose respectability is all on the surface, it is a question how long the deceit will escape discovery. In the present design the carvings and mouldings are not only worked out in the solid wood, but the absence of screws, nails, and glue is apparent; stout wooden pins and tennon-joints, such as were used in mediæval framing, being substituted.

Fig. 20.—Sideboard.

We must certainly condemn one appendage, usually considered indispensable, to this piece of furniture—the marble top. A sideboard is intended for the deposit of glass and delicate china. Now, the idea of having frail wares banged down on an unyielding piece of adamant is something revolting in these days of interest in ceramic art. Marble tops were originally intended to protect the wood-work from dampness caused by the water dripping from an ice-pitcher. This might spot varnish and blister veneers; but with solid wood no such precaution is necessary. As a substitute for the marble top, let soft mats be used. These act as a cushion for fragile ornaments.

The custom of displaying specimens of fine china-ware in our rooms as works of art suggests the propriety of providing shelves on the principle of an *étagère* over the sideboard and mantel-piece. These may be cov-

---

leather, a shelf is arranged for ornamental pottery. The doors below are glazed with bevelled glass, and the cupboard encloses a fire-proof safe for keeping silver, the depth of which is increased by the sideboard being built a number of inches into the wall.

ered and backed with leather, which, if of a color complementary to the china, forms an agreeable background. Stamped leather of ornamental designs may be easily procured, and if the spaces underneath the shelves are treated on a cove plan, resembling that of a canopy, they present a very attractive appearance.

This method of decoration is likely to become popular from the fact that painting on pottery is now a fashionable pastime. The ornaments may possess an additional interest from being specimens of the owner's handiwork.

CHAPTER X.

FIREPLACES.

Mantels.—Marble Mantel.—Wooden Mantel.—Open Fireplaces.—The Crane.—Hearths.—
Tile.—Tile in Furniture.—Screens.

MANTELS of wood are, as a general thing, more artistic and attractive than those of marble. Indeed, the specimens of the latter
found in our modern dwellings frequently exhibit such poverty of design
as to be positively ugly. There can be but one objection urged against

Fig. 21.—Marble Mantel.

wood, and that is its liability to catch fire. This difficulty is, however,
easily overcome by placing a border of stone or tile between the grate
and the wood-work, to serve as a protection to the inflammable material of
which the mantel is constructed. Yet, as it will probably be some time

before wooden mantels are by any means universally popular, examples of both kinds are given in the accompanying illustrations.

In Fig. 21, I have shown a design for a marble mantel somewhat elaborate in character, the style being that common in the last century. Fig. 22 shows a wooden mantel of the same period, over which shelves are arranged for ornaments. Naturally, much of the effect depends upon

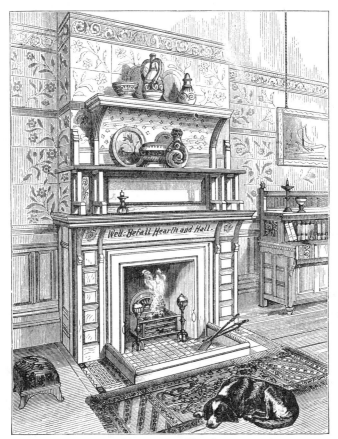

Fig. 22.—Wood Mantel.

what these may be. In the case of wooden mantels, French clocks and ordinary vases should be avoided. Brass-work and pottery are much more suitable. If, however, a timepiece be desired, there are the "cathedral clocks," so called from the resemblance which their striking tones bear to the sound of a distant bell. They are enclosed in a case of bevelled glass, through which the works are distinctly visible.

In the mantel shown in our picture there is a border of stone around the fireplace, which projects beyond the wood-work, and shields it from any mischief likely to be wrought by the heat. This border is also continued as a coping around the hearth, and serves the purpose of a fender. In this way are defeated the nefarious designs of the carpet-man, who delights in rendering an open fire impossible, if by so doing he may display an extra yard of Axminster or Brussels.

To speak of our firesides seems absurd in these days of furnaces. If we have a fireplace at all, it seldom has a fire in it, and is frequently put up as an unmeaning ornament, without even possessing a flue. It is to be hoped, however, that the furnace may soon be a thing of the past, and the cheerful and cheering fire may again illumine the hearth around which, literally, we may form our social circle. We can hardly expect, in these days of anthracite, to revive the delightful old custom of wood fires; still, fire-dogs need not be discarded. An ingenious contrivance in the way of a grate for burning soft coal is now in vogue. It resembles a basket, which is set on andirons in the same manner that we would adjust a back-log, and may be lifted off any time that a wood fire is preferred.

The ancient crane has also its tender associations. I remember seeing a very picturesque arrangement in the studio of one of our New York artists. It consisted of a genial mass of blazing coals, confined in a three-cornered basket, and swinging merrily from a crane suspended above the hearth.

These fireplaces were very common about the time of the Revolution, and may yet be found in some of the old colonial houses. At this time of Centennial reminiscences, it would seem fitting to revive the fashions of "those good old colony days," and let the rising generation see the wainscoted chamber of the ancient manor-house, with oaken floors and the traditional old chimney-piece, with its quaint, pictorial tiles around the border. Interiors such as these have been the theme of many artists of the present century, prominent among whom is Mr. E. Wood Perry, whose pictures are mostly drawn from the real. One of these, entitled "Fireside Stories" (Fig. 23), we have taken the liberty of engraving.

It has been suggested elsewhere in this volume that in library or sitting rooms the mantel should be placed opposite the windows, so that, when facing the fire, the reader's back may be toward the light. But in a dining-room it is better to place the mantel at the end; for, unless this apartment is unusually wide, there will not be sufficient space between the table and the fire, either for the comfort of those seated on that side or for the convenience of the waiter.

Hearths should be a subject of serious consideration. The ordinary

marble hearths, an inch and a quarter thick, which have hitherto been
attached to our mantels, are utterly inadequate to resist the heat of a wood

Fig. 23.—" Fireside Stories."

or even a grate fire. For this reason, it has been found necessary to construct a fender combined with a metal hearth, in order to screen the real
one from the heat which it is itself unable to bear. These false contrivances seem, in our day, too trivial to be tolerated; for, if we have a hearth,
why not let it be of a material which would actually stand the fire, and
dispense altogether with these metal makeshifts which have so long dis-

graced our firesides? Tile, like terra-cotta, from the fact of its having been exposed to a high degree of heat in its manufacture, is capable, above any other material, of resisting the influence of fire, and the glaze upon its surface is of such a nature that it may undergo, for years, the roughest treatment without showing the slightest scratch. Tile is really not much more expensive than marble or slate, and it is both durable and easily cleaned. Not only is it an improvement over white marble as regards utility, but affords a relief in color, and enhances the beauty of our rooms. In this way tile may be made to play its legitimate part in household decoration. But to attempt to use such a material in furniture or elsewhere seems singularly inappropriate. Tile is especially adapted for the lining of bath-tubs, or for a wainscoting back of a washstand, or in any position where hardness is required, as in a floor; but to make the top of a table of tile, as if it were a rostrum to stand upon, rather than a place upon which to put delicate china or glass, is one of those follies that we can only excuse on the plea of ignorance.

Fig. 24.—Screen Panel.

The introduction of tile into wood panels is another instance of the absurdities into which some manufacturers have fallen while displaying their zeal in promoting the revival of ancient fashions.

Screens can often be employed with great advantage, as well as effect, in a dining-room, where that apartment is of sufficient size. I give an illustration of one (Fig. 21), in which the panels are filled up with embroidery, consisting of flowers and birds.

Fig. 24, from the catalogue of Messrs. Cox & Sons, represents on a larger scale a panel ornamented with a Japanese design.

CHAPTER XI.

COLONIAL FASHIONS.

Fashion in Furniture.—Dining-room.—High-back Chair.—Dining-table.—Dining-rooms treated in Dark Colors.—Table-cloth.

HERETOFORE it has been the custom to buy new furniture in accordance with the latest caprice of fashion, just as a lady selects a new bonnet. But now the revival of styles prevalent in the days of our ancestors may induce some of the present members of old Puritan and Knickerbocker families to bring down from the garret long-discarded and forgotten heirlooms. At the Lady Washington tea-parties given in fashionable society, our belles delight to appear in the dresses and jewels worn by their grandmothers at the receptions of Washington and Lafayette. Certainly the honor which is done these ancient costumes might be appropriately extended to such articles of furniture as remain to us

Fig. 25.—Some Examples of Modern Upholstery.

from the same age. Many of them, if placed in a modern drawing-room, would put to shame the meretricious upholstery which a perverted taste has made fashionable. As examples of the latter, let us take the sofa and chair shown in Fig. 25, which are fair types of modern extravagance. Clearly, they are constructed in violation of all correct principles, and of fend against good taste. Not only do they have the *appearance* of weakness, but they are in reality unfit to stand ordinary usage for any length of time. Figs. 26 and 27, specimens of the reformed school, are offered in contrast.

All flimsy, magnificent attempts at furniture, too delicate for use, too uncomfortable for repose, foster the idea of shutting up our drawing-rooms except on state occasions, when the conventionalities of society are carried out in a formal and ceremonious manner. When the entertainment is over, much to the relief of both host and guests, the grand room is again closed, and the family seek more home-like apartments in a less pretentious portion of the house, where, perhaps, some of the ancestral mahogany is still in use.

Fig. 26.—A Chair of the New School.

In some sections of the country where certain peculiarities of style, prevalent for many years, appear to have stamped their impress upon the buildings, it seems ridiculous to introduce anything entirely new and foreign. For example, in Rhode Island, Pennsylvania, New Jersey, and other States, there are certain distinctively local modes of building. If these can be accepted by the architect, they may be frequently rendered in a very satisfactory manner, and, when the work is completed, it will appear in harmony with its surroundings. In accordance with this idea, I give, in Fig. 28, a view of a dining-room which formed part of a design prepared for the residence of Mr. Lawrence Waterbury, of Westchester. The style is that of the last century, and is characteristic of some of the old mansions that were built prior to the Revolution. Stained glass is employed in the upper sash of the windows, and the walls and ceilings are treated in harmonious colors. The floor is of inlaid woods, relieved by rugs of Oriental pattern. The dado is of India matting, which gives a certain warmth and softness to the room, and produces all the effect of porcelain, without having the appearance of rigidity which characterizes tile. The sideboard and fireplace, more fully illustrated in Figs. 20 and 22, accord with the rest of the fittings, and are types of the Jacobean period.

We know that the high-backed chair has been frequently condemned on the ground that it is old-fashioned and barbarous. That it is old-fashioned, and contrary to recent ideas, is a fact too patent to be contradicted; but that it is barbarous and unfit for modern use I must dispute. There is something solid and comfortable in these high backs, as if they were

Fig. 27.—Specimens of the Reformed School.

meant to be leaned upon. The design shown in Fig. 16 is a good one for chairs of this description. It is the same as that already given in the dining-room interior.

It is frequently remarked that new houses have a stiff, uncomfortable look, and that people moving into them are continually conscious of their newness and want of home-like feeling. The practice, however, of reviving old fashions does away with much of this. I recently built a house modelled upon ancient styles, and the lady who was its occupant told me that she was particularly struck with its home-like effect; that the old-fashioned fireplace and general finishing and furnishing were such as to immediately produce a sense of "at-homeness;" and, far from realizing that she had come into a newly completed dwelling, she felt as if she had lived there for years. A greater compliment to the Colonial style, as adapted to modern domestic purposes, could not have been given.

There is no necessity that the dining-table should be of a very elaborate design, as it is generally hidden by a cover; but its construction is a matter of much importance. A table standing on four legs is to be recommended in preference to those of the "pedestal" style, having but one support in the centre. This not only suggests a sense of insecurity, but is æsthetically wrong; for this pedestal, if used in the ordinary extension-table, must, whenever the table is drawn out, be cut in two, showing two incomplete standards. Now, this is only endured from the fact that custom sanctions it; but regarding it from an artistic point of view, it is as bad as if a piano-leg were divided in the centre. If, therefore, we are compelled to have these telescopic tables, let them, by all means, have four legs, in which case the evil is modified to some extent.

Eastlake, with justice, condemns these "rattletraps" altogether as unconstructional, and recommends the old system of placing two tables fitted with flap-leaves end to end, when dinner-parties are given. Square tables he considers preferable to round, as from them the cloth hangs in more graceful folds, and the corners are valuable in the way of affording extra room.

Dining-rooms, as a general thing, should be treated in dark colors, so that their walls may form an agreeable background for the table-cloth and

Fig. 28.—Dining-room Interior.

fixtures. A white table-cloth is generally too glaring in its effect, and out of keeping with the surroundings. For general purposes, one of a cream tint is preferable.

Figs. 13, 14, and 15 represent furniture designed for Mr. G. E. Hamlin's house. See Design 15.

CHAPTER XII.

BOOKCASES AND PIANOS.

Light in Library.—Bay-windows.—Hooded Chimney-piece.—Music-stool.—Music-stand.

ONE of the most conspicuous articles of furniture in a house is the bookcase, and there are several requirements connected with it that are frequently lost sight of. The old bookcases, running eight feet high, the upper shelves of which could not be reached without a step-ladder,

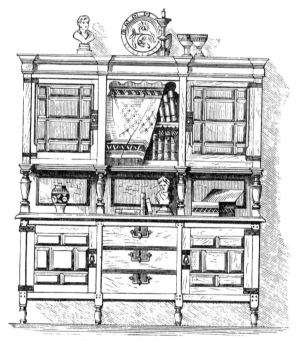

Fig. 29.—Neo-Jacobean Bookcase.

have mostly gone out of date, and others of a more convenient height are substituted. It is obvious that this change, at least, is favorable, for we are enabled to use the top for bronzes and other ornaments, while the wall space above is left free for pictures. Some even go so far as to keep the top of uniform height with the mantel. There is a certain advantage in this, as it seems to carry out the wainscoting, and, indeed, may be made a part of it. One objection, however, is that such an alignment seems to

Fig. 30.—The Library.

give an appearance of stiffness to the room. If glass doors are used, the squares should be small; when made of thick glass, they are greatly improved by bevelling. Much expense may be spared, however, and an agreeable effect produced, by curtains. In fact, a compromise might be made between curtains and glass, as shown by our illustration. By this plan the more valuable books may be locked up, while the plainer kind or works of reference are protected by the drapery.

I have stated that the windows in the library should be generally opposite the fireplace, so that the light may be at the back of the occupant when sitting before the fire. In the illustration (Fig. 30), however, there is a slight deviation from this rule. A small bay-window, containing a plant cabinet, is arranged at the left; but the glass, being in the depth of the recess, is partially screened from the reader by the projecting chimney.

Should a greater degree of shade be required, a sliding curtain beneath the transom will prove effectual.

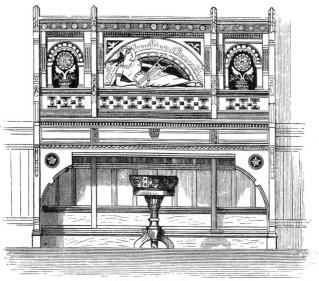

Fig. 31.—Upright Piano.

These bay-windows often have a most pleasing effect, making a cosy corner for plants and birds. In this instance there is a decorated panel introduced in the wainscot, and the upper part of the sash is illuminated with stained glass.

The hooded chimney-piece, constructed entirely of light freestone, and

Fig. 32.—English Design of Grand Piano.

terminating with a carved bracket, on which may be displayed specimens of pottery, is a conspicuous object in the room.

The bookcase is somewhat similar in character to that shown in Fig. 29. It has no doors; but a simple border of leather, attached to each shelf by means of silver nails, serves to protect the books from dust.

Perhaps the piece of furniture which has undergone the least reform is the piano. Not only is there great barrenness of design apparent, but it would seem as if manufacturers had despaired of being able to work any change. All continue in the same groove, the few attempts at improvement being so insignificant as to make little or no impression. Whether square or upright, grand or concert, all pianos, both in this country and Europe, look as if manufactured on the same plan.

Fig. 33.—Music-stand.

Fig. 31 is a design for an upright piano similar to one prepared for Mr. G. E. Hamlin, intended to be inlaid with woods of different colors, the motive of which was taken from a design of Mr. J. Moyr Smith.

Fig. 32 shows an English design of a grand piano, which, I think, exhibits some very beautiful detail. There is, however, an objection to the stool, on account of the legs being curved across the grain, and, consequently, weak. The music-stand also seems to be equally objectionable, as it is not in any way adapted to the accommodation of large books.

Fig. 33 shows two articles of this kind, which are, I think, an improvement. In the first the books can be more easily adjusted, and can also be protected by lock and key. The music-stool, which is sufficiently long for a duet, can be easily raised or lowered by means of a ratchet.

CHAPTER XIII.

PLANTS.

Flower Decoration.—Swiss Scene.—Miniature Conservatory.—Buckingham Hotel.—
Pottery and Wooden.Chests in Fireplaces.

THERE is one very simple and economical method of decorating a room, and that is by the introduction of plants and vines. By this, I do not mean that it is necessary to have an elaborate conservatory, or even a collection of plants in a bay-window; but in certain nooks, which seem difficult to furnish, a healthy plant has often a finer effect than showy furniture or costly hangings. The rude flower-stands formerly used are now superseded by artistic ones of wood or metal, the sides of which are filled in with illuminated tile. Fig. 34 illustrates a flower-stand similar to that shown in the sketch of the library (Fig. 30), but having a small aquarium in the centre, which, being portable, can be removed

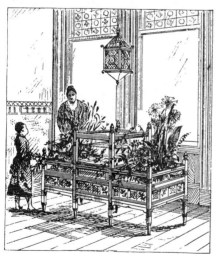

Fig. 34.—Flower-stand.

at pleasure, leaving the entire stand free for plants. The top is lined with zinc, in order to prevent the water dripping through, and is capable of holding a large number of pots. These are often ornamental in themselves, being frequently of faience or majolica, and may be either grouped or placed in single stands.

Fig. 35 illustrates a single vase and stand, which is the same as that shown in the dining-room interior (Fig. 36).

Another inexpensive method of decoration is the introduction of flowers, according to a system quite common in England, but only recently introduced here. It consists of an arrangement of plants in the fireplaces in summer. Of course, in a position like this, where the sun cannot reach them, there are only certain plants which would thrive, as, for instance, the English ivy, or some varieties of fern. If cut flowers, which can be changed as they fade, are added, the effect will be as bright and cheerful as that of a wood or sea-coal fire in winter. This also does away with the fireboard, or that American invention, the summer-piece, which is in keeping with so many of the shams to which custom has given sanction. There is nothing to be ashamed of in an open fireplace even in summer-time, especially if the sides and back are made ornamental. In laying out grounds, it is a common expedient to plant trees thickly between the house and any eyesore in the landscape, and this principle can be as readily carried out in our houses. Even if the fireplace is besmeared with smoke, the introduction of plants is a very legitimate method of hiding the blemish. This system may also be called

Fig. 35.—Flower-vase.

into service in case the windows of our living-rooms overlook some domestic portion of the grounds, such as a kitchen garden or a farm stable. In fact, I have seen a window looking simply into a vacant court made to serve as a frame to a miniature Swiss landscape, by the introduction of rock-work and a few ferns, which, being reflected in a diminishing mirror, had precisely the appearance of distant mountains and trees.

Speaking of flowers and vines in the fireplace reminds me that here is an excellent place for pottery; for, while being a picturesque nook, it also is a safe deposit for treasures of this kind. A high Japanese jar in the centre, and a pair of smaller ones at the sides, will have a pleasing appearance. I have also seen antique wooden chests, with ornamental straphinges and curious locks, in fireplaces. They not only relieve the barrenness, but, if in a bedroom, serve as most convenient receptacles for small articles. In a dining-room they may be used as a liqueur-case, or made to perform some other useful service.

Many people seem to think that it is impossible to have plants without going into an elaborate system of greenhouses or conservatories, with water-pipes, furnaces, and a professional gardener at the head. There are other means, however, by which they may be cultivated on a modest scale without expense and with but little trouble. A miniature conservatory may be arranged by means of a simple glazed frame, shaped some-

what like a bay-window. This, being made the size of the window, is screwed on to the outer side, taking the place of the blinds, which are not required in the winter season. By opening the sash top and bottom, the warm air of the apartment circulates among the plants, which shut out the dreary landscape and give a fresh, summer-like appearance to the room. I have, in the middle of January, entered a room furnished in this manner, and the effect of the green foliage with the window-sashes open was such as to drive away all thoughts of the winter outside.

Fig. 36.—Glimpse of the Dining-room.

I was much impressed by an arrangement at the Buckingham Hotel, New York, where plants were made a prominent feature. The lofty ceilings gave ample scope for huge palms and orange-trees; and, as the visitor entered the spacious hall-way, the effect of these, with the singing of birds and the plash of a fountain, was such as to make him fancy himself in a tropical garden. There was also a corridor of plate-glass connecting two wings of the building, where tile boxes filled with brilliant foliage were arranged along the sides. These afforded an agreeable surprise, being unusual in our city hotels.

CHAPTER XIV.

BEDROOM FURNITURE.

Fashionable Furniture.—Architect designing Furniture.

IN the illustration (Fig. 46) we have several articles of bedroom furniture, modelled after the style of the seventeenth century, which recommends itself by its characteristic simplicity and honesty of treatment. The bed has a canopy framework, from which curtains are suspended, the cove being covered with stamped leather. The decoration in the panels may be inlaid, or painted simply in stencil pattern.

Fig. 47 shows a dressing-table of the same period, which, in some respects, answers the purpose of a bureau, being liberally supplied with drawers. There is, also, a corner cabinet, intended for a jewel-case, back of which a small burglar and fire-proof box may be inserted in the brickwork, and entirely masked by an inner door. Medicine-cases are often constructed in this manner.

Figs. 48 and 49 are a wash-stand and commode of the same school. Fig. 37 is a hanging cabinet, similar to the one in the library (Fig. 30).

One great difficulty in the way of introducing furniture of this description is, that people do not know where to find it. They usually go to a fashionable dealer, and are compelled to choose from what they see before them. It is true that several of our manufacturers have attempted to offer something better in the way of design, and with considerable success and profit. But their great mistake has been that, knowing they had the monopoly, they made their prices so high that few could afford to deal with them, thus confining the possibility of exercising good taste to wealthy persons alone. There is really no reason why this furniture should be more expensive than any other. That fashionable upholsterers should subordinate art to sordid and mercenary considerations indicates a short-sighted policy; for the wider the diffusion of art culture among the people, the greater will be the demand for furniture of artistic design. If one of their patrons desires anything new, they will usually prepare a design, and with it submit a price; but should he ask to retain the drawing in order to get further estimates, the privilege is promptly refused, and the statement usually vouchsafed that they are not in the habit of allowing other manufacturers to profit by their brains. One is, therefore, compelled to take an inferior design from another establishment, or pay the price of the original estimate, exorbitant as it may be. There is a simple remedy for all this which, as I have mentioned before, is coming into practice.

Fig. 37.—Hanging Cabinet.

After the house is completed, instead of abandoning the architect, and submitting to the tender mercies of an upholsterer, let him who has thus far given satisfaction, prepare designs for the furniture also. He will be able, not only to give drawings upon which several estimates may be obtained, and the advantage of competition thereby gained; but if he be possessed of ability, he will so arrange that every article shall be in harmony with the rest of the building.

CHAPTER XV.

METALS.

Locks.—Bolts.—Handles.—Hinges.—Imitation in Metals.—Sconce.—Mirror.—Chandelier.

METAL, if artistically wrought, may contribute largely to the adornment of our dwellings. It is important that all designs should be consistent with the material in which they are to be executed. Models are not infrequently prepared for cast iron which can only be properly executed in wrought, from the fact that they possess certain distinctive features which fitly belong to the latter. This comes of the spirit of imitation, which is the most subtle enemy of true art, and which must be eradicated before the first steps toward true reform can be taken. It is the height of folly to keep on casting and recasting the wretched forms, unworthy the name of designs, which, unfortunately, crowd our foundries, and then, perhaps, add insult to injury, by painting and sanding these horrors so as to imitate stone. We will not here speak of iron for external use; but metal-work for interiors is greatly in need of reform. Hitherto it seems to have been hidden as much as possible, perhaps on account of the realization of its ugliness. Locks, for instance, instead of being in sight, are buried within the wood-work, which is cut away for their accommodation, so as to materially lessen its strength.

Now, the ancient idea of a lock was to display it, and, therefore, they were made artistically ornamental, as shown in Fig. 38. Here, the metal face not only appears, but is elongated, in order to serve the additional purpose of a finger-plate. Fig. 39 represents a drawer lock, where the entire face is displayed, to which is also attached the handle. Fig. 40 represents a small drawer handle, and Fig. 41 a door bolt, both of which display ornamental faces.

The old system of embellishing the hinge, and making it appear a constructive feature of the door, seems to be entirely lost sight of in these days of modern deception. The present aim is to bury the hinge, which has degenerated into a flimsy article known as the "butt." Fig. 42 is a design for a metal hinge intended to extend the entire width of the door.

This differs materially from the old hinges as seen on church doors, which, however appropriate for public buildings, appear out of place in dwellings. Fig. 43, which serves the same purpose, shows a lighter hinge, such as was used in the days of the Georges.

The buildings erected by the British Government on the Centennial Grounds at Philadelphia showed how much this honest treatment is regarded in England. Even the nail-heads, instead of being covered with putty and paint, were exposed to view and ornamented. This substantial method of construction attracted much attention, and many persons were heard to declare that if our country-houses were built on the same plan, a vast improvement would be the result.

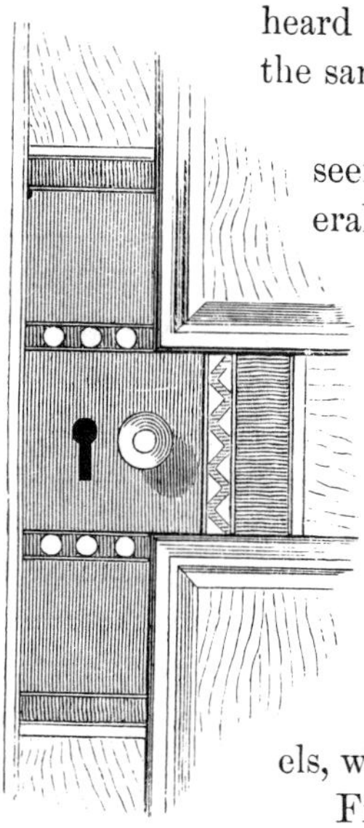

Perhaps the most prominent pieces of metal-work seen in our rooms are the chandeliers, which, as a general thing, are too heavy and also inartistic in shape. The thinness, which is one of the legitimate conditions to be observed in the treatment of metal, seems utterly lost sight of, and heavy castings, apparently strong enough for the anchor of a man-of-war, are continually produced. To invest metal with forms which might equally well be executed in stone or wood, is absurd. The idea that chandeliers and brackets are simply tubes for the conveying of gas is apparently forgotten. Even huge pedestals are sometimes placed on top of stair newels, which seem to groan beneath their weight.

Fig. 38.—Door Lock.

Fig. 44 is a design of a chandelier, by Archer & Pancoast, in which the tubular construction is apparent. The work is so open in character as not to obstruct the view of the opposite wall, and the effect is pleasing in the extreme, relieving the room of the cumbersome appearance so frequently presented by the ordinary chandelier.

Apparently, this complaint which I make against gas-fixtures which obstruct the view has suggested itself to architects to whom the placing of signs on buildings has been intrusted. Instead of fastening them flatly against the walls, an invisible screen of wire is arranged to project some inches from the building, and on this the gilt letters are placed. In this way no part of the wall is concealed, and the letters, instead of marring the architecture, become graceful ornaments.

Fig. 45 shows a side bracket, generally known as the "sconce." It consists of a sheet of plate-glass, bevelled at the edges, and set into a very legitimate frame of brass or ormolu, before which candles were formerly placed. Gas jets may be arranged in the same way with an equally good effect. Gas, however, I do not regard as the pleasantest mode of lighting. Candles, although not so brilliant, give a much softer and more becoming light, and oil or kerosene is less trying to the eyes. The old Carselle lamp was one of the pleasantest lights for reading, but this is now rather expensive, and difficult to manage. The

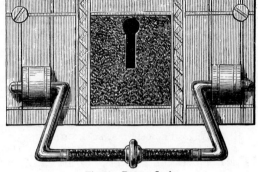

Fig. 39.—Drawer Lock.

German student lamp is, however, a fair substitute, and its form partakes strongly of the character of the chandelier above described.

Fig. 40.—Drawer Handle.

We would not usually recommend the use of gas in the country, unless a supply can be had from some public works. Too much machinery in a house is liable to make trouble. Repairs are almost sure to be needed, and great annoyance is caused by the remoteness of mechanics. Gas is by no means so indispensable an article as some of our countrymen might suppose. In the large cities of Europe it is excluded, in a great measure, from private houses, and in the palaces and dwellings of the nobility it is not used except for inferior purposes. At fashionable parties in our cities it is often superseded by wax-candles.

Bevelled mirrors, with metal frames, were also quite common at one period; but instead of reaching from floor to ceiling, as if intended

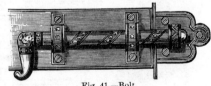

Fig. 41.—Bolt.

to delude the visitor into the belief that the reflection of the room was another apartment, they were seldom larger than ordinary pictures. The one above the fireplace rarely exceeded a foot or eighteen inches in height, but extended along the length of the mantel.

CHAPTER XVI.

HOME ART.

Gentlemen as Amateur Cabinet-makers.—Ladies as Wall Decorators.—Imitation Stained Glass.—Home-made Curtains.—Rods and Brackets.—Fret or Bracket Saws.—Burlaps Hearth-rug.—Impromptu Sconces.—Grouping of Flags.—Renewing Picture-frames.

THE possession of works of art is often looked upon as the exclusive privilege of a favored few, whose incomes allow them a surplus over and above the expenses of living. For people in moderate circumstances to purchase pictures or artistic furniture is, according to popular notions, an unwarrantable extravagance. Yet a doctrine such as this would frequently have the effect of debarring from the enjoyment of beautiful surroundings precisely those persons who are most able to appreciate them. In this country wealth is in many cases possessed by individuals who, having amassed it suddenly, lack the cultivation that would alone enable them to use it properly, while refinement and taste are the attributes of others whose poverty denies them all chance of gratifying their

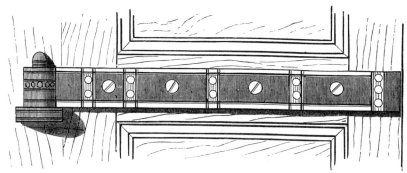

Fig. 42.—Hinge.

finer instincts. Occasionally, however, we find persons whose passion for beauty is not to be crushed or controlled by the want of a liberal income. Their desire for artistic surroundings will lead them to master the arts themselves, and produce with their own hands objects that rival in attraction any for which the rich man ignorantly and carelessly exchanges his money.

I have in mind a gentleman who, having considerable leisure, amused himself an hour or two each day in an amateur workshop, whence he produced a number of very artistic pieces of furniture. He told me he did not rely entirely upon his own taste, but had the designs made full size by an architect. All he had to do then was to cut out the wood as drawn on the paper, and exercise his skill in finishing. By this means he was enabled to adorn his house with furniture of an artistic character, the cost of which would otherwise have been beyond his means, while at the same time he combined an agreeable amount of exercise with an employment that became more and more fascinating as he pursued it.

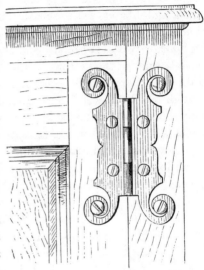

Fig. 43.—Lighter Hinge.

Another gentleman, who had just completed an artistic cottage, was asked where he was going to get his furniture, when he astonished his friends by asserting that the only apartment he intended to furnish completely at first was his workshop. Although fully occupied by professional duties, he managed to furnish his principal room in the course of twelve months. His operations were facilitated, however, by an accidental circumstance, resulting from an act of benevolence. A man who was destitute of means applied to him for work. After being for some time the recipient of charity, he was finally intrusted with odd jobs, in the performance of which he showed so much ingenuity that he was soon permitted to assist his benefactor in various mechanical pursuits. The gentleman in question made a practice of devoting one day of every week, usually Saturday, to what he called his " work of recreation." He soon discovered in his assistant an apt scholar, who could be trusted to carry out practically the plans arranged by his master during the hours of the latter's holiday. If more of our business community would adopt the same plan, they might secure for themselves a healthful and remunerative pastime. Such examples are also likely to have a good effect on mechanics as a class, inducing them to regard their labor as something above mere drudgery, and to infuse some artistic sentiment into their work.

The wife of this gentleman, who also possessed a kindred talent for artistic work, distinguished herself in the way of color, her desire to relieve the whiteness of the walls of her dwelling having induced her to make the subject of decoration a special study. She commenced in a simple way with some of the less important apartments, venturing on something more artistic as she gained experience, and reserving the living-rooms for her last and best efforts. The work finally produced in the parlor, dining-room, and library was so chaste and original as to command the admiration of all who saw it. Upon the parlor alone she spent a year, painting an hour or two every day. She began with the early flowers of spring as models, and, as the seasons changed, gathered fresh leaves and blossoms, until the characteristic growth of every month in the year was represented. Wild flowers were apparently her favorite subjects, being not only more easily obtained than others, but producing a more satisfactory effect when painted upon the wall. The commonest plants, such as flags and clover, oats and cat-tails, were not despised by our artist. These were made to grow out of an apparent *jardinière*, painted to represent tile, as the upper member of the dado, and now and then a lady-bug or beetle

Fig. 44.—Chandelier.

would obtrude itself in the midst of the garden, adding life and interest to the scene.*

In the course of a personal interview with this lady, she told me she had much regretted not being able to afford stained glass, and had imagined that this was a luxury that circumstances would compel them for the present to forego. Within a short time, however, she had read of a method common in France by which paper, prepared by a new process of lithography, could be transferred to glass. The materials required were a few sheets of tin-foil, a bottle of transparent varnish, a roller, and some brushes. This, together with the designs, and glass to work upon, included all that was necessary. A short time since, I learned from her husband that she had been able to undertake the experiment, which had proved a great success.

The resources of this lady seem inexhaustible. On the occasion of a recent visit to her house, she showed me some very novel and striking cur-

---

* A room was recently decorated in a manner similar to that just described, for Mr. George A. Hoyt, of Gray Rock, Stamford, Connecticut, by Miss Mary W. M‘Lain, a young lady who has developed some original ideas in decoration, and is making this art a profession.

tains, which I thought at first were raw silk. Blue and red bands, relieved with narrow lines of black, were woven in top and bottom, which, in contrast with the warm cream-colored ground, produced a delightfully bright and cheerful effect. Upon closer examination, I was astonished, as well as delighted, to find the whole curtain made of the simplest domestic material. The ground was of unbleached muslin, with stripes of blue and red flannel sewed upon its surface, and the black lines were narrow velvet ribbon. These curtains were suspended from a wooden rod, with turned ends—as brass at five dollars a window was considered too expensive—and in place of metal rings, loops of red ribbon, tied in tasteful bows, were substituted.

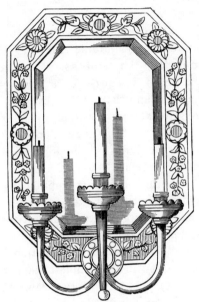

Fig. 45.—A Sconce.

Even in metal rods and rings, the taste of the upholsterer is opposed to reform. An attempt at display is made by having these rods, which are intended to support a few yards of drapery only, of a size apparently sufficient to sustain a ton weight. The excessive ornamentation might also be avoided; and instead of the rods being broken up by surface decoration of elaborate, and not always the most chaste, design, it would be better to observe simplicity, allowing the plain surface to give a broad reflection, relieved only by the rings. Another point wherein upholsterers are apt to run ornamentation to excess is in the terminals. The ends of these poles are usually too elaborate, and present a heavy and awkward effect.

But to return to the description of the wonders achieved by the lady concerning whom so much has been said. As metal brackets for the support of the curtain-rods were also impracticable on account of the expense, a wooden scroll was designed, which she herself cut out with a bracket-saw.

These little saws open another channel for woman's industry. The difficulty heretofore has been the miserable patterns in the shape of what is called "scroll-work," offered with the machines. Any lady interested in this work, would find a great advantage in learning to design the patterns so as to have something original. Very beautiful effects of inlay may be produced by means of the scroll-saw. For instance, take veneer of different colors—say rosewood and holly—with a vine or geometrical pattern traced upon its surface, and let the two be sawed out at once.

Fig. 46.—Bedroom Furniture.

The leaves of the holly are then secured into the corresponding spaces of the rosewood, and *vice versa.* When glued into their places, the effect is that of two strips of inlay. These veneers, when artistically executed, are easily disposed of to furniture manufacturers; and, considering that the scroll-saw is not a quarter of the price of a sewing-machine, and that, with a little exercise of artistic talent, an operator can make her labor much more profitable, the industry should receive encouragement.*

A hearth-rug in a gentleman's study recently attracted my attention. The Oriental effect was so peculiar that I expressed my admiration, when, to my astonishment, he told me that it was made by his little daughter, a child of seven or eight years. On a minute examination I found the ground to be common burlaps, worked in the simplest manner with black and colored worsted. The border consisted of two rows of flannel, harmonious in color, the edges of which projected one beyond the other.

In the room of a gentleman in which were displayed a number of ingenious contrivances, I saw a pair of sconces made by himself. He had come across a plate-glass establishment, where they had a thrifty way of utilizing the broken pieces which usually go to waste, by squaring and bevelling their edges, and putting them into simple wooden frames as mirrors. He purchased a pair of these at a nominal cost, and, after decorating the frames in color, he attached to their lower sides three clay pipes with curved stems. These he colored with liquid bronze in such a

---

* This scroll-sawing, although mechanical in itself, has proved the germ of some happy artistic efforts. The work of the carving-tool is often displayed upon the surface of the wood; as, for instance, in the case of vine-work, where the veins may be in relief or intaglio, with rounded stems and berries.

manner as to give them the appearance of metal brackets. Upon the top of each he placed a cut-glass saucer—such as are used with candelabra. These held the candles; and, when completed, at the expense of a few shillings, the whole sconces compared favorably with those of extravagant cost at fashionable establishments.

Another picturesque arrangement in the same apartment was the grouping together of quite a number of small flags of different nations, gathered by their stems, and radiating upward. A Japanese banner about twelve inches wide, containing a human figure, was suspended from the mantel, reaching to within a foot of the floor. This not only had the effect of screening the grate when it contained no fire, but gave a bright effect to an otherwise uninteresting portion of the room.

Fig. 47.—Dressing-table and Cabinet.

I lately saw an improvised china closet in the parlor of a lady in Stamford which is worth describing. There were doors originally on either side of the mantel, one of which was never used, having been placed there merely for symmetry. This was removed, and a semi-octagon recess was constructed, with back and shelves covered with crimson baize, relieved to some extent with gilt mouldings and brass nails. On these were displayed a choice collection of Wedgwood and Dresden china. The whole arrangement was of so simple and effective a character that it seemed especially worthy of commendation. Such might be introduced with admirable result into many a sombre room.

CHAPTER XVII.

ART-SCHOOLS FOR WOMEN.

Woman's Carving School of Cincinnati.—Royal School of Art Needle-work.—Industrial
Arts taught in our Schools.—Artists decorating Walls.—Adapting Curious Workmanship.—Trousseau Chest and Old Mantel.

THE Woman's Pavilion at the Centennial Exhibition showed clearly
what can be accomplished by female artists. A complete set of furniture was there exhibited, carved with infinite skill and delicacy, the work
having been performed at a school for women recently instituted at Cincinnati. Indeed, the real artistic spirit with which they seemed to have
entered into their work might put most of the sterner sex to the blush.
In England, owing to the influence of the South Kensington teaching,
ladies in some of the highest ranks in life have made fresco-painting a
study, and have excelled their mas-
ters in the art. Such efforts on the
part of ladies of rank to elevate an
employment whereby women may
earn a livelihood is philanthropic in
the extreme. There is, indeed, no
reason why women should not become proficient, and be employed in
all the industrial arts where physical
strength is not required. The Royal
School of Art Needle-work in London is one, where the Queen is both
a worker and patron; H.R.H. the
Princess Christina is president; and
the Duchess of Northumberland and
the Marchioness of Waterford are
members, with a large retinue of the

Fig. 48.—Wash-stand.

nobility as counsel. The school is founded for the purpose of restoring
ornamental needle-work for secular purposes to the high place it once
held among the decorative arts. They advertise to fill orders for dec-

orative needle-work of all kinds, and solicit designs from the ablest artists and architects, with the assurance that their instructions will be carefully carried out.

If our ladies would give more attention and encouragement to the useful arts, they would increase their own accomplishments, and at the same time do a missionary work, the fruits of which might be reaped by a large class of our industrial community. We might then hear less of the tyranny of shopkeepers and manufacturers in compelling girls to be on their feet from morning until night, destroying both mind and body in the endeavor to earn an insignificant stipend.

Why should not these industrial arts be taught in our schools and seminaries? Take painting on china, for instance. When some of our ladies of wealth have become proficient themselves, what a field of industry they might establish for a worthy and highly gifted set of women, who simply want instruction to excel in something better and higher than what has hitherto been conceded as woman's sphere of labor!

The Cincinnati school was founded by Mr. Henry L. Fry and his son, William Fry, whose exquisite work at the residence of Mr. Nicholas Longworth, Jr., induced that gentleman, in connection with several others, to establish a school for the instruction of women in the art of carving. Another member of the Longworth family came nobly forward with an endowment of one hundred thousand dollars for its support. The enthusiastic manner in which nearly a hundred pupils embraced this opportunity seems to give the strongest assurance of its success. A similar movement, we are rejoiced to see, is now set on foot by some of the representative, though not "strong-minded," ladies of New York and Boston. Judging by the character of its officers, we may expect to see the happiest results from this noble enterprise, in which instruction not only in carving, but in painting on pottery, and also in needle-work of all kinds, is included.

One noticeable fact in this period of business depression is, that many artists who formerly devoted their time exclusively to the work of the studio have been induced to exercise their talents in a field of practical, though artistic, industry. The decoration of private houses and public buildings has thus received a new impulse from the genius of some of our most excellent artists. Mr. Lafarge's work, in the interior of Trinity Church, Boston, is a good example of this, and we sincerely hope that a large amount of the artistic talent of the country, which has heretofore been devoted exclusively to the canvas, will now find opportunities for expression in those branches of industrial art which have been, to a great extent, monopolized by a set of men whose ignorance has only been exceeded by their conceit.

Another method of producing novelties in the way of art is frequently accomplished by adapting some curious piece of workmanship to a different use. Sir Walter Scott converted the pulpit formerly used at Dryburgh-Abbey into a console table, which was worked into the wainscot in one of his principal apartments. Here it retained all its traditional interest, and at the same time performed a useful part, so that the room it occupied was not begrudged.

A gentleman, who had developed considerable talent in this line, showed me a most elaborately carved mantel, which looked as if it might

Fig. 49.—Commode.

have cost a large sum to manufacture. He was in the habit of attending the bric-à-brac auctions at Leavitt's, and among other things picked up what was formerly an old trousseau chest, but which, from want of care, had become pretty well demolished—so much so, indeed, that, like some antique china, the pieces were all that remained. The collector appreciated these, however, and, perceiving their capability, devised an original plan for their reconstruction; and his library mantel proved how successfully it was realized. In another room he showed me an equally artistic mantel, which he said was in the original kitchen of his house, now converted into the dining-room. It was composed of simple boards and rude moulding, originally painted black. Over this he painted, with his own hands, a coat of chocolate, which served as a good groundwork for some beautiful effects in polychrome.

The fireplace proper he had simply faced up with Philadelphia brick. A pair of old fire-dogs, and a fender which he had found stowed away in the garret, were brightened up and made to adorn the hearth.

Even where wealth is missing, there are many pleasant devices by which rooms may be made attractive. The effort to discover means whereby artistic effects may be produced, without the expenditure of large sums of money, has an educating and refining influence, added to which is the satisfaction attendant upon the overcoming of difficulties. A little study, aided by patience and industry, will often serve to develop grace and beauty out of the poorest materials; while, if taste be lacking, the richest ornamentation will only produce a disagreeable and annoying effect.

THE END.

Index to Country Seats & Modern Dwellings

INDEX

INDEX

INDEX

INDEX

INDEX

INDEX

INDEX

INDEX

INDEX

INDEX

INDEX

INDEX

INDEX

INDEX

INDEX

INDEX

INDEX

INDEX

INDEX

INDEX

v